Curriculum Development for Adult Learners in the Global Community

Volume I
Strategic Approaches

Curriculum Development for Adult Learners in the Global Community

Volume I
Strategic Approaches

Edited by
Victor C. X. Wang

KRIEGER PUBLISHING COMPANY
Malabar, Florida
2008

Original Edition 2008

Printed and Published by
KRIEGER PUBLISHING COMPANY
KRIEGER DRIVE
MALABAR, FLORIDA 32950

FROM A DECLARATION OF PRINCIPLES JOINTLY ADOPTED BY A COMMITTEE OF THE AMERICAN BAR ASSOCIATION AND A COMMITTEE OF PUBLISHERS:
This publication is designed to provide accurate and authoritative information in regard to the subject matter covered. It is sold with the understanding that the publisher is not engaged in rendering legal, accounting, or other professional service. If legal advice or other expert assistance is required, the services of a competent professional person should be sought.

Library of Congress Cataloging-In-Publication Data

Curriculum development for adult learners in the global community / Victor C. X. Wang, editor.
    p. cm.
ISBN 978-1-57524-296-5 (volume 1 : alk. paper) — ISBN 978-1-57524-300-9 (volume 2 : alk. paper)
1. Adult learning. 2. Curriculum planning. I. Wang, Victor C. X.
LC5219.C87 2008
375'.001—dc22

                                       2008024734

10 9 8 7 6 5 4 3 2

To Anthony Wang, my son who has filled my days with love and joy and is such an adorable, smart little boy. To my teenage daughter, Anni Wang, who has recently won a Presidential Award and will go to the best middle school because of her academic achievements, I should have allowed her more play time. And finally, to Katie Wang, a heartfelt thank you for encouraging me and for your continued tolerance in my personal and academic journeys.

Contents

Acknowledgments

As editor of the book, I must express my heartfelt thanks to many people in the field. As soon as I finished composing the proposed chapter titles, I sent them to scholars and practitioners (who have taught adult learners around the globe) in the field of adult education. To my great surprise and delight, I received responses within two weeks from many of our first-rate professors and practitioners in the field. Therefore, I wish to thank my friends, colleagues, and mentors who contributed to this volume. Without your contribution, this book would not be a reality. It has been my utmost pleasure working with each and every one of you and I am so proud of your insightful chapters. A special thank you goes to Kathleen P. King and John A. Henschke who invited Patricia Cranton and Edgar Boone to provide reviewer letters. Patricia Cranton and Edgar Boone are experts' experts in the field. Their letters definitely confirm the value of this book.

I extend a huge thank you to Shannon Ryder of Krieger Publishing Company for her timely encouragement and support. The users and our students should be happy about the professionalism our publisher can provide! Worthy of note is the fact that Krieger Publishing Company is one of the authoritative publishers in publishing books in adult education around the globe. Not only are they professional, but they also provide first rate editors (Mary Roberts is one of them) for books in the field of adult education. Their efforts will undoubtedly add to the quality of our book. Thank you again, Shannon and Krieger Publishing Company! May our cooperation continue for many years.

Victor C. X. Wang

The Editor

Victor C. X. Wang, Ed.D., is an assistant professor/credential director of vocational and adult education at California State University, Long Beach. Wang's research and writing activities have focused on workforce education, the foundations of adult education, adult teaching and learning, training, transformative learning, cultural issues in vocational and adult education, distance education, and curriculum development. He has published more than 10 books and dozens of chapters and refereed journal articles and has been a reviewer for three journals. He has won many academic achievement awards from different universities in China and in the United States. He taught extensively as a full professor in China in places such as universities, radio stations, and China Central TV (CCTV) prior to coming to study and work in the United States in 1997. He has taught adult learners English as a second language, Chinese, computer technology, vocational and adult education courses, research methods and curriculum development for the past 18 years in university settings. In addition, he has served as a translator/narrator for national and international leaders both in China and in the United States. The videotapes and DVDs he published for national and international leaders are played all over the world for both educational and investment purposes. He coedited two books (*Comparative Adult Education Around The Globe; Innovations in Career and Technical Education: Strategic Approaches Towards Workforce Competencies Around the Globe*) with Fordham University's Professor Kathleen P. King, which have been adopted as required textbooks by major universities in the United States and in China.

The Contributors

Claretha H. Banks is an assistant professor who holds a Ph.D. in career and technical education from Virginia Institute of Technology. She teaches human resource development and adult education courses at University of Arkansas, Fayetteville. Her research interests also focus on the vocational and adult education/human resource development (HRD) area. She holds graduate faculty status and advises graduate students with an interest in vocational and adult education and human resource development. She has extensive professional experience in business and industry and continues to serve as a consultant to international, national, and state organizations.

Lisa M. Baumgartner, Ed.D., is an associate professor of adult education at Northern Illinois University, DeKalb. Her research and writing focus on adult learning and development and women's contributions to the field of adult education. A recipient of the W. K. Kellogg Foundation Cyril O. Houle Scholars Research Grant for Emerging Scholars in Adult Education, she completed a study on civil rights activist Septima P. Clark's lifelong contributions to social justice adult education. In addition, she coedited *Adult Learning and Development: Multicultural Stories* with Sharan Merriam (2000) and is a co-author of *Learning in Adulthood: A Comprehensive Guide* (3rd ed.) with Sharan Merriam and Rosemary Caffarella (2007). She has served on the steering committee for the annual North American Adult Education Research Conference. She is a consulting editor for the *International Journal of Qualitative Studies in Education*, *The Qualitative Report,* and *Adult Education Quarterly.* In 2004, she received the Commission of Professors of Adult Education Early Career Award which honors individuals in the early stages of their academic career who have made significant contributions in scholarship and service to the field.

Laura L. Bierema is an associate professor and program coordinator of adult education in the Department of Lifelong Education, Administration, and Policy at the University of Georgia. She holds an Ed.D. from the University of Georgia, a master's degree in labor and industrial relations from Michigan State University, and a B.A. also from Michigan State University. She teaches courses in adult learning, organization development and change, human resource development, and group dynamics. She has published numerous articles and book chapters and is the author or coauthor of three books. Bierema is a Cyril O. Houle Scholar in Adult and Continuing Education, and a Lilly Fellow. She is also the 1998 recipient of the Richard A. Swanson Excellence in Research Award, and the Academy of Human Resource Development's "Cutting Edge" Award, for one of the 10 best papers presented at the 1997, 2002, and 2004 conferences.

Renée L. Cambiano is an associate professor of education in the Department of Educational Foundations and Leadership at Northeastern State University in Tahlequah, Oklahoma. Her research interests include adult learning preferences and motivation, specifically within distance and online learning environments, traditional classrooms, and prisons, about which she has written numerous articles. She is the 2007 recipient of the Circle of Excellence Award in Research at Northeastern State University. She is the program director of the Master in Education in Teaching program, which is designed to promote "Master Teachers" through the use of learning styles. Cambiano earned her B.S. in fisheries biology from Northeastern State University, her M.S. in curriculum and instruction from the University of Memphis, and her Ed.D. in adult education from the University of Arkansas in Fayetteville.

Judith A. Cochran, Ph.D., is an Endowed Professor at the University of Missouri, St. Louis. She teaches courses in literacy, administration, and program development of adult and community education. Cochran directs the E. Desmond Lee Regional Institute of Tutorial Education which is a collaborative of six universitities, community agencies, and public school systems improving academics in underserved areas. She has been a Visiting Scholar at the University of Texas and the University of Arizona in addition to being an invited speaker at the Fulbright International Conference in Budapest, Hungary, and the Pacific Rim Early Childhood Conference in South Korea. She is currently writing a second book on international education.

Sandra R. Daffron is the director of the Continuing and College Education Masters program, Woodring College of Education, Western Washington University. She brings an extensive background in adult education and continuing professional education, with an Ed.D. from Northern Illinois University in adult and continuing education, an M.S. in special education from Southern Illinois University and a B.S. in home economics education from Eastern Illinois University. Daffron has 27 years of experience in graduate school instruction, and in providing training, conferences, workshops, and staff development for teachers, lawyers, judges, court staff, physicians, Army trainers, and correctional education personnel. In addition to her academic experience, Daffron has served as an assistant dean for IIT Chicago Kent College of Law, as the vice president and executive director of the American Judicature Society (a court reform organization), and served two years as chief of party, for a Rule of Law project for USAID in West Bank and Gaza.

Gail M. Goulet is the president and CEO of two companies: Career Connections Training Centre Inc. (CCTC) and Data Connect Information Services Inc. (DCIS). CCTC, established in 1993, is an accredited a private post-secondary educational institution in British Columbia, delivering government-sponsored programs to the South Fraser communities and developing customized training for the private and nonprofit sectors. DCIS, established in 1998, is a software development firm that provides customized software solutions for educational and training institutions. She completed a master's degree in adult and higher education from Western Washington University.

John L. Gray is the police chief for the City of Arlington, Washington, and was previously the police chief for Lake Stevens, Washington, for a total of 11 years. He has 30 years of experience in policing, working for city, county, and federal agencies. He earned his master's of education from the Woodring School of Education at Western Washington University, and his bachelor's degree from San Diego State University. He has instructed for Northwestern University's School of Police Staff and Command, the Washington State Criminal Justice Training Commission, and Everett Community College. He is a member of the Board on Law Enforcement Training, Standards and Education for Washington State and the Everett Community College Criminal Justice Advisory Board. He has published articles in *Police Chief Magazine* published by the International Association of Chiefs of Police, and *Law and Order Magazine*.

Vivian W. Mott is a professor of adult education and chair of the Department of Counselor and Adult Education at East Carolina University, College of Education, in Greenville, North Carolina. She holds a Ph.D. from the University of Georgia, an M.S.Ed. from the University of Tennessee, and certificates of advanced study in gerontology and ethnic studies. She is a recipient of the *2007 Centennial Women of Distinction* award from East Carolina University and the W. K. Kellogg Foundation Cyril O. Houle Scholars Research Award. Her research interests follow her long-standing professional work on the development of professional expertise, reflective practice, multicultural issues, and ethics in education and business.

Recent research projects have involved Native American women, higher education faculty, multinational corporations, public school teachers, counselors, and retired women. Her work has been published in the *Journal of Transformative Learning, Continuing Studies in Education, Noetic Sciences Review,* the *New Directions on Adult and Continuing Education* series, and numerous book chapters.

Fredrick M. Nafukho is an associate professor of human resource development and chair, HRD Program of the Department of Educational Administration and Human Resource Development, College of Education and Human Development, Texas A & M University. He holds a Ph.D. in human resource development, Louisiana State University, where he was a Fulbright Scholar, an M.Ed. (economics of education), and B.Ed. (business education and economics) from Kenyatta University, Kenya. In his 16 years of experience working in higher education, he has also served as associate professor and assistant department head, University of Arkansas, Fayetteville, and head, Department of Educational Administration and Curriculum Development, Moi University, Kenya. Nafukho has published over 120 articles, chapters, and books. His primary area of research has been aligned with investment in human capital, enrollment modeling and prediction in higher education, E-learning, and performance improvement. He served as proceedings editor and chair of the Academy of Human Resource Development Annual Conferences, 2006-2007. He is a board member of the AHRD Executive Board, and serves as an editorial board member of *Human Resource Development Quarterly, Advances in Developing Human Resources,* and *Journal of Eastern Africa Research and Development.* He teaches courses in adult education and human resource development.

Jason X. Viada is a member of the detective division at the police department for a small city in northwest Washington State. He has been a police officer since 1994. He is currently a graduate student and is earning a master's degree in continuing and college education from the Woodring School of Education at Western Washington University. He received his bachelor's degree in law and justice from Central Washington University. Viada's primary role at the police department is that of criminal investigator. He is involved in adult education and provides training for other officers on several topics. He is a certified instructor in many areas such as firearms, empty hand control tactics, electro-muscular disruption, chemical munitions, specialty impact munitions, oleoresin capsicum aerosol spray, noise-flash diversionary devices, and field training.

Mary Ziegler, Ed.D., serves as an associate professor in the Educational Psychology and Counseling Department at the University of Tennessee, Knoxville. She is the former director of the Center for Literacy Studies where she received numerous grants for research. Her doctorate is from Columbia University in adult education and she teaches courses, makes presentations, and consults in this area. She has numerous publications in adult literacy, workplace learning, and professional development. Recently, she collaborated on the publication of studies that focus on learning through narrative.

Introduction

Victor C. X. Wang

As a common Chinese proverb goes, without rice, even the cleverest house-wife cannot cook (Yuan, 2007). The implication is that without the right material, no matter how good you are as a cook, you may not accomplish the cooking task. Similarly, Westerners posited that knowledge of curriculum is, by definition, central to the professional teacher and an essential orientation for all professional responsible beginners (as cited in Print, 1993, p. 1). Two lines of thought from totally different cultures have confirmed the importance of curriculum development for professional teachers. What are the compelling reasons why adult learners want to teach others? Over the years, adult learners have accumulated such a rich reservoir of experience that they are ready to obtain teaching credentials from a university in order to teach their occupational skills to others. Without teaching credentials, they are not authorized to teach others. By teaching their knowledge, skills and attitudes to others, adult learners become professional teachers and trainers. However, having sheer knowledge in one's occupation does not automatically grant a person the power to teach in the field. A great deal depends on one's knowledge in curriculum development. This is probably why a course in curriculum development in all vocational and adult education credential programs is offered in almost every state in the United States. By credential laws and regulations, all teachers are required to be equipped with knowledge in curriculum development.

Curriculum development can be considered as both art and science although most scholars consider curriculum development as a process that can be described as more akin to art than science (Iwasiw, Goldenberg & Andrusyszyn, 2005, p. 2). Further, it is a complex process characterized by interaction, cooperation, change, and possibly conflict (Iwasiw et al., 2005, p. 2). Some argue that curriculum development has neither beginning nor end, indicating that curriculum is an ongoing activity in any established field (Iwasiw et al., 2005, p. 2). It is also true that curriculum development is influenced by personal interests, philosophies, judgments, and values. As I continue to teach courses such as the core course titled "Curriculum Development for Designated Subjects" in the state of California, I have examined and compared many books regarding curriculum development

1

available in the field of vocational and adult education including some international books in this field.

What I have found about these books on curriculum development is the sheer fact that most books reflect behavioral philosophy in curriculum development. These books address traditional aspects of curriculum development such as planning, designing, managing, and evaluating for a sound lesson plan. These approaches support behavioral philosophy in curriculum development. Some books even address Bloom's 1956 taxonomy, needs assessments, task analysis or even the four steps of instruction (e.g., motivation, presentation, homework, and follow-up). It is obvious all these approaches work well with behavioral philosophy. While behavioral philosophy in curriculum development is a well-established method, other philosophies, judgments, and values have been virtually ignored. In the field of vocational and adult education, not only do we need behavioral philosophy in guiding our teachers and/or administrators to develop curriculum, but also we need other philosophies such as humanistic, progressive, liberal, radical, and analytic philosophies. Although our adult learners do not oppose a behavioral philosophy, they embrace other philosophies such as humanistic and progressive philosophies. As adult learners learn to develop curricula to teach other adult learners, theories of adult learning can offer to help them develop sound curricula for other adult learners. Leaders in adult education indicate *andragogy* (*the art and science of helping adults learn*) reflects humanistic and progressive teaching philosophies. Therefore, other adult learning approaches together with the use of andragogy in curriculum development should be considered given the nature of our adult learners. This book has been written to provide a current, practical, international, and adult learning based approach to designing and developing curriculum in the field of vocational and adult education.

The demands of both public and private schools in America and society today are such that teachers with international, adult learning based curriculum skills are highly valued and this book seeks to provide a vital source for teachers who wish to develop their skills in the field of curriculum design and development in the larger field of vocational and adult education. As Zumwalt suggests, "Given the view that professional teachers should have the knowledge to enable them to create sound educational programs . . . it is essential that teachers have knowledge of some planning process that enables them to think about curriculum beyond the individual lesson" (as cited in Print, 1993, p. 93). To go beyond the individual lesson, professional teachers need to take into consideration different variables and models that can help them with their planning process. With this goal in mind, the contributors and editor of this book have addressed in detail how these variables and models can equip professional teachers with knowledge and skills to build sound, practical, adult learning based curriculum for adult learners.

In addition, this book seeks to address:

- How do you design meaningful curriculum for economically and culturally disadvantaged adult learners?
- How do you derive curriculum from adult learners themselves?
- What are the fundamentals of curriculum development?
- What are the generic models that can be applied to adult learners?
- What do you do to design and implement E-learning curriculum for adult learners?
- How do you use principles of adult learning to develop curriculum for adult learners?
- What about learners in the global community? How do they challenge curriculum developers in vocational and adult education?

These are but a few of the many questions we ask our adult educators when they are engaged in developing curriculum for other adult learners in the field. To help adult learners receive their teaching credentials and to enable them to teach their occupational skills to others in the field, such questions need to be addressed in detail. This book has provided answers to the above and other questions related to curriculum design and development in the larger field of vocational and adult education.

One final factor to consider when developing curricula for adult learners is that we draw adult learners from around the globe. These adult learners from the global community come to adult educators not just for teaching credentials. More importantly, they come to adult educators to acquire the basic knowledge and skills of curriculum development. To develop meaningful and practical curriculum for adult learners in the global community, one has to take into consideration theories and principles of adult learning—powerful approaches other than just a behavioral philosophy. As globalization brings different cultures together, adult learners are positioned in a global community, defying existing curriculum development approaches that may not serve them well. Over the years, the theories of adult learning have been applied to various fields. Why not use them for the sake of curriculum development in the field of adult education itself? They can prove to be a powerful tool in assisting curriculum developers design useful curricula for adult learners.

As I continue to teach curriculum development in the field, I also notice one phenomenon, that is, books on curriculum development have not been written by experts in the field of adult education. They have been written by people in other fields. To paint the picture bleaker, courses in curriculum development are not taught by people with a background in adult education, rather by people from other educational fields. Small wonder only behavioral philosophy has been taught. Should such a situation continue, we will definitely fail to serve both our educators of adults in training and our adult learners. To rectify such a situation in the field, both scholars and practitioners (who have taught adult learners around the globe) have contributed chapters to this book and to Volume II.

Chapters in Volume I focus not only on traditional approaches of curriculum development, but also on using principles of adult learning to develop curriculum for adult learners. Bierema (Chapter 1) discusses how effective educational design for adults considers multiple variables and requires reflective practice and environmental sensitivity. Her chapter addresses considerations for designing education for adults and proposes a holistic framework that considers the educator, the learner, the process, the context, and the method. In addition, she includes theoretically sound, practical recommendations for designing instructional programs for adults throughout.

Baumgartner (Chapter 2) discusses andragogy's place in curriculum development and instruction in a global community. She also explores approaches to curriculum development for adult learners in the global community.

Mott (Chapter 3) presents a unique approach to curriculum development, that is, to derive programs, courses, and syllabi from or with adult learners themselves. This chapter considers ways in which traditional curriculum development can be adapted to support learner involvement in the development process. The chapter begins with a brief overview of how social learning theory, constructivism, and collaborative learning models support learner-derived curriculum development. Case studies are then presented as successful examples of learner-derived curriculum development in informal, nonformal, and formal adult learning venues.

Banks and Nafukho (Chapter 4) seek to demonstrate how curriculum should be developed to distinguish among the various conditions that singularly or in combination attribute to the adult learners with diverse background needing special assistance. In addition, the chapter analyzes and synthesizes the place and function of the practice of education for adults with special needs in the global community. Their chapter also addresses specific models that adult educators can employ to develop curriculum for adult learners with special needs.

Cambiano (Chapter 5) addresses the importance of sequencing instruction in global learning environments. In doing so, she explores the theories, types and implications involved with sequencing instruction for adult learners in global learning communities. In addition, the following principles are addressed: (1) the educator's role in the teaching and learning process; (2) selecting content appropriate for adult learners; (3) sequencing instruction and its relationship to adult learning; and (4) sequencing instruction to promote learning through effective learning environments for adult learners in global learning communities.

Ziegler (Chapter 6) explores fundamental models of curriculum development and how the use of these models supports the work of adult educators in the global community. The chapter includes a description of a few different models and how these are applied in practice situations.

Daffron, Goulet, Gray, and Viada (Chapter 7) present strategic approaches of curriculum development for police officers and fire fighters who depend upon proper training, which can mean the difference between life and death for the public safety workers themselves and the public at large. Their chapter investigates what models are working and what changes ought to be made in the curriculum for these professionals.

Cochran (Chapter 8) discusses instructional strategies that are based on pragmatic and behaviorist theories. She discusses how the behaviorist instructional strategies associated with ADDIE (analyze, develop, design, implement and evaluation) have disappeared from international instruction. In doing so, Cochran shows that a relatively new learning theory, principles, and instructional strategies can provide educational processes that may be culture-free and effective in engaging adults in their own learning.

We will learn that curriculum development takes on new meaning according to educators' individual and collective values and beliefs about education, teaching, and learning. Our contributors maintain that curriculum development is shaped by contextual realities, and even politics. As globalization has become a reality, it is becoming all the more important that we address developing curriculum development for adult learners by crossing cultural boundaries, instructional design and the transactional adult learners, and curriculum development for other major cultures such as in China. As decentralization remains the norm in curriculum development in the Western culture, what about centralization that is extensively implemented in other cultures? Both American adult learners and adult learners from other countries need to be equipped with knowledge in curriculum development from other cultures.

Once adult learners have acquired the knowledge and skills on how to develop meaningful curriculum, they need to learn how to teach adult learners in the global community. They also need to learn methods of helping adults learn in the 21st century. Can the theories of adult learning be implemented in every culture around the globe? Such topics make this book especially relevant and compelling for today and the future.

This book is designed for the teacher-practitioner and is written from both a scholar and practitioner's perspective. The book falls naturally into two volumes.

Individual chapters can be selected according to readers' specific needs and interests.

References

Iwasiw, C. L., Goldenberg, D., & Andrusyszyn, M. A. (2005). *Curriculum development in nursing education*. Sudbury, MA: Jones & Bartlett Publishers.

Print, M. (1993). *Curriculum development and design*. Australia: Allen & Unwin.

Yuan, H. W. (2007). *Chinese proverbs*. Retrieved August 30, 2007, from http://www.wku.edu/~yuanh/China/proverbs/q.html.

Chapter 1
Principles of Instructional Design and Adult Learners
Laura L. Bierema

Abstract

Instructional design is not as simple as following a linear model of creating a lesson plan or discovering the perfect planning formula. Effective educational design for adults considers multiple variables and requires reflective practice, respect of learners, and environmental sensitivity. This chapter will address considerations for designing education for adults. It will propose a holistic framework that considers four key variables of the learning episode: the educator, the learner, the process, the context, and how the design and development methods can attend to these four variables. The chapter will challenge educators to be self-reflective and aware of how their values translate into designing and delivering instruction. It will bring the learner to the forefront and identify strategies for giving learners voice in instructional design. The chapter will address the process of learning and provide strategies for creating instruction that resonate with learners on multiple levels. The chapter will also attend to key issues of context that affect instructional design such as power relations, positionality, and place. Finally the chapter will speak to actual methods of instruction and how the variables of the educator, learner, process, and context come together in instructional design. The chapter will include theoretically sound, practical recommendations for designing instructional programs for adults throughout.

Introduction

There are plenty of traditional models that provide roadmaps of instructional design (e.g., Caffarella, 2002; Houle, 1974; Knowles,1950; Mager, 1997; Noe, 1999; Robinson & Robinson, 1995; Tyler, 1949). Mastering the ability to analyze learning needs, design, develop, implement, and evaluate an educational program are basic competencies for adult educators and human resource developers. What is less obvious and straightforward is authentically attending to diverse and sometimes competing needs and objectives. Educational contexts are dynamic, contested spaces characterized by power differentials and historical scars related to race, gender, and class. As educators, we have a responsibility to know our own values, biases, and positionalites, and understand how they intersect with other stakeholders in the instructional process. This chapter begins the conversation around instructional design for diverse adult learners. It is not intended to introduce the next model of instructional design, but rather to make the one(s) that you use more robust, humane, representative, and responsible.

Introduction of the Framework

This chapter introduces a framework that brings adult learners' and educators' concerns to the forefront in the instructional design process. It considers the educators and how their values and being impact instructional design decisions and implementation. The framework reveres the learners and strives to understand their motivations, challenges, and goals. It also considers the process of learning and how best to foster it for a range of diverse learners and learning goals. The framework acknowledges the power of context and the importance of attending to interpersonal and social dynamics in educational programming. Finally, the framework is built around considering the educator, the learner, the process, and the context in the selection of instructional design and delivery methods. It is at the point of design all of these variables converge. The goal is to meld them in a way that facilitates optimal learning for diverse learners.

Although adult learning has been systematically studied since the 1920s, there is no single explanation or theory of adult learning, nor is there a single preferred instructional design method. This chapter integrates a range of adult learning theories and shows how they can be applied in practice. Educators seeking to deepen their theoretical knowledge should consult *Learning in Adulthood: A Comprehensive Guide* (Merriam, Caffarella, & Baumgartner, 2007) for a thorough explanation of adult learning theory. Robinson's (1995) *Helping Adults Learn and Change* is also a practical resource. This chapter presents a framework organizing adult learning theory according to five categories including the educator, learner, learning process, context, and program development and delivery. This framework is an artificial structure proposed to enhance our understanding of relevant theory and practice. Adult learning is a complex process that may involve all of these categories at the same moment. The framework is summarized in Table 1.1.

The Educator

The educator is one of the "who's" of instructional design, the learner being another. Being an effective educator is not an end. Rather, it is a process that high-

Table 1.1

Framework for Adult Education

The Educator (The "Who")	The Learner (The "Who")

• Reflective Practice
• Self-Knowledge
  o Beliefs
  o Values
• Educational Stance
  o Philosophical insight
  o Teaching style
• Lifelong Learning
	• Participation and Motivation
	  o Life focused
	  o Intrinsic motivation
	• Characteristics of Adult Learners
	  o Andragogy as preferred learning mode
	  o Relevant and timely learning
	  o Self-directed learning
	  o Experiential learning
	  o Diverse learning styles

The Learning Process (The "How")	**The Learning Context (the "Where")**

• Coping with Change
• Making Meaning out of Ideas and Experience
  o Critical reflection
  o Transformative learning
• Whole Person Learning
  o Spirituality
  o Affect and emotion
  o Somatic, embodied learning
  o Narrative learning
	• Place
	  o Physical
	  o Psychological
	• Positionality
	  o Fluid, changing
	  o Acknowledges we are all raced, classed, and gendered
	• Power
	  o Exercised through relationships
	  o All have a degree of it
	• Pedagogy
	• Multicultural Issues
	• Inclusiveness

The Program Design and Delivery **(the "Who, What, Where and How")** Instructional techniques integrating the educator, learner, learning process, and context.	

quality educators pursue throughout their lifetimes. The best educators embody Shon's (1983) reflective practitioner stance through their continual examination and adjustment of practice. This reflective practice gives the educators a keen sense of self and how their values translate into educational thought and action. Effective adult educators understand and continually asses their educational stance which includes philosophical insight and teaching style.

Self-knowledge

Reflective practice and self-knowledge are fundamental competencies of effective educators. The adult education literature is biased more toward learners and learning than educators. Notable exceptions include the work of Elias and Merriam (2005) and Zinn (1991) on educational philosophy, Brookfield's (1995) work on becoming a critically reflective educator, and Daloz's (1986, 1988, 1999) work on mentoring. The reflective work of educators should be a continual process that helps them be cognizant of their philosophy, values, mental models, and positionality. Palmer (1998), in his inspiring book, *The Courage to Teach,* observes:

> *Teaching, like any truly human activity, emerges from one's inwardness, for better or worse. As I teach, I project the condition of my soul onto my students, my subject, and our way of being together. The entanglements I experience in the classroom are often no more or less than the convolutions of my inner life. Viewed from this angle, teaching holds a mirror to the soul. If I am willing to look in that mirror and not run from what I see, I have a chance to gain self-knowledge—and knowing myself is a crucial to good teaching as knowing my students and my subject.*
>
> *In fact, knowing my students and my subject depends heavily on self-knowledge. When I do not know myself, I cannot know who my students are. I will see them through a glass darkly, in the shadows of my unexamined life— and when I cannot see them clearly, I cannot teach them well. When I do not know myself, I cannot know my subject—not at the deepest levels of embodied, personal meaning. I will know it only abstractly, from a distance, a congeries of concepts as far removed from the world as I am from personal truth.*
>
> *The work required to "know thyself" is neither selfish nor narcissistic. Whatever self-knowledge we attain as teachers will serve our students and our scholarship well. Good teaching requires self-knowledge: It is a secret hidden in plain sight.* (pp. 2-3)

Self-knowledge is not enough, and this aspect of the framework also requires the educator to be continually engaged in self-development and growth. That means learning new things, acknowledging and learning from mistakes, reflecting on practice, changing one's practice, and continually stretching one's teaching self to be an example for learners.

Educational Stance

In addition to cultivating self-knowledge, effective educators consider how their philosophy and style affect their teaching. Merriam and Brockett (1997) explain that "A philosophy of education is a conceptual framework embodying certain values and principles that renders the education process meaningful" (p. 28). Elias and Merriam (1995) observe:

> *The educator is generally more interested in skills than in principles, in means than in ends, in details than in the whole picture. The philosophy of adult education does not equip a person with knowledge about what to teach, how to teach, or how to organize a program. It is more concerned with the why of education and with the logical analysis of the various elements of the educational process.* (p. x.)

Elias and Merriam (1995) argue that understanding educational philosophy distinguishes professional educators from paraprofessionals and beginning teachers. True professionals not only know what to do, but also why they do it. They seamlessly merge theory and practice and embody truly reflective practice. Being more cognizant of philosophy also helps bridge theory and practice (Merriam & Brockett, 1997). Educators interested in assessing their individual philosophy should refer to Zinn's (1991) Philosophy of Adult Education Inventory (PAEI). This instrument will give insight as to philosophical teaching inclinations according to liberal, progressive, behaviorist, humanistic, or radical orientations.

The educator is the first aspect of the framework that also considers the learner, the learning process, the learning context, and how program design and development can address these variables. Effective educators are committed to an ongoing process of reflective practice that yields self-knowledge and builds their educational stance. Effective educators are the epitome of lifelong learners and through their learning engagement continually improve their ability to serve learners.

The Learner

The learner makes up another "who" of instructional design and next aspect of the framework. To effectively value learners and meet their needs, it is important for instructional designers to understand why adults participate in adult education, and what they need.

Participation in Adult Education

Participation in adult education activities is widespread in the United States and has steadily increased since the late sixties. Boshier (1991) has developed the Education Participation Scale (EPS) which provides insight to motivational orientations of adult learners. Merriam et al. (2007) note that the profile of the typical adult learner has remained consistent since participation was first systematically studied in 1965 by Johnstone and Rivera. Participants in formal education tend to be white, middle class, employed, younger and better educated than the nonparticipant, and seeking employment-related learning.

According to the National Center for Education Statistics (2004-2005), 44% of adults reported participation in formal adult educational activities over a 12-month period ending in spring 2005, excluding full-time only enrollments in college/university or vocational/technical credential programs. The majority of participation reported was work-related courses or training to maintain or improve current skills or knowledge, or to attain new skills. Adults also engage in English as a second language (ESL), adult basic education (ABE), general education development (GED), credential programs, apprenticeship programs, and personal development courses. ESL and GED participants reported taking classes to improve how they felt about themselves and to make day-to-day living easier as the key reasons for doing so. The survey also asked participants about distance education and informal learning activities for personal interest. Approximately one-third (32%) of adults reported using some type of distance education. From the survey we can conclude that the majority of adult learning is work-related to either enhance current skill or gain new knowledge, ESL and GED education is important to a sense of self-efficacy, and increasingly adults are using distance education in meeting their learning goals.

Characteristics of Adult Learners

Adults have high expectations for timely and relevant learning. The concept of andragogy has influenced scores of adult educators and instructional designs. Adult learning tends toward self-direction and is highly experiential. Although adult learning has common characteristics, the diversity of learning styles and needs must be acknowledged and valued in the learning process. Adulthood is full of multiple demands so learning will most likely be sought when it is relevant to a life issue or problem. The learning must also be about something adults care about and find useful. Adult motivation to learn is likely to be intrinsic, that is, they are learning to meet unmet needs, resolve unwanted conditions, or reach desired goals. Robinson (1995) suggests five purposes for adult learning: (1) personal growth and development, (2) personal and social improvement, (3) organizational effectiveness, (4) cultivation of the intellect, and (5) social transformation.

Early theoretical work in adult education focused on describing the learner. These contributions dominated from the 1960s through the 1980s and include Houle's (1961) work on understanding learner goals, Knowles' (1970) popularization of the andragogy concept, the advancement of self-directed learning as a key feature of adult learning (Knowles, 1975), and the development of lesser known theories such as Knox's (1977) proficiency theory, and McClusky's (1950) theory of margin. For a full discussion of adult learning theory see Merriam, Caffarella, and Baumgartner (2007).

Much of adult learning theory and practice is grounded in the concept of andragogy (Knowles, 1970), a process of catering to adult learners that is contrasted with pedagogy which has traditionally focused on child learners. Pedagogy expects passive learner dependence on the teacher who takes full responsibility for making decisions regarding learning (what should be learned, when, how, and why). Learners have little experience to use as a resource for learning and thus defer to the experience of the teacher and other educational resources. Pedagogy expects learners to become ready to learn when told since they are viewed as externally motivated. The learning topics will be subject-centered and selected by the teacher.

Andragogy, on the other hand, views the learner as self-directed, capable of making decisions about what should be learned, as well as actively constructing meaning rather than passively receiving it from others. The term *andragogy* was popularized by Malcolm Knowles and its practices are grounded in humanism and the idea that learners are autonomous and desiring of self-development and improvement. Andragogy acknowledges that learners perform a variety of life roles and have a vast reservoir of experience from which to draw for educational resources. Andragogical educators strive to honor and include learner experience in the learning process. They recognize that adult learners become ready to learn when they experience a need to know something in order to perform more effectively in some aspect of their lives and the focus of their learning is life-centered, not subject-centered. Motivation to learn comes from internal motivators (self-esteem, recognition, quality of life, confidence, etc.) and each individual has a unique way of learning. Andragogy has been critiqued for being individualistic in nature, ignoring social context, and lacking a social change imperative, yet it has had a major impact on the design and delivery of adult education programs. Refer to Table 1.2 for a summary of key points related to adult learners.

In addition to understanding the various theories and practices that provide insight about adult learners, we can also be informed by understanding learning styles. Jarvis (2006) suggests that learning begins with the senses (sound, sight, smell, taste, and touch) and that these sensations are transformed into knowledge, skills, attitudes, values, and emotions. Adults tend to have a sensory learning style preference such as visual, auditory, or tactile, and Kolb (1991) has suggested that there are experiential learning styles as well. Kolb presents a learning cycle where learners involve themselves fully, openly, and without bias in new experiences (Concrete Experience), reflect on and observe these experiences from many perspectives (Reflective Observation), create concepts that integrate their observations in to logically sound theories (Abstract Conceptualization), and use these

Table 1.2

Major Principles and Practices of Adult Learning

- Adults can and do want to learn, regardless of their age.
- Adults have a rich background of knowledge and experience. They tend to learn best when this experience is acknowledged and when new information builds on their past knowledge and experience.
- Adults are motivated to learn by a mixture internal and external factors.
- All adults have differing preferred styles of learning.
- For the most part, adults are pragmatic in their learning. They tend to want to apply their learning to real life.
- Adults are not likely to willingly engage in learning unless the content is meaningful to them.
- Adults come to a learning situation with their own personal goals and objectives, which may or may not be the same as those that underlie the learning situation.
- Adults prefer to be actively involved in the learning process than be passive recipients of knowledge. In addition, they want the opportunity to be supportive of each other in the learning process.
- Adults learn both in independent, self-reliant modes and in interdependent, connected, and collaborative ways.
- Much of what adults learn tends to have an effect on others (for instance, on work colleagues and family).
- Adults are more receptive to the learning process in situations that are both physically and psychologically comfortable.
- Adult life roles affect what, how, and where adults learn.
- Adults are often internally asking the questions, *"Why am I learning this?"* and *"How will I use this in the future?"* Be sure that this information is covered.
- Adults need time built in for reflection.
- Adults expect the content to resonate with their experience. Often the learners will make these connections themselves, if given the reflection space.
- Adult learning needs are diverse. One size does not fit all.
- Adults will give you feedback on the learning if asked. Conduct frequent process checks to ensure that learning needs are being met. Ask, "How could your learning be better supported by yourself? Your colleagues? Your learning facilitators?" Be sure to respond to any feedback offered by the participants.
- Adults need a varied format to attend to multiple learning styles.
- Adults expect to have input to the design and flow of the learning.
- Adults like to link their learning to a wider context. Incorporate this need into your design.

Adapted in part from Caffarella (1994).

theories to make decisions and solve problems (Active Experimentation). Tendency toward various locations within the learning cycle results in a learning style. Strategies for addressing both learners and learning styles will be revisited in the final section of the framework. Much has been written about experiential learning. Fenwick (2003) should be consulted for a critical review of these theories.

So far, this chapter has introduced "the who" with its focus on the educator and learner as key participants in the instructional process. Understanding the learner's motivation and characteristics is important to creating educational experiences that resonate with the learner. Many adult educators' knowledge of adult learning stops with their understanding of learner participation and principles of andragogy. Although necessary knowledge, it is not sufficient for creating effective instructional design. The next aspect of the framework introduces "the how" or process of learning, key information for serious educators.

The Process

The process aspect of the framework describes "the how" of learning. The learning process is usually inspired by change and is a key coping strategy for adults. Learning can be psychomotor, cognitive, or affective. Robinson (1995) suggests that the learning process begins with awareness of a need or problem followed by investigation of how the problem might be resolved (reading, taking a class, or talking with someone). Next the learner mentally practices the new behavior weighing the advantages and disadvantages of adopting a new way of thinking, feeling, or acting. Next the learner tries out the new thinking, feeling, or acting, and finally the learning is solidified and becomes learned behavior.

Five orientations to learning include behaviorist, humanist, cognitivist, social cognitivist, and constructivist (Merriam et al., 2007). All of these theories have influenced adult education and have a role in instructional design. Constructivism heavily influences adult education, particularly experiential learning, transformational learning, reflective practice, communities of practice, and situated learning (Merriam et al., 2007). The learning process is also most effective when it engages the whole person: body, mind and soul. Jarvis (1992, p. 11) explains, "Learning . . . is about the continuing process of making sense of everyday experience." Adults employ myriad strategies to create this sense-making process throughout their lifetimes. Illeris (2002) suggests that the process of learning involves three learning dimensions: cognition, emotion, and society. The cognitive aspect involves knowledge and skills and the emotional aspect involves feelings and motivation. The social dimension accounts for the interactions with others and how they impact the learning process.

Coping with Change

When considering adult learning, we must acknowledge the role of change in adult life. Adulthood is characterized by constant change which may create identity crisis, challenge relationships, and impact a person's sense of legacy. Learning is often in anticipation of or in response to change and is a fundamental coping mechanism when confronted with change. Life changes that might inspire learning include: leaving home for the first time, becoming a college or graduate student, falling in love, leaving a relationship, losing a loved one, awakening to a cause, starting a family, receiving a promotion, getting fired, experiencing a change in financial circumstances, traveling abroad, reorganizing or downsizing at work, and the list goes on. Some of these changes could be described as transformational, that is, they evoke a process of change and shift an adult's way of thinking and being in the world. Change often requires adults to engage in a process of understanding the meaning of their new life circumstances. Given the shifting workplace environment and the significant number of adults who engage in work-related learning, there is no shortage of change-inspired learning that occurs through organization development interventions and workplace changes.

Meaning Making

Adults learn through making meaning of life situations and reorganizing their understandings of ideas, and at times changing their behaviors and beliefs as a result of learning. When adults construct meaning, they engage in a process of critical reflection. Sometimes the learning can even be transformational. Transformational learning changes how we think and act by causing our mental models or assumptions to be challenged and changed. Several models and theories exist to explain the learning process. These include change theories; transformative learning; formal, informal and nonformal learning; spirituality; affective learning; brain function and cognition; somatic or embodied learning; and narrative learning. Merriam et al. (2007) provide a comprehensive review of these contemporary learning theories.

One of the most popular theories describing the learning process is transformational learning (Freire, 1970; Merriam 1993, 2001; Mezirow, 1978, 1990, 2000). Transformational learning centers on change and learning that produces change. Transformational learning changes how we know and view ourselves, versus informational learning which changes what we know, while the view of self remains intact. Transformational learning can be gradual or sudden. When we think of the process of transformational learning, we are interested in how changes occur that cause transformation. Although transformation is an attractive prospect for instructional designers, it is not something easily designed for or predictable. Educational design aimed at fundamentally changing learner's thoughts or actions also raises several ethical issues.

Taylor's (2000) conclusions about transformative learning offer important insights for facilitating the learning process, whether or not it is transformative. Taylor concluded from research on Mezirow's model that feelings play a key role in transformative learning. He also surmised that relationships are very important to process and that context and culture play an important role in transformative learning.

Whole Person Learning

New perspectives on the process of adult learning are burgeoning. They extend beyond cognitive learning and include spirituality, affective or emotion-based learning, somatic or embodied learning, and narrative. Strategies for each are listed in Table 1.3.

Spirituality in adult education means responding to the human need to find meaning, understand the self, and connect with the natural world. Adult educators have a role to play in facilitating the active engagement of learners with crucial life questions, justice, and meaning. Spirituality does not mean creating a platform for proselytizing and is not necessarily religious. It means connecting learning to what one values and using it to deepen meaning.

Considering emotion or affect is important to adult learning because emotions can either motivate or impede learning. "Rationalist doctrine" influences most educational programs. In other words, emphasis is placed on factual information and the use of reason and reflection to learn from experience. Stimulating the affective dimension of learning is vital for adult education. In fact, some believe that adult education is affective learning, the purpose being to help adults draw meaning out of life experiences (Lindeman, 1961). Therefore, the adult educator's understanding and integration of the affective domain in program development is paramount.

Somatic learning explores the connection between learning and the body by integrating "as an existential whole, the experiential history of individuals with their current experience. It implies an education that trusts individuals to learn from their ability to attend and to listen to the information they are receiving from the interaction of self with the environment" (Sellers-Young, 1998, p. 176). This is counter to how most adults have been taught to use only their minds in learning. Somatic or embodied knowing is experiential knowledge that involves senses, perception, and mind/body action and reaction (Matthews, 1998). Western culture has been dominated by the separation of cognitive knowledge from embodied knowledge and the distrust and denigration of bodily knowing (Simon, 1998).

Table 1.3

New Adult Learning Theory Applications

Creating Transformative Learning Conditions	Creating Safe Spaces for Spiritual Learning
• Create safe, open, trusting space. • Allow for participation, collaboration, exploration, critical reflection and feedback. • Educator relinquishes "position power." • Use first names. • Identify learning styles. • Foster group ownership and individual agency. • Place self and other educators at center of own learning in critically reflective social group. • Process feelings. • Critically reflect. • Discuss value-laden content. • Adopt a teacher-learner-centered approach versus a learner-centered or "learning-centered" approach. • Further explore the teacher-learner relationship. • Learn more about educational helping relationships. • Manage power differentials productively. (Taylor, 2000)	• Make space to explore spiritual learning. • Practice dialogical communication. • Give learners a choice—not everyone may want to focus on the spiritual. • Share your own spiritual experiences with learning. • Cultivate a deep sense of trust. • Engage learners cognitively, effectively and spiritually. • Consider the sociocultural aspects of learners' being (the personal, the cultural, the structural, the political, and the sacred). • Bring our own authentic selves with us to the learning environment as instructors.
Resources and Ideas for Affective Learning	Starter Ideas for Somatic Learning
• Critical questioning • Role-playing • Simulations • Journaling • Silence	• Build a model of a process or procedure. • Physically manipulate components of a process or system. • Create large pictograms and peripherals.

Resources and Ideas for Affective Learning—continued

- Reading materials
- Reaction paper—immediate reaction to an issue
- Reflection
- Critical incidents
- Service-learning activities
- Process checks
- Sensory-based learning activities
- Drawing
- Singing
- Paper mache or playdough
- Use of symbols (art, imagination, dreams, metaphors, etc.)
- Memory and imagination exercises
- Improvisation
- Case studies
- Field trips
- Ropes-type courses
- Story-telling
- Educational biographies
- Challenging physical adventures

(Meier, 2000)

Starter Ideas for Somatic Learning—continued

- Act out a process, system, or set of concepts.
- Have an experience and then talk about and reflect on it.
- Complete a project that requires physical activity.
- Do an active learning exercise (a simulation, a learning game, etc.).
- Take a field trip and then write, draw, and talk about what was learned.
- Interview people outside the class.
- In teams, create active learning exercises for the whole class.

Narrative Learning

Storytelling has been used throughout time to transfer knowledge and culture. There are many indigenous cultures where knowledge is exclusively transferred through the oral tradition of stories. Storytelling is enjoying a renaissance within many organizations. Storytelling helps us:

- Unearth and transfer knowledge resident in the minds of the people who are working with processes day to day.
- Reinforce and grow certain aspects of organizational culture and behavior, as well as to plant the seeds for changing others.
- Infuse people with a vision that inspires creativity and aligned action.
- Build stronger work relationships.
- Build understanding and bridges between diverse populations.
- Discover how people perceive and interact with specific issues.
- Fan the flames of what is working within groups and organizations.

More recently, developments in mind/body research (Weiss, 2001) and feminist and postmodernist discourse (Davis, 1997; Green, 2000) have turned the attention of adult educators to somatic learning. Our bodies are a source of knowledge if we listen to them. Somatic learning strategies include helping learners tune into the physicality of learning.

Narrative learning parallels a resurgence of interest in the power of story, not only in our communities but in our organizations as well. We are discovering story as a way to uncover, create, and share knowledge. Leaders are exploring using story to reinforce and transform culture. There is renewed interest in how story might be used to build bridges between diverse groups and cultures, as our technologies move us more and more into the reality of global community and interdependence.

The "how" or process of adult learning helps adults cope with change through meaning making and attending to the whole person in the learning situation. This chapter has now considered "the who" of instructional design, including the educator and learner, as well as "the how" of learning by attending to the processes by which adults cope with changes and create meaning. Next we turn to the context that examines the sociocultural location of learning and how that impacts adult learners.

Context

Context is the social system that permeates the thinking and actions of all human beings within a particular social situation such as a classroom, school, organization, community, or nation. Context has several attributes including place, positionality, power, and pedagogy. Place (or environment) is a multifaceted physical and psychological space in which social action is situated. It may incorporate physical conditions, political conditions, economic conditions, power dynamics, and other influences that impact the people occupying that space. Place may also require its inhabitants to modify their thinking and action when they are occupying the space.

Positionality is the way "people are defined not in terms of fixed identities, but by their location within shifting networks of relationships, which can be analyzed and changed" (Maher & Tetreault, 1994, p. 164). Positionality refers to: ableness, age, class, culture, gender, power, race, religion, sexual orientation, and so forth. It is "a concept that acknowledges that we are all raced, classed, and gendered, and that these identities are relational, complex, and fluid positions rather than essential qualities" (Martin & Van Gunten, 2002, p. 46). We all live framed by socially constructed positions, wanted or not. Such automatic categorization is embedded in our society and is at work in adult education. A person's success within a given context depends on interaction with other individuals in the context. For instance, a woman of color may find her efforts to advance in an organization being constantly thwarted by a culture that functions to promote and protect white men. White male participants in training may be given more attention by the instructor who calls on them more often, makes eye contact more frequently, and encourages their participation more regularly than the women.

Power has been defined as the ability to impose one's will on others, even amid resistance. More positive definitions of power assume that it is the ability to influence others or to bring about change. The exercise of power happens through relationships. All individuals have some degree of power, although it may be equal or unequal, stable, shifting, or changing. Power takes various forms and is fluid, shifting depending on place and positionality. Power is reciprocal, although not usually equally so. An employer has certain power to control wages and working conditions. Employees can reciprocate through absenteeism, work slowdowns, or union formation, but these reciprocal exercises of power may not be equal to the employer's ability to affect the worker's job status.

Instructional designers have an opportunity to attend to contextual issues through pedagogy that acknowledges and accounts for the dynamics of social interaction: place, positionality, and power. When designing instruction, it is important for educators and learners to understand various positionalities in their learning environments (Tisdell, 1995). Positionality may result in an individual being marginalized or privileged, depending on the context.

The concept of positionality has led many scholars in adult education to examine their own positions (Brookfield, 1990; Johnson-Bailey & Cervero, 1998, 2001; Tisdell, 1995, 2001). Such studies (Johnson-Bailey & Cervero, 1998, 2001; Tisdell, 1995, 2001) have examined the social positions of gender, race, class and sexuality in various combinations, because positionality is not an identity, it is how identities work together to affect a person's social status. Unfortunately, when we address sociocultural contexts and the social roles of individuals in adult higher education, key factors are often ignored. Merriam and Caffarella (1999) observe "not everyone wants to admit that the issues of race, ethnicity, gender, and sexual orientation have or should have any educational relevance" (p. 127). Social context and positionality are important issues to consider in contemporary education and in the learning process of adults because they impact adult life. Some people are oppressed by other individuals or society because of their social positions. It is, therefore, necessary to acknowledge them in education. Some questions worthy of considering as you consider your own role as an educator would be: What is your positionality? How does your positionality impact your learning? How does your positionality impact your teaching?

Although contexts and experiences differ, they hold the potential for learning and in even organizing our learning as described by Merriam and Caffarella (1999):

Adult learning in context has a structural dimension which acknowledges that our society has become highly multicultural and diverse and that political and economic conditions often shape the learning experience. It is no longer a question of whether in adult learning situations we need to address issues of race, class, gender, culture, ethnicity, and sexual orientation, but rather a question of how should we deal with these issues, both in terms of who presently constitutes the majority of learners, at least in formal adult learning activities, and who should be involved. We need to know the backgrounds and experiences of our learners, as individual learners, but also as member of socially and culturally constructed groups such as women and men; poor, middle-class, and rich; and black, white, and brown. These socially constructed notions of who our learners are and we are as educators and subsequent power dynamics should be given the same attention in teaching and learning, planning, and administrative functions of the technology of our practice. (p. 196)

Effective instructional designers will consider contextual factors in their work. There are also strategies for promoting inclusive learning contexts that deserve notice. Mindful educators must take account of both their individual positionality and that of their students and how privilege and power play out in the learning experience. When designing with respect to context, educators need to be mindful of Tisdell's (1995) *Levels of Inclusivity of Curriculum and Pedagogy*. She suggests that instructors should create programs that address all three levels. Level 1 reflects the diversity of participants in the learning activity. Level 2 attends to the diversity of the institutional context that is sponsoring the activity, as well as the wider and immediate contexts in which the participants live and work. Level 3 reflects in some way the changing needs of an increasingly diverse society.

There is an increasing body of multicultural adult education literature. Within the context frame, educators must acknowledge that curricular decisions are political and that decisions about content and materials is driven by the instructor's philosophical outlook, values, and positionality. Creating inclusive environments for adults requires that educators consider the specific learning environment, the institution sponsoring the educational activity, society at large, and the relationship of these contexts to one another (Tisdell, 1995). To achieve inclusive adult education, educators must think about what "inclusive" means and carefully consider curriculum design for given learning activities. Curriculum should be evaluated to asses how it implicitly or explicitly contributes to challenging structured power relations based on class, gender, and race, and to assess whether materials examine issues form the viewpoint of unequal power relations. Materials should also be evaluated to see whether they include diverse content with regard to race, class and gender. Teaching strategies also deserve scrutiny to evaluate whether they are contributing to challenging structured power relations based on gender, race and class or if they are simply reinforcing the status quo. Teaching methods should be incorporated that facilitate inclusive learning among diverse learners (Brookfield, 1987; Caffarella, 1992; Cassara, 1990; Merriam, Caffarella, & Baumgartner, 2007; Shor, 1992; Tisdell, 1995). Finally it is important to reflect on how your own unconscious behavior in the learning environment contributes to challenging or reproducing society's unequal power relations.

Tisdell offers the following strategies for creating inclusive learning environments:

1. Integrate affective and experiential knowledge with theoretical concepts.
2. Pay attention to the power relations inherent in knowledge production.
3. Be aware that participants are positioned differently in relationship to each other and to the knowledge being acquired.
4. Acknowledge the power disparity between the teacher/facilitator and the students.
5. Identify all stakeholders and their positionality in the educational program.
6. Consider the levels of inclusivity and the levels of contexts involved in the educational activity.
7. Consider how curricular choices implicitly or explicitly contribute to challenging structured power relations.
8. Adopt emancipatory teaching strategies.
9. Be conscious of the ways in which unconscious behavior contributes to challenging or reproducing unequal power relations.
10. Build a community based on both openness and intellectual rigor to create a democratic classroom.

Attending to context in instructional design is imperative in increasingly diverse and global settings. Instructional designers must consider the dynamics of place, positionality, and power when creating learning experiences and rely on a pedagogy that promotes inclusion and sensitivity to diversity. The next section addresses how to put the framework into practice through program development and delivery.

Program Development and Delivery

Lawson (1998) notes that successful program development depends on taking a systematic approach to delivering programming that is effective for both the participants and the organization. Programs designed to correspond with the

Table 1.4

Comparison of Program Planning Models

Tyler's Questions (1949)	Knowles's Model (1970)	Houle's Framework (1974)	▶
1. What educational purposes should the school seek to attain? 2. What educational experiences can be provided that are likely to attain these purposes? 3. How can these educational experiences be effectively organized? 4. How can we determine whether these purposes are being attained?	1. Assess needs and interests in program planning. 2. Define purposes and objectives. 3. Design a comprehensive program. 4. Operate a comprehensive program. 5. Evaluate a comprehensive program.	1. Identify a possible educational activity. 2. Make a decision to proceed. 3. Refine and identify objectives. 4. Design a suitable format. 5. Fit the format into larger patterns of life. 6. Put the plan into effect. 7. Measure and appraise the results.	▶

organization's strategy and employees' needs are most effective. Attention paid to the elements of the framework proposed in this chapter (educator, learner, process, and context) will facilitate this process. These variables converge in the planning where educational programs are designed, developed, and delivered. As instructional designers, we must consider our intended outcomes of the educational program. Typical purposes include encouraging individual growth and development, addressing practical problems and issues of adult life, preparing for current and future work opportunities, adapting to change, and examining societal and global issues.

Nearly all instructional models incorporate the classical steps of analyzing needs and selecting solutions, designing and developing non-training solutions, deriving instructional outcomes, designing and developing instruction, implementing instruction, and monitoring and improving the process (Mager, 1997). The instructional design that is the framework of programming is rooted in program planning theory. Classical, rational program planning models developed by Ralph Tyler (1949) and Malcolm Knowles (1950) have been widely influential in

Table 1.4

extended from previous page

Instructional Systems Development (ISD) or ADDIE Model	Sork's Summary of Models (1997)
1. Analyze. 2. Design. 3. Develop. 4. Implement. 5. Evaluate.	1. Honor the learners' experience, perspective, and expectations. 2. Recognize the importance of diversity. 3. Involve stakeholders in planning. 4. Understand the importance of context in which planning occurs. 5. Base programs on the needs of learners. 6. Clarify the aims or goals of the workshop. 7. Incorporate workshop processes that actively involve learners. 8. Choose facilitators or instructors and instructional resources with great care. 9. Promote application of learning as a central themes. 10. Attend carefully to administrative details. 11. Care for the physical and emotional needs of participants. 12. Assess program outcomes in addition to learner satisfaction.

the practice of designing instructional programs. Refer to Table 1.4 for a summary of instructional design models.

This chapter does not intend to offer yet another instructional design model. Rather, its goal is to address issues of import when designing education for adult learners. Several models exist that more-or-less propose the following prescribed steps of analysis, design, implementation, and evaluation. As mentioned at the beginning of this chapter, following these steps is a basic educational design competency. Yet, models for design do not begin to capture the complexity of designing education for adults. Cervero and Wilson (1994) have criticized these classical instructional design models for being too technical and rational. Their concern is that these models do not accurately reflect reality because they ignore the human element of power dynamics and the negotiation of interests in the planning process. Cervero and Wilson argue that the program planner's role is to negotiate often disparate and incompatible interests while simultaneously mitigating power dynamics. Nowhere in the Tyler or Knowles models is such haggling addressed. For instance, management may want to organize a training to address a performance problem, when in reality training will not resolve the issue because it is a result of a bad managerial decision. Program planners often find themselves confronted with the delicate task of investigating underlying assumptions that educational programming is an appropriate course of action. When educational programs are not the best choice, planners must diplomatically nudge clients toward alternative interventions, which can be a political tangle. Finally, even when everyone agrees on the purpose of a program, the content and instructional design are often compromised to satisfy the interests of all stakeholders.

Cervero and Wilson (2006) follow the traditional design process, but inject the democratic negotiation of interests and power relations into their model as summarized below.

1. Negotiate the program's needs assessment.
    - Decide whose interests matter and assess their needs.
    - Connect stakeholders needs to the historical and social context.
    - Anticipate how power relations frame assessment.
    - Democratically negotiate needs.
2. Negotiate the programs educational, management, and political objectives.
    - Prioritize educational, management and political objectives.
    - Negotiate objectives before, during and after the program.
    - Anticipate how power relations frame the negotiation of objectives.
    - Democratically negotiate objectives.
3. Negotiate the program's instructional design and implementation.
    - Manage the politics of selecting and organizing content.
    - Manage the politics of selecting formats and instructional techniques.
    - Manage the politics of selecting and preparing instructional leaders.
    - Democratically negotiate the instructional design and implementation.
4. Negotiate the program's administrative organization and operation.
    - Finance the message.
    - Market the message.
    - Use program location to work the message.
    - Democratically administer programs.
5. Negotiate the program's formal and informal evaluation.
    - Evaluate programs based on educational, management and political objectives.
    - Manage the politics of evidence and criteria.
    - Anticipate how power relations frame program evaluation.
    - Democratically evaluate program objectives. (pp. 105-106)

No single formula exists for creating powerful programs that will maximize learning for all learners. Yet, planners can do several things to ensure that each participant has an opportunity to learn from the experience. I work to answer three simple questions or what I call the "POP" (purpose, outcomes, process): *What is the overarching purpose of the educational program?* The *purpose* is the overarching goal and should be established with the learners and context in mind. *What are the key learning and institutional objectives?* The *objectives* should attend to needs of the learner, educator, and context and incorporate the various learning domains and orientations (affective, behavioral, and cognitive) and accommodate diverse learning styles (sensory or experiential). *What is the best process for attaining the purpose and objectives that is sensitive to diverse learners and learning needs?* The *process* should maximize different learning procedures as outlined under "The Process" section of this chapter and be sensitive to adult learners and context.

Concurrent with determination of purpose, outcomes, and process for the educational program, it is important for the designer to consider the elements of the framework (the educator, learner, process, and context). One easily overlooked means of doing this is in the creation of learning objectives. Planners tend to favor cognitive learning objectives with less focus on behavioral or affective goals. This is a mistake that will leave most adults dissatisfied with their learning experience. To tend effectively to diverse learners and learning processes, a blend is imperative. In addition to favoring cognitive learning goals, most instruction does not incorporate reflection which aids in constructing meaning. The opportunity to reflect on learning is key for adults and should be built into the learning objectives as an important affective goal.

We have already discussed the importance of providing a diverse array of instructional strategies. Adult learners do not respond favorably to constant lecture. Research has also shown that passive instructional strategies, such as lecture, are less effective at helping learners retain information. We can also think about instructional techniques according to goals outlined in Table 1.5 according to affective, behavioral, and cognitive learning domains.

According to Caffarella, instructional techniques can also be selected according to the activity level, which should be varied. A blend of low, medium, and high activity levels during the session will keep learners active and engaged with the process as outlined in Table 1.6.

Learning style should also be considered when designing education. Designers should pay attention to the senses in the learning process, balancing visual, auditory, and tactile learning activities. Consideration should also be given to enhancing experiential learning for a range of learners. Kolb's Learning Style Inventory (1991) provides useful insight and has implications for instructional design, based on the learning cycle.

Table 1.5

Instructional Strategy Based on Learning Goals

Affective	Behavioral	Cognitive
Critical incident	Case study	Lecture
Debate	Game	Panel
Reflective practice	In-basket	Group discussion
Observation	Demonstration	Buzz group
Dialogue	Simulation	Reaction panel
Silence	Trial and error	Screened speech
Role playing	Skill practice	Symposium
Dialogue	Behavior modeling	Listening group
Simulation	Observation	Dialogue
Group discussion	Experimentation	
Storytelling		
Metaphor analysis		
Games		
Exercise		

Table 1.6

Activity Level of Instructional Techniques

High	Medium	Low
Group discussion	Reaction panel	Lecture
Buzz group	Screened speech	Panel
Case study	Listening group	Symposium
Game	Behavior modeling	Demonstration
Simulation	Role playing	
In-basket	Storytelling	
Structured experience	Silence	
Critical incident	Observation	
Trial and error	Reflective practice	
Metaphor analysis	Dialogue	

Adapted from Caffarella (1994)

Conclusion

The goal of this chapter was to introduce a framework for instructional design that caters to adult learners. It identified key theoretical and practical principles according to the educator, the learner, the process, and the context, and then addressed how to integrate these variables in instructional design and delivery. Educators must begin with themselves in the instructional process through an ongoing process of cultivating self-knowledge and philosophical insight. This awareness is facilitated through engaging in reflective practice, committing to continuous improvement in teaching, challenging one's teaching repertoire through innovation in the design and delivery process, talking with learners about educator challenges such as positionality and authority in the classroom, and seeking ongoing feedback on teaching.

Adults seek learning to cope with change or to address problems in life. They are problem- and life-centered in their learning and expect instruction to be relevant and timely. Adult learners must be respected and see the value in what they are learning. The educator must work to create environments comfortable for diverse learners; use a variety of teaching strategies to reach various learning styles; build in varied activities to accommodate diverse learning styles, needs and goals, and activity levels; honor and use experience of participants; and facilitate reflection on lessons learned to aid in meaning construction.

Adults construct meaning and use learning as a means of adopting different ways for thinking, feeling, or acting. This can be attended to in instructional design by incorporating opportunities for reflection, building trusting relationships and learning spaces, challenging learners to expand beyond their comfort zone, creating environments conducive to learning, layering learning by tapping all the senses, and addressing the whole person in the instructional design. Instructional designers must give the context careful consideration and attend to social, economic, political, and cultural differences of learners. Positionality must be acknowledged for its impact on the educator, learners, and process. Educators should be tuned in to power relations and how they play out in the instructional process. Educators should also be willing to discuss authority and power issues with learners and continually evaluate instruction for inclusivity. Teaching strategies should also be emancipatory and democratic.

Finally, the framework of educator, learner, process, and context converges with program design and delivery. The goal of the framework is to synthesize these aspects of the framework into meaningful, active, and experiential learning for adults. Instructional designers should consider the aspects of the frame as they plan programs and negotiate democratically in the spirit of Cervero and Wilson (2006).

This chapter has argued that instructional design is not as simple as following a linear model of creating a lesson plan or discovering the perfect planning formula. Although anyone can follow the analyze, design, develop, implement, and evaluate formula for creating instruction, effective educational designers go far beyond those steps to consider multiple variables that affect the learning process with respect to the educator, learner, process, and context. The integration of these variables into the design process demands more of educators than merely following a boilerplate design. It demands that they are continually engaged in self-discovery and growth themselves, and that they revere adult learners and understand and facilitate their unique process of learning. Incorporating the framework into design also challenges educators to be aware of their positionality, biases, and power, and to endeavor to mitigate these factors thus creating more inclusive educational experiences for adults. Through a more mindful process of educational design and delivery, adult educators ensure that instruction is robust, respectful, and inclusive.

References

Boshier, R. (1991). Psychometric properties of the alternative form of the education participation scale. *Adult Education Quarterly, 41*(3), 150-167.

Brookfield, S. (1995). *Becoming a critically reflective teacher.* San Francisco: Jossey-Bass.

Brookfield, S. D. (1990). *The skillful teacher.* San Francisco: Jossey-Bass.

Caffarella, R. S. (1994). *Planning programs for adult learners: A practical guide for educators, trainers and staff developers.* San Francisco: Jossey-Bass.

Caffarella, R. S. (2002). *Planning programs for adult learners: A practical guide for educators, trainers and staff developers* (2nd ed.). San Francisco: Jossey-Bass.

Cervero, R. M., & Wilson, A. L. (1994). *Planning responsibly for adult education: A guide to negotiating power and interests.* San Francisco: Jossey-Bass.

Daloz, L. (1986). *Effective teaching and mentoring: Realizing the transformational power of adult learning experiences.* San Francisco: Jossey-Bass.

Daloz, L. (1988). The story of Gladys who refused to grow: A morality tale for mentors. *Lifelong Learning: An Omnibus of Practice and Research, 11*(4), 4-7.

Daloz, L. (1999). *Mentoring guiding the journey of adult learners* (2nd ed.). San Francisco: Jossey-Bass.

Davis, K. (Ed.) (1997). *Embodied practices: Feminist perspectives on the body.* Thousand Oaks, CA: Sage.

Elias, J. L., & Merriam, S. B. (1995). *Philosophical foundations of adult education* (2nd ed.). Malabar, FL: Krieger.

Elias, J. L., & Merriam, S. B. (2005). *Philosophical foundations of adult education* (3rd ed.). Malabar, FL: Krieger.

Fenwick, T. (2003). *Learning through experience: Troubling orthodoxies and intersecting questions.* Malabar, FL: Krieger.

Freire, P. (1970). *Pedagogy of the oppressed.* New York: Herter and Herter.

Green, J. (2000). Social somatic theory, practice, and research: An inclusive approach in higher education dance. In J. Crone-Willis & J. LaPointe-Crump (Eds.), *Dancing in the millennium conference proceedings*, comp (pp. 213-217). Congress on Research in Dance, Dance Critics Association, National Dance Association, Society of Dance History Scholars.

Houle, C. O. (1961). *The inquiring mind.* Madison, WI: University of Wisconsin Press.

Houle, C. O. (1974). *The design of education.* San Francisco: Jossey-Bass.

Houle, C. O. (1996). *The design of education* (2nd ed.). San Francisco: Jossey-Bass.

Illeris, K. (2002). *Three dimensions of learning.* Roskilde, Denmark: Toskilde University Press/Leicester, UK: NIACE

Jarvis, P. (1992). *Paradoxes of learning: On becoming an individual in society.* San Francisco: Jossey-Bass.

Jarvis, P. (2006). *Towards a comprehensive theory of human learning: Theory and practice.* London and New York: Routledge/Falmer Press.

Johnson-Bailey, J., & Cervero, R. M. (1998). Power dynamics in teaching and learning practices: An examination of two adult education classrooms. *International Journal of Lifelong Education, 17*(6), 389-399.

Johnson-Bailey, J., & Cervero, R. M. (2000). The invisible politics of race in adult education. In A. L. Wilson & E. R. Hayes (Eds.), *Handbook of adult and continuing education* (New ed., pp.147-160). San Francisco: Jossey-Bass.

Johnstone, J. W. C., & Rivera, R. J. (1965). *Volunteers for learning: A study of the educational pursuits of adults.* Hawthorne, NY: Aldine de Gruyter.

Knowles M. S. (1950). *Informal adult education.* New York: Association Press.

Knowles, M. (1970). *The modern practice of adult education: Andragogy versus pedagogy.* New York: Association Press.

Knowles, M. (1986; 1990). *The adult learner: A neglected species.* Houston: Gulf.

Kolb, D. (1991). *Learning styles inventory.* Boston: McBer & Company.

Lawson, K. (1998). *The trainer's handbook.* San Francisco: Jossey-Bass/Pfeiffer.

Lindeman, E. C. (1961). For those who need to be learners. In S. B. Merriam (Ed.), *Selected writings on philosophy and adult education* (2nd ed.) (pp. 31-36). Malabar, FL: Krieger.

Mager, R. F. (1997). *Making instruction work or skillbloomers: A step-by-step guide to designing and developing instruction that works.* Atlanta: The Center for Effective Performance, Inc.

Maher, F. A., & Tetreault, M. K. T. (1994). *The feminist classroom: A look at how professors and students are transforming higher education for a diverse society*. New York: Basic Books.

Martin, R. J., & Van Gunten, D. M. (2002). Reflected identities: Applying positionality and multicultural social reconstructionism in teacher education. *Journal of Teacher Education, 53*(1), 44-54.

Matthews, J. C. (Spring 1998). Somatic knowing and education. *Educational Forum, 62*(3), 236-242.

McClusky, H. (1950). The organization and administration of adult education. *Review of Educational Research, 20*(3), 224-229.

Meier, D. (2000). *The accelerated learning handbook*. New York: McGraw-Hill.

Merriam, S. (1993). *An update on adult learning theory*. New Directions for Adult and Continuing Education. San Francisco: Jossey-Bass.

Merriam, S. B., & Brockett, R. G. (1997). *The profession and practice of adult education: An introduction*. San Francisco: Jossey-Bass.

Merriam, S. B., & Caffarella, R. C. (1999). *Learning in adulthood*. San Francisco, CA: Jossey-Bass.

Merriam, S. B., Caffarella, R. S., & Baumgartner, L. M. (2007). *Learning in adulthood: A comprehensive guide* (3rd ed.). San Francisco: Jossey-Bass.

Mezirow, J. (1978). Perspective transformation. *Adult Education, 28*(2), 100-110.

Mezirow, J. (1990). *Fostering critical reflection in adulthood: A guide to transformative and emancipatory education*. San Francisco: Jossey-Bass.

Mezirow, J. (1991). *Transformative dimensions of adult learning*. San Francisco: Jossey-Bass.

Mezirow, J. (2000). Learning to think like an adult: Core concepts of transformation theory. In Mezirow & Associates (Eds.), *Learning as transformation: Critical perspectives on a theory in progress* (pp. 3-33). San Francisco: Jossey-Bass.

National Center for Educational Statistics Adult Education Participation in 2004-2005. *Participation in adult education activities*. Retrieved July 31, 2007, from http://nces.ed.gov/pubs2006/adulted/01.asp.

National Center for Educational Statistics Adult Education Participation in 2004-2005. *Reasons for participation*. Retrieved July 31, 2007, from http://nces.ed.gov/pubs2006/adulted/02.asp.

National Center for Educational Statistics Adult Education Participation in 2004-2005. *Distance education & informal learning activities for personal interest*. Retrieved July 31, 2007, from http://nces.ed.gov/pubs2006/adulted/06.asp.

Noe, R. A. (1999). *Employee training and development*. New York: McGraw-Hill.

Palmer, P. J. (1998). *The courage to teach: Exploring the inner landscape of a teacher's life*. San Francisco: Jossey-Bass.

Robinson, D. G., & Robinson, J. C. (1995). *Moving from training to performance: A practical guidebook.* San Francisco: Berrett-Koehler.

Robinson, R. D. (1995). *An introduction to helping adults learn and change* (Rev. ed.). West Bend, WI: Omnibook Co.

Schon, D. A. (1983). *The reflective practitioner: How professionals think in action.* New York: Basic Books.

Schor, I. (1992). *Empowering education: Critical teaching for social change.* Chicago: University of Chicago Press.

Sellers-Young, B. (1998, September). Somatic processes: Convergence of theory and practice. *Theatre Topics 8*(2), 173-187.

Simon, S. (1998). *Subjectivity and the experiencing body: Toward an ecological foundation for adult learning.* Doctoral dissertation, Portland State University.

Sork, T. J. (Winter, 1997). Workshop planning. In J. Fleming (Ed.), *New Directions for Adult and Continuing Education*, No. 76, (5-17). San Francisco: Jossey-Bass.

Taylor, E. (2000). Fostering Mezirow's transformative learning theory in the adult education classroom: A critical review. *Canadian Journal for the Study of Adult Education, 14*(2), 1-28.

Taylor, E. W. (1997). Building upon the theoretical debate: A critical review of the empirical studies of Mezirow's transformative learning theory. *Adult Education Quarterly, 48*(1), 34-60.

Tisdell, E. J. (1995). Creating inclusive adult learning environments: Insights from multicultural education and feminist pedagogy, Information series No. 361. Columbus, OH: ERIC Clearing House on Adult, Career and Vocational Education.

Tisdell, E. J. (1999). Women teaching for social change in adult education: The spiritual and cultural dimensions of "teaching across borders." Paper presented at the Adult Education Research Conference. DeKalb: Northern Illinois University.

Tisdell, E. J. (2001). The politics of positionality: Teaching for social change in higher education. In R. M. Cervero & A. L. Wilson (Eds.), *Power in practice: Adult education and the struggle for knowledge and power in society* (pp. 145-163). San Francisco: Jossey-Bass.

Tyler, R. W. (1949). *Basic principles of curriculum and instruction.* Chicago: University of Chicago Press.

Weiss, R. P. (September, 2001).The Mind-Body Connection in Learning. *T+D 55*(9), 61-67.

Zinn, L. M. (1991). Identifying your philosophical orientation. In M. W. Galbraith (Ed.), *Adult learning methods* (pp. 39-77). Malabar, FL: Krieger.

Chapter 2
Andragogy: An Introduction and Implications for Curriculum and Instruction
Lisa M. Baumgartner

Abstract

The purpose of this chapter is to explore approaches to curriculum development for adult learners in the global community. The chapter concerns andragogy's place in curriculum development and instruction in a global community. I will provide an introduction to andragogy including its history, the six assumptions of andragogy, and critiques of the assumptions. Next, andragogy's application to curriculum and instruction will be addressed. Namely, I will discuss curricular considerations in light of andragogy's assumptions. In addition, I will provide practical classroom practices that reinforce the assumptions of andragogy that may be modified in light of cultural differences.

The History of Andragogy

Although the term *andragogy* has been associated with U. S. adult educator Malcolm Knowles, who believed that adults learn differently from children, its origin is European. *Andra* comes from the Greek *aner* meaning "man, not boy" and *agogos* means "leader of" (Davenport, 1987, p. 17). Though Socrates, Plato and Aristotle believed in lifelong learning, it was John A. Comenius, a 17th-century Czech educator, writer, and Protestant bishop, who "urged the establishment of special institutions . . . and methods and teachers for work with adults" (Savicevic, 1991, p. 180). The European industrial revolution created a need to educate adults. Mechanics institutes, trade unions, and societies for teaching literacy to the masses sprang up across Europe in the 18th and 19th centuries (Draper, 1998; Savicevic, 1991). By 1833, Alexander Kapp, a German schoolteacher, had coined the term *andragogy* to make a distinction between the teaching of adults and the teaching of children. However, the term was synonymous with adult education. It did not describe specific assumptions about adult learners (Draper, 1998).

During the 1800s, Europeans' rejection of "authoritarianism," and a memorization and lecture approach to learning "encouraged a number of people to think of education for adults as different from the education of children" (Draper, 1998,

p. 7). A humanistic philosophy emerged that "focused on the dignity and autonomy of human beings . . . It encouraged learners to be self-directing" (p. 8). Danish philosopher and theologian N. F. S. Grundtvig (1783-1872) purported andragogical principles during this time (Warren, 1989). Grundtvig believed that schools should "serve people" (Warren, 1989, p. 216). He founded Danish folk schools that were based on andragogical principles. Namely, learning was student-centered, teachers engaged in dialogue with students, and teachers and students learned from each other (Warren, 1989).

By the early 20th century, the progressive philosophy was becoming part of the educational landscape in the United States and in 1926 Eduard Lindeman, who was strongly influenced by Grundtvig, published "Andragogik: *The Method of Teaching Adults*" in the *Worker's Education Journal* and also published his book *The Meaning of Adult Education* where he used the term andragogy *synonymously* with adult education (Draper, 1998, p. 12).

It would take until the late 1960s, for Knowles to popularize the term *andragogy* and create a set of assumptions about adult learners in the United States. First, Knowles had to *learn* about adult learners. After graduating from Harvard in 1934, Knowles worked from 1935-1940 as a director of training for the National Youth Administration of Massachusetts where he talked with people in the community to see what skills employers were looking for and he arranged classes to teach those skills to young adults (Knowles, 1989). Knowles enrolled at the University of Chicago and completed a master's degree in adult education in 1949. He was influenced by Lindeman's The *Meaning of Adult Education,* Edward L. Thorndike's *Adult Learning* which stated a revolutionary idea at the time—that adults could learn—and Lewin's *Resolving Social Conflicts* which helped Knowles understand "that forces in social systems operate to facilitate or inhibit learning" (Knowles, 1989, p. 75). For his master's thesis, Knowles extracted 13 "Principles of Adult Teaching" which included: "Students should want to learn . . . There should be a friendly and informal climate in the learning situation . . . Physical conditions should be favorable . . . The students should participate and should accept some responsibility for the learning process . . . Learning should be related to and should make use of the students' experience . . . The teacher should be enthusiastic about his subject and about teaching it (Knowles, 1950, pp. 32-35). These principles later formed Knowles's six assumptions about adult learners.

By 1960, after receiving his doctorate in adult education from the University of Chicago, Knowles was "experimenting with . . . adult oriented strategies in the hope that this would lead to theoretical insights" (Knowles, 1989, p. 78). He helped learners share responsibility and diagnose their own learning needs. He stated, "I experimented with such other strategies as self-evaluation, setting a classroom climate that was conducive to learning, and using learning contracts" (p. 78).

In 1967 Knowles met Yugoslavian adult educator Dusan Savicevic who informed Knowles that he was practicing andragogy (Knowles, 1989; Savicevic, 1998). Knowles defined andragogy as "the art and science of helping adults learn" (Knowles, 1980, p. 43). Knowles first used the term in an article he wrote in 1968 titled, "Androgogy, Not Pedagogy" in the journal *Adult Leadership* (Knowles, 1989, p. 80). By 1970, Malcolm Knowles published *The Modern Practice of Adult Education: Andragogy Versus Pedagogy*. He presented them as "separate and opposing educational ideologies, saying that pedagogy is based on a now obsolete premise—that is, the idea that the purpose of education is to transmit culture" (Draper 1998, p. 14). By 1980, Knowles modified his stance saying that pedagogy and andragogy were on a continuum. Pedagogy referred to teacher-directed learning and andragogy referred to self-directed learning (Draper, 1998).

Knowles's 13 principles of adult teaching became six assumptions about adult learners. These assumptions follow: Some of Knowles's 13 principles of adult teaching put forth in his master's thesis were solidified in the six assumptions about adult learners that were developed in the 1960s and 1970s. These six assumptions follow (Knowles, 1989, pp. 83-84):

1. "Regarding the need to know: Adults need to know why they need to learn something before undertaking to learn it." Sometimes learners have to be made aware of why they need to know something—similar to the consciousness raising of Freire (1970).
2. "Regarding the learner's self-concept: Adults have a self-concept of being responsible for their own lives (the psychological definition of adult)." Knowles noted that many adults expect to be taught using teacher-centered, pedagogical methods and it is incumbent upon the adult educator to help adults transition from dependent to self-directed learners.
3. "Regarding the role of the learner's experience: Adults come into an educational activity with both a greater volume and a different quality of experience from youths." Adults have different learning styles, motivation, goals and needs than youths so they need individualized teaching strategies (Knowles, 1989). Knowles believed that learners possessed their own best resources for learning. Therefore, experiential techniques that helped the learner tap into those experiences such as "group discussion, simulation exercises, problem-solving activities, case method, and laboratory methods" were best.
4. "Regarding readiness to learn: Adults become ready to learn those things they need to know or to be able to do in order to cope effectively with their

real-life situations. An especially rich source of readiness to learn is the developmental tasks associated with moving from one developmental stage to the next."

5.   "Regarding orientation to learning: In contrast to children's and youths' subject-centered orientation to learning (at first in school), adults are life centered (or task centered or problem centered) in their orientation to learning." Hence, a course titled "Consumer Mathematics: What Every Consumer Needs to Know to Get the Best Buy for Your Money" is more appealing than "Basic Math I."

6.   "Regarding motivation to learn: While adults are responsible to some extrinsic motivators (better jobs, promotions, salary increases, and the like), the more potent motivators are intrinsic motivators (the desire for increased self-esteem, quality of life, responsibility, job satisfaction, and the like)."

European Conceptions of Andragogy

While Knowles's notions of andragogy frame this chapter, it is worth noting different ideas of andragogy in Europe. All of these conceptualizations occurred after World War II. Savicevic briefly delineates the various meanings of andragogy in European countries. For example, Germany has several meanings of the term. Terms such as *adult pedagogy* with subset terms *college pedagogy* and *vocational pedagogy* appear in the literature (Savicevic, 1991, pp. 185-186). German literature on andragogy discusses the need to "establish a scientific discipline focusing on adult education and learning" (p. 186). In contrast, France does not appear to have a science of adult education but instead "pedagogy is extended to encompass research problems relative to adult education and learning" (p. 187). The Dutch idea of andragogy, purported by Ten Have in the 1960s, considered the idea of adult learning processes and "social work and other forms of guidance [for the adult]" (p. 187). The social work aspect of this definition fell out of favor and now andragogy applies to adult learning. As for the British, in the 1970s, an andragogical group at the University of Nottingham took a more Freireian social justice approach to andragogy and saw "andragogy as a function of helping adults to become the driving force behind their own thoughts and feelings" (p. 188). In the British literature there is a dispute as to whether andragogy is a theory of adult learning or "a special kind of ideology" (p. 190). The Finnish believe that pedagogy and andragogy are part of the field of educational science whose theoretical base is only starting to be created. In Russia, andragogy is synonymous with the term *adult pedagogy*. Subsets of knowledge under this term include literature on the psychology and sociology of adults as well as instructional methods for adults (Savicevic, 1991). In Poland, the terms *andragogy* and *adult pedagogy* are synonymous. Andragogy is "a scientific discipline focusing on the study of all problems relating to adult education and learning" (p. 194) and adult education is very different from children's' education in subject, method of instruction, and function. Hungarian scholars consider andragogy as a "scientific discipline" that concerns the education of adults in all contexts (Savicevic, 1991).

In sum, there are several schools of thought on the concept of andragogy. Some consider andragogy and pedagogy as part of the science of education. Others consider it a "process of education and learning but also other forms of guidance and orientation" (Savicevic, 1991, p. 198). Still others see andragogy as a way teachers and adult students should interact—more of a set of prescriptive rules. Another view does not see adult education as a science but says it is taking its ideas from other socio-scientific areas of psychology, sociology, and the like. Finally, some consider it a science, such as in Germany, Poland, Hungary, and the Netherlands (Savicevic, 1991).

Critiques of Andragogy

Whereas Knowles's conception of andragogy "became a rallying point for those trying to define the field of adult education" (Merriam, Caffarella, & Baumgartner, 2007, p. 85), it also received critiques over the years. It is important to explore some of these critiques before discussing andragogy's application to the curriculum.

Elias (1979) believed that there was no basis for a differentiation between how children and adults learn. First, he disagreed with Knowles's assumption that people move from a state of dependence to that of self-direction. He said the process of independence began before adulthood and cited the works of developmental psychologists Erikson, Freud, and Piaget to support his point. Second, Elias acknowledged that adults have a greater quantity and different quality of experiences than children which can be a rich resource for learning, but he failed to see how this distinguished andragogy and pedagogy since "Dewey based his theory of education [of children] on experience" (1979, p. 253). Third, Elias noted that both children and adults have developmental tasks which create a readiness to learn. Children may have *different* developmental tasks but the learning process is the same. Last, Elias posited that children are as problem-centered in their learning as adults. He concluded that andragogy and pedagogy, "present two different approaches to the education of children and adults. Dewey called these two approaches traditional and progressive" (1979, p. 255).

Pratt (1988) disputed Knowles's idea that adult learners are self-directed. Self-direction is a "situational variable" influenced by the adult learners' "competence, commitment and confidence" (p. 165). Learners low in any of these areas may need support and direction. Self-directed learning is not only for adults. He stated, "Adult educators ought to acknowledge states of dependency as potentially legitimate because, like self-directedness, dependency is a situational attribute and the product of a specific person-situation interaction" (p. 170).

Hartree (1984) had many critiques of Knowles's theory. She asked, "Is Knowles presenting a theory of teaching or a theory of learning? . . . Are the assumptions about the adult learner descriptive or prescriptive—statements about what the adult learner should be like rather than a mirroring of his real nature?" (p. 206). Hartree (1984) concluded that Knowles's assumptions concerned the learner and did not address all aspects of a theory including how, what and why adults learn. Therefore, Hartree considered Knowles's work a set of assumptions based on "a philosophical conception of man and his existence in the world" (p. 209). Pratt (1993) added that andragogy helped adult educators understand adult learners but it did not help "expand or clarify our understanding of the process of learning" (p. 21). He viewed andragogy as a "philosophical stance with regard to the purposes of adult education and the relationship of the individual to society" (pp. 21-22). Knowles (1980) conceded, "I don't see andragogy as an ideology at all but as a system of assumptions about adult learners that needs to be tested out for different learners in different situations" (p. 59).

More recent critiques of andragogy centered on its universality and white Western bias. Pratt (1993) remarked that Knowles's assumptions implied that everyone wants to participate in a teaching/learning transaction that privileges individuality over community. African scholar Bangura (2005) noted that andragogy was founded on a Western conceptualization of humanism that denied the importance of religion which is of great importance in Africans' learning process. Bangura asserted that the African educational paradigm of ubuntugogy, which includes the importance of religion, consensus, and dialogue in the teaching and learning process, was a more culturally appropriate method of educating adults. Roberson (2002) agreed that spirituality did not appear to be part of andragogy. Further, Lee (2003) stated that Knowles failed "to discuss the role of cultural contexts in his construction of andragogy" (p. 20). Yet, it was clear from studies conducted on the "meaning making of Taiwanese Chinese immigrants" (Lee, 1999) and the "learning experiences of Anglophone Caribbean immigrant women in postsecondary institutions" (Alfred, 2003; Lee, 2003, p. 20) that contexts determined how learners view themselves and how they engaged in learning. The teacher/student relationship, issues of power in the classroom, and communication are all culturally transmitted. Knowles considered none of this, according to critics.

Grace (1996) believed that Knowles ignored the influence of power and the socio-political context, and overall he stated that andragogy "does not operate from a critical social agenda" (p. 389). Though Knowles's assumptions are based on individual freedom, Knowles does not acknowledge that "organizational culture and social structures and relations impact on individual freedom. The individual cannot be seen as the isolated and insulated self whom Knowles defines as an autonomous, self-directed learner" (Grace, 1996, p. 390). Last, Misch (2002) took issue with Knowles's assumption that adults are more internally motivated to learn than children. He stated that few people really knew their true motivation for learning since they have subconscious motivations. Further, in his context, a U.S. medical school, people who parroted back answers provided by their instructors were rewarded. Ultimately, argued Misch (2002), circumstances matter. "Internal and external motivators are not dichotomous; they interrelate with, and act upon, one another in a complex fashion. Malcolm Knowles's . . . wish that adult learners be internally motivated causes a warm, fuzzy glow that turns out to be ephemeral upon closer scrutiny" (p. 159).

Clardy (2005) summarized the main problems with andragogy. First, "Andragogical theory does not adequately reflect the full nature and range of adult learning experiences" (p. 13). It ignores the context. Second, saying that adults learn differently from children is misleading. Andragogy and pedagogy are really just two different ways of learning. Third, not all adults have the same learning needs, motivations, and requirements. Fourth, "Autonomous, self-directed learning is a special, not a universal condition" (p. 19). While some adult learners may be irritated if the teacher is in full authority, the teacher just can't abandon the learners if they don't have the skills.

Recent Research

Recent research on andragogy conducted primarily in the United States, Taiwan, and Hong Kong affirms some of Knowles's assumptions. Kember, Kwan, and Ledesma (2001) interviewed 17 lecturers across three departments (engineering, social sciences, and paramedical) at a Hong Kong university concerning their perceptions of differences between adult students and traditional students, their definitions of good teaching, and the methods they employed in the classroom. Teachers confirmed Knowles's assumptions that adult students were more practical, task centered (and less theoretically oriented) and they had a richer work experience compared to traditional college students. Those instructors who taught in a learner-centered, andragogical way tried to remediate students' weaknesses while those who taught in a pedagogical way tried to teach to the learners' strengths or treated adults and traditional college students the same.

Ray and Chu (2005) used andragogy as a conceptual framework to see if students at a United Epitaxy Company (UEC) Extension Center in Taiwan preferred a more student-centered or a learner-centered teaching style. They also wondered what kind of teaching style Taiwanese teachers of adults would use and what effect "the role of eastern culture playing in adult classrooms" (p. 102). In the study, 309 learners completed a survey questionnaire. Researchers made observations of classrooms and interviewed students and teachers. Researchers found that teachers used andragogical methods in their teaching. Students confirmed Knowles's assertion that adults want to know the relevance of their classes to their lives. They came with a great deal of experience and wanted the instructor to have students share experiences with each other. Students also noticed that instructors tried to set an easy-going climate where students were seen as peers. However, students were very reluctant to speak up in class even though they wanted each other to do so. They respected the teacher's authority and this prevented them from sharing their experiences. The researchers concluded that more research needs to be conducted on "which particular aspects of a Confucian environment—power distance, collectivism, uncertainty avoidance, social harmony, fear of losing face or the like—offer the greatest hindrance to more classroom participation by students" (p. 107).

Rachal (2002) reviewed 18 empirical studies published between 1983 and 2001. These quasi-experimental or experiential studies examined the usefulness of pedagogy and andragogy as an instructional design and by learner outcomes. The results were mixed. Rachael cited numerous methodological shortcomings of the study including the lack of differentiation between adult students and others used in studies, learner control in planning the objectives and learning strategies, the use of predetermined objectives in the learning activity, and the use of paper-and-pencil tests to measure learning (Rachal, 2002). Rachal offered seven criteria for future studies that investigate andragogy including: voluntary participation of the learners, using only adult learners in studies instead of mixing adults and traditional students, course objectives that are collaboratively determined, a psychologically and physically comfortable learning environment, and a "performance-based assessment of achievement" (p. 221). Taking Rachal's (2002) advice, Wilson (2005) isolated the experiences of adult learners in her study and found that andragogical concepts did not influence learning but they did influence adult students' satisfaction with the course and with the instructor.

In sum, the idea that adults needed to be taught differently from children has existed for several centuries. In the 1800s, Grundtvig's Danish folk schools utilized principles of andragogy. Malcolm Knowles popularized the concept in the United States in the 1960s. His six assumptions of andragogy received criticism over the years including andragogy's lack of attention to social context and the idea that the assumptions do not apply to children.

Now that the reader has a solid grounding in the history of andragogy, its conceptualizations in Europe, Knowles's six assumptions of andragogy and criticisms, let us explore andragogy's application to the curriculum. First, the assumptions will be delineated and their general application to the curriculum will be briefly discussed. Next, the andragogical assumptions will be broken down into principles that should guide and organize andragogical learning. Last, a practical application of the six assumptions to the classroom will be discussed.

Andragogy and the Curriculum

In a truly andragogical setting, the learners would plan their own curriculum. They would decide the courses, their content, the organization and sequence of content, and they would evaluate themselves on their learning. The facilitators would provide learning contracts, help students become more self-directed, utilize the learner's own experiences to help them plan their goals, assess their needs, and plan a course of action.

Formal educational settings, such as university settings, require that a curriculum is planned by the instructor (or a curriculum committee) and implemented by the instructor/facilitator. For example, the faculty may decide the courses necessary for those pursuing a master's degree in adult education. In this case, the curriculum is set. Often, a departmental committee determines the course objectives. However, andragogical concepts can still be utilized throughout the curriculum. Some general curriculum considerations in light of andragogy's assumptions follow:

1. "Regarding the need to know: Adults need to know why they need to learn something before undertaking to learn it" (Knowles, 1989, p. 83). A curriculum that demonstrates Knowles's "need to know" assumption would provide both course objectives and the practical relevance of the course material and objectives to learners' lives. Teachers/facilitators could draw on learners' experiences to draw out course relevance. Sometimes the teacher's role is to help the learner recognize the gap between what they know and what they want to know. Hence, some consciousness-raising techniques such as facilitators using critical questioning or learners' assumptions could be embedded in the curriculum.

2. "Regarding the learner's self-concept: Adults have a self-concept of being responsible for their own lives (the psychological definition of adult)" (Knowles, 1989, p. 83). Knowles noted that many adults expect to be taught using teacher-centered, pedagogical methods, and it is incumbent upon the adult educator to help adults transition from dependent to self-directed learners. The idea of guiding individuals to be more self-directing could be infused into the curriculum. However, the teacher should be sensitive to the cultural

context. Different techniques can be used for those from group-oriented cultures and individual-oriented cultures. (More specifics on exactly how to accomplish this in the classroom appear later in this chapter).

3. "Regarding the role of the learner's experience: Adults come into an educational activity with both a greater volume and a different quality of experience from youths" (Knowles, 1989, p. 83). Adults have different motivations, goals, and needs than youths so they need individualized teaching strategies (Knowles, 1989). Knowles believed that learners possessed their own best resources for learning. Therefore, a curriculum rich in experiential techniques that help learners tap into those experiences such as "group discussion, simulation exercises, problem-solving activities, case method, and laboratory methods" work best (Knowles, 1989, p.84). Each course in the curriculum could have an experiential component.

4. "Regarding readiness to learn: Adults become ready to learn those things they need to know or to be able to do in order to cope effectively with their real-life situations. An especially rich source of readiness to learn is the developmental tasks associated with moving from one developmental stage to the next" (Knowles, 1989, p. 84). Each course in the curriculum could provide objectives that connected to developmental challenges faced by learners.

5. "Regarding orientation to learning: In contrast to children's and youths' subject-centered orientation to learning (at first in school), adults are life centered (or task centered or problem centered) in their orientation to learning" (Knowles, 1989, p. 84). Curriculum planners would need to recognize a balance between theory and application. Hence, a course titled "Consumer Mathematics: What Every Consumer Needs to Know to Get the Best Buy for Your Money" is more appealing than "Basic Math I." Courses in the curriculum would need to have practical application.

6. "Regarding motivation to learn: While adults are responsible to some extrin_ sic motivators (better jobs, promotions, salary increases, and the like), the more potent motivators are intrinsic motivators (the desire for increased self--esteem, quality of life, responsibility, job satisfaction, and the like)" (Knowles, 1989, p. 84). The curriculum would need to intrinsically appeal to learners' self-esteem or have the potential to enhance a learner's quality of life. Teacher/facilitators could help learners recognize this appeal.

Andragogical Principles

In the previous section, andragogy's implications on the curriculum were noted. Now, the author will explore some basic principles that can be extracted from Knowles's six assumptions. Then practices and procedures that occur in an andragogically based classroom will be discussed. Clardy (2005) describes eight principles that should guide and organize andragological learning. Each principle is followed by the andragogical needs being addressed:

1. The adult learner must be able to define what they want to learn (autonomy, personal need, reasons, intrinsic motivation).
2. The plans for the learning program should be made jointly between "teacher" and "student" (autonomy, personal need, reasons).
3. The adult must be involved in the evaluation of the learning program (autonomy, intrinsic).
4. The climate of the learning program must be safe and nonthreatening (experience).
5. The program should relate to an include the adult's existing experience and cognitive structure (experience).
6. Learning activities should be experiential and "hands on" rather than passive and pedagogical (personal needs, pragmatic, experience).
7. Learning should lead to practical solutions to experienced problems. The curriculum should be problem rather than subject based (personal needs, pragmatic).
8. The proper role of teacher is one of process facilitator and co-learner rather than content expert (autonomy). (p. 10)

Andragogy in Practice: Its Application to the Classroom

Clardy (2005) delineates practices and procedures that derive from the principles of andragogy. Each practice and its application to the classroom will be discussed.

Give students the tools to become increasingly self-directed. If Knowles's assumptions about adult learners are true, then any curriculum that focuses on adult learners should include self-directed learning. Some practical suggestions regarding how to assess students' self-directed learning readiness and how to facilitate self-directed learning in the classroom follow.

First, an assessment of students' self-directed learning readiness may be in order. Some popular tools for such a task include Guglielmino's (1977) Self-Directed Learning Readiness Scale (SDLRS). This scale is based on psychological qualities associated with self-directed learning such as self-discipline, curiosity, independence, goal orientation, and persistence in learning. Another popular assessment tool for self-directed learning is the Oddi Continuing Learning Inventory (OCLI) (Oddi, 1986). This instrument also measures self-direction as a personality trait. Adult educators should be aware, however, that these inventories were created in the United States and although the SDLRS has been administered in many countries (Guglielmino & Associates, 2006), any instrument may be somewhat culturally biased.

A second assessment of students' self-directed learning readiness can be achieved through personal observation and discussion with learners. Grow's (1991) four-stage Self-Directed Learning model describes a learner's level of self-direction and corresponding teaching techniques. Dependent Learners (Stage One) are low in self-direction and they need the teacher to tell them what to do. They respond best to lectures, drills, coaching, and frequent behavioral reinforcement (Grow, 1991). Stage Two learners may consider themselves good students but may not be familiar with course content. The instructor motivates students, leads discussions, demonstrates tasks, and provides guided practice on that task. Those learners at Stage Three, the involved learners, have confidence and some familiarity with the material. The teacher is a facilitator at this level. Students enjoy group projects and collaborative learning. Stage Four learners are high in self-direction. The teacher is a guide on the side and a mentor to students.

After the students' self-directed learning readiness is assessed, teachers use several techniques to increase learners' self-direction. Learners lower in self-direction need support to reach the next level of development. This type of instruction is known as scaffolding. The instructor provides activities that may model a task, define a task, or simplify a task so the learner can, with the help of the teacher, achieve the goal. In addition, the instructor may motivate the learner to learn the task (Ellis, Worthington, & Larkin, n.d.). Through modeling, the teacher makes explicit the thinking and action on the task. In short, the teacher may talk through the task and model it until the learner can do the task independently. As the learner gains competence and confidence in his or her skills and moves up to Grow's stages three and four on self-directed learning, the scaffolding or support can be removed. Although scaffolding can increase learners' self-direction, there are limitations. First, scaffolding is very labor intensive as each student's needs differ (Ellis, Worthington, & Larkin, n.d). Second, scaffolding requires an empathic teacher. Third, some teachers may have trouble with allowing students to make mistakes as they learn. Learners can really benefit, however, from this type of instruction to increase self-direction.

Self-directed learning is not necessarily an individualistic activity. Cooperative and collaborative learning are other methods that can be used to move learners toward self-direction. Cooperative learning is considered more structured than collaborative learning but both methods encourage active learning, view teaching and learning as an interaction between the students and teacher, balance lecture and small group activities, and see the teacher as a coach (Matthews, Cooper, Davidson, & Hawks, 1995, as cited in Millis & Cottell, 1998). In cooperative learning, the students often have a common group activity. They engage in "positive interdependence" (Millis & Cottell, 1998, p. 11). In short, people realize that cooperation benefits the group and the individual. The group's success depends on the contributions of the individuals. The group generally needs to solve a problem. Each member of the group has interdependent roles and members learn from each other in the problem-solving process. In cooperative learning there is individual accountability. In addition, group members develop social skills and small group skills.

Techniques that structure cooperative learning can encourage deep thinking and people can construct knowledge together. In this process, they can gain confidence about the subject matter and can become more self-directed. "Think-pair-share" is a technique used in cooperative learning (Millis & Cottell, 1998, p. 72). The instructor poses a question that does not have one "correct" answer. Students think about an answer for a couple of minutes on their own. They pair with another student to discuss their thoughts and then the instructor asks groups to share their responses. Another cooperative learning technique that encourages brainstorming is "roundtable" (p. 72). The instructor poses a question or problem and students get in a circle and respond verbally and in written form to the question. Cooperative learning can increase people's confidence in the material. Students can learn together and perform alone as they construct knowledge. Vygotsky notes, "What children can do together today, they can do alone tomorrow" (as cited in Adams & Hamm, 1996, p. 3). In addition, cooperative or collaborative learning may appeal to group-oriented cultures.

In short, self-directed learning concepts and ideas should be sprinkled throughout the course curriculum. Exercises and activities that promote self-directed learning should be encouraged. Ideally, then, the learner can become self-directed and can design his or her own curriculum for a given project. Self-directed learning is not a solitary activity. Cooperative learning can also promote self-directed learning.

Create a comfortable psychological and physical climate for learning. Pay attention to issues of safety, trust, and respect. Creating a comfortable psychological climate implies that safety, trust, and respect are part of that atmosphere. To create an open atmosphere, teachers can elicit and honor students' experiences. During the first class session, students can pair up and introduce each other. Next, they can spend part of the class writing a couple of paragraphs explaining how the course has relevance to their lives, what they expect to learn, and what they can contribute to the discussion based on their experiences (Robinson & Kakela, 2006). These exercises help the learner and teacher value each others' experience. The learners realize they each have things to offer in the teaching/learning transaction. In addition, course assignments can require that learners tie course material to their experiences. For example, learners in an adult learning theory course may be asked to write about their best and worst learning experience and tie these experiences to course readings on motivation, participation, or learning styles.

Exercises that encourage students to connect new information with what they already know build learners' confidence in their knowledge of course material which creates a comfortable psychological climate for learning (Robinson & Kakela, 2006). This can be accomplished by having students write reflection papers on various issues or pair up and discuss a topic. For example, in teaching Gardner's (2006) multiple intelligences, the instructor may ask students, "What is the best way you learn things?" Students may say, "When I was in a human anatomy class, I made up songs to remember all the bones in the body." Or "I need to DO an activity to remember things. I have to be active." The instructor can say, "You already know how you best learn" and can introduce Gardner's concepts of musical intelligence and kinesthetic intelligence.

Students feel safer in a learning environment when they know that their preferred way of learning is respected and valued. Teachers that create activities that appeal to students' preferred ways of learning help learners know that their ways of being and learning are accepted and encouraged. This helps them feel safer. Gardner (1995) describes eight types of intelligences. He states, "An intelligence is a capacity . . . that is geared to a specific content in the world (such as musical sounds or spatial patterns)" (pp. 202-203). For example, to appeal to those with a high linguistic intelligence, who learn best through words, class activities and assignments that incorporate storytelling or journal writing would be appropriate (Armstrong, 2000). Kinesthetic learners would prefer hands-on activities such as working with objects or making things with their hands while those with interpersonal intelligence would respond best to concepts used in cooperative learning, simulations, or board games (Armstrong, 2000).

Teacher authenticity also contributes to a comfortable psychological climate. Authentic teachers gain students' trust and respect. According to Cranton and Carusetta (2004), authenticity includes: (1) Knowing oneself as a teacher and person; (2) Critically reflecting on one's practice to know the origins of one's values and assumptions; (3) Awareness of how the teaching context constrains instruction and the ways this influences our actions; (4) Understanding learners' preferences and characteristics and how they differ from our own; (5) Developing open and genuine relationships with learners.

Cranton (2006) offers several strategies for fostering authentic relationships. The first strategy, self-awareness, can be promoted through taking psychological inventories such as the Myers-Briggs Type Inventory or creating an art project that represents your personality. Second, knowing others and how they differ from you can be accomplished by simply chatting with students about their families and interests. Additionally, asking for feedback from students or having students take learning inventories can assist teachers in knowing about others. Third, Cranton lists three types of student-teacher relationships. She suggests that instructors must develop relationships that are comfortable and authentic for them. The "respectful distance" relationship between a student and teacher is characterized by trust and respect (p. 9). Learning is the focus of the relationship. Emotional support and telling personal stories to each other are not part of the relationship. The collegial relationship is characterized by "mutual sharing of experience and expertise" (p. 10). The teacher views the student as a future colleague and may socialize with the student. In the "close relationship" students and teachers know each other inside and outside the classroom (p. 10). They rely on each other for emotional support. They are involved in each others' lives. Fourth, the teaching context constrains authentic teaching. She lists several constrains, such as a "mandatory curriculum" and "grading policies" (p. 11). Cranton (2006) recommends being "open with students about the policies and social norms that influence or inhibit your practice" and "Becom[ing] familiar with written and unwritten policies and procedures and question[ing] those that have the potential of interfering with good relationships" (p. 11). Last, critical reflection on teaching can be facilitated by keeping a teaching journal, blogging with others about teaching, or talking to students about the classroom experience.

It should be noted that different cultures have different ways of acting and being authentic (Lin, 2006). For example, in a culture that values humility and harmony, individualism and standing up for one's beliefs may not be appreciated. So, recognizing the teaching context and making choices in expressing one's authentic self is important. There is a balance between personal values and context (Lin, 2006). For example, when the author taught English to adults in Japan, her authentic way of teaching in the United States included inviting students to challenge her statements and to speak rather directly. She learned that students did not want to challenge her statements because they did not want her to lose face and that their method of communication was less direct than she was accustomed to so she modified her teaching style to fit into the school's teaching culture.

Last, grades are often required in formal educational learning settings. The use of grades as a criterion for achievement sometimes creates a less than optimum psychological climate for learning. In informal or nonformal learning settings, Knowles advises against grades. He states, "The use of grades introduces an element of formality and competition that runs counter to the very spirit of andragogy" (Knowles, 1970, p. 183). However, some settings require grades. In order to take the focus off the grade, instructors have used a variety of techniques. Some instructors create a contract where the student must complete a certain number of various assignments at a satisfactory level to achieve a particular grade. For example, for an "A" the student must write four 15-page papers and lead one class discussion during the course of the semester. A student who contracts for a "B" may have to only complete three 10-page papers. Another strategy that lessens the pressure of grades is to provide students the opportunity to redo assignments until they are satisfied with their grade.

The remaining practices and procedures that evolve from andragogy concern the learner's self-directed learning needs. These needs can be met through the use of learning contracts, which are written agreements between teachers and learners. The learning objectives, strategies, and resources used to achieve the objectives, and the evidence and criteria used to assess learning are all negotiated between the teacher and learner (Anderson, Boud, & Sampson, 2004). Learning contracts help learners develop skills such as "objective setting, communication, and negotiation" as well as project evaluation (Anderson et al., 2004, p. 11).

The learner and teacher need to plan what needs to be learned. The first step in writing a learning contract is establishing the student's learning needs. A discussion between the teacher and learner as to "what the learner wants to learn, what the learner could learn and what the learner should learn" should take place (Cross, 1992, as cited in Anderson et al., 2004, p. 17). In addition, learning needs can emerge as the learning occurs (Anderson, et al., 2004). Methods used to stimulate learning needs include examining course materials, looking at class activities, and having discussions with peers. Knowles (1986, as cited in Anderson et al., 2004), says that learners should draft their learning needs and talk with peers. Evaluating one's long term goals and objectives as well as taking interest inventories also help the learner determine what needs to be learned. Anderson et al. (2004) suggest that teachers and learners seek out lectures, workshops, or readings that may stimulate learning interests. Sometimes, what needs to be learned emerges from the work context. For example, a person who conducts personal health history interviews for an insurance company encounters unfamiliar health-related terms during the interview. She may want to create a learning contract that increases her knowledge of medical terms and conditions so she can conduct a better interview.

Sometimes the learner does not exactly know what he or she needs to learn. In this case, the teacher may be more responsible for creating the learning objectives and the learner may chose *how* the objectives are going to be achieved (Anderson et al., 2004). If the learner has little experience in the area, the teachers may need to be more directive.

In conjunction with the teacher, the learner needs to identify competencies and abilities and complete a self-assessment. Two questions can help the learner identify competencies and complete a self-assessment. First, "Where have I been?" (Anderson et al., 2004, p. 18). This question helps learners assess what they already know and what skills they already have. Second, "Where am I now?" The student and teacher can evaluate students' strengths and weaknesses in "knowledge, skill, and experience" (p. 18). Depending on the subject to be learned, perhaps exams on the subject can be administered. For example, if the person wants to improve his or her writing abilities, an English proficiency exam, similar to those administered to incoming college freshmen in the United States could be administered. Alternatively, the student could write an essay on a particular subject and it could be evaluated on several criteria including sentence structure, complexity of thought, grammar, spelling, and level of detail.

The learner should be involved in establishing learner objectives, the sequence and nature of the learning experiences, and the resources used. The learner needs to help establish objectives. First, the learner should develop goals from which objectives can be written (Anderson et al., 2004). For example, a goal could be to learn more about public speaking. The learner could watch films of famous public speeches or read books on speech making and perhaps talk to speech or communication instructors to get an idea of what things she or he may want to learn. From those conversations, the learner could pinpoint the learning objectives. Learning objectives have to contain a "learning intention" (p. 20). An objective would not be "to read books about great speech makers." An objective, in the case of the person wanting to become a better public speaker, may be "to identify key components of a good speech."

Objectives should "reflect the learner's perceived needs but they must also be manageable and achievable given the time and resources available" (Anderson et al., 2004, p. 21). For example, if the person has one month to become a better speaker some reasonable objectives could be: (1) to identify three different types of speeches (e.g., demonstration, informational, persuasive), (2) to analyze effective techniques used in these three types of speeches, (3) to write and present a 5 minute speech from a category of one's choice.

The sequence of learning can be co-constructed by the learner and teacher. Preferably, the learning experiences can build on each other. For example, identifying different types of speeches is necessary before a person analyzes the content and techniques used in those types of speeches. In addition, the resources and strategies used to obtain those resources should be taken into consideration. Students generally realize that books and journals are good resources for learning but they sometimes fail to recognize that people are resources also. Course handouts, films, CDs, internet sites, librarians, work sites, friends, family, and people working in a particular field are all resources. "Developing a learning strategy involves identifying sources of information and determining suitable methods for accessing them" (Anderson et al., p. 41). When people are the resources, it is best to decide how to approach them and the method used to obtain information. Will people have time to be interviewed? Would they prefer that the person gives them questions to answer by e-mail? Would interviewing a focus group of people who have a similar expertise work?

The teacher needs to serve as the facilitator by helping learners organize resources, clarifying learning expectations, and asking questions in a Socratic manner rather than providing expert answers. The teacher acts as the guide on the side. In organizing resources, the teacher and learner create a plan of action that guides the learner in knowing what to look for, who to talk to and how to do that, how to get materials, and how to prioritize resources (Anderson et al., 2004). The teacher needs to make sure the learner knows what he or she is supposed to produce and the assessment procedures used in assessing the learning products such as papers, artwork, etc.

Determining the criteria for assessment is also important. The criteria for assessment depend on the objectives. Skill objectives may require the person to perform a skill in a certain amount of time with a particular amount of accuracy (Anderson et al., 2004). An essay exam or written essay may require a certain word count, be formatted in a particular style, and have a thesis statement and arguments to support that thesis statement. Some questions to ask while determining the criteria for assessment are: "Does the student want written and/or oral comments?" "Should the teacher use a rating scale or check list?" "[Are] marks, grades or merit ratings useful or irrelevant? If they are to be used, what will be the specific criteria for each level of achievement?" (p. 24).

Teachers and facilitators sometimes worry about the quality of work done under learning contracts as being inferior to professor-determined coursework. This is why learning contracts and criteria for assessment need to be held to some standards. For example, assessment criteria should include: "(1) evidence of analysis and critical thinking; (2) use of multiple sources; (3) references to appropriate literature; (4) use of argument supported by evidence; (5) some element of personal reflection; (6) logical development and structure" (Anderson et al., 2004, p. 53).

The learners should evaluate their learning outcomes. Learners can evaluate their outcomes. One method for doing this is to have the learner write a paper that explains the following: (1) the objectives they pursued, (2) the evidence used to show the objectives were met, (3) the criteria used to judge the evidence, (4) a reflection and judgment on the quality of the work they did, (5) further work they need to do to achieve the objectives to their satisfaction (Anderson et al., 2004). Evaluation can take many forms including a self-evaluative paper, students can assign a letter grade to their work and explain why they chose that grade, or they can reflect on each objective and write how well they thought they demonstrated that objective and what they would do differently.

Andragogy in Action: St. Olaf's Paracollege

These practices are not especially evident in higher education. Higher education institutions are known for teaching in pedagogical ways. Generally, there is a fairly prescribed curriculum and students choose a college major and fulfill the requirements for the degree. However, St. Olaf, a private Lutheran school in Northfield, Minnesota, instituted a Paracollege in 1969 where students could design their own majors. One of its goals was to "impel students to assume more responsibility for their own education" (Saint Olaf College, 1971, p. 2). Students met with a tutor and planned a course of study. Although the college required general courses such as a freshman seminar and requirements in religion, creative arts, physical education, and a teaching requirement, students could fulfill these requirements in a variety of ways as long as they received approval from the appropriate authorities. For example, to fulfill the creative arts requirement, students could participate in a choral group, band, or drama group. Alternatively, they could take private music lessons, a regular college course, or any other approved creative arts activity. Students were required to take a general examination that covered content from the natural and social sciences as well as the humanities (Saint Olaf College, 1971). A senior project and a comprehensive examination, written by a committee and the student, in the major area of study were also required. Grades were assigned to exams and in required courses only. Students were expected to meet with their tutor a minimum of half an hour every other week. The tutor and the student were to decide assignments and participate in discussions.

Although students put together their own educational programs in conjunction with a tutor, they were expected to utilize the available learning strategies. Students could attend seminars which explored "the liberal arts and the relationships among traditional academic disciplines" (The Paracollege, St. Olaf Catalogue 1996-1997, para.7). Tutorials, based on the traditions at Oxford and Cambridge, were another option. Students and the tutor agreed on a course of reading and writing. Workshops, which taught a particular topic or skill, and often lasted less than a semester, were also utilized. Last, students could attend regular college classes.

The Paracollege program as described above closed in 2000. In "By Chance and By Design, Incidents of Learning" (1999) David Booth reflects that the Paracollege was student centered, interdisciplinary, and community based. He noted, "There was extraordinary involvement of students in the elaboration of theory and practice in the Paracollege" (para. 7). The Paracollege philosophy, and that of andragogy, was/is that learning arises from "accidental encounters among people, texts, art works, disciplines and personal experiences" (para. 13). As with andragogy, the Paracollege valued discourse—the experiences of the teacher and learner were intertwined so that both could learn. Discourse among students and faculty were highly valued. The Paracollege demonstrated the overall andragogical concepts of learner self-direction. It was presumed that students could design an academically sound concentration and that they could make their own meaning out of the things they were exposed to.

Andragogy: A Summary and Concluding Thoughts

The idea that adults learn differently from children has been around a long time. In the 1800s, N. F. S. Grundtvig founded Danish folk schools that utilized andragogical concepts. Malcolm Knowles popularized the term *andragogy* in the United States in the late 1960s and created a set of assumptions about adult learners. Over the years, critics noted the universality and white Western bias of andragogy and its lack of attention to cultural context. Recent research shows that adult students in Taiwan preferred a more student-centered teaching style but were reluctant to dialogue with each other and the instructor although they wanted their classmates to participate in class discussions. Hence, perhaps whereas the assumptions about adult learners may apply in non-Western cultures to some extent, the application of andragogy may differ in the classroom. For example, the idea that learners move from dependent to more independent learners is a tenet of andragogy. In fact, helping the learner to become more self-directed is a goal of the instructor. In collectivist cultures where the group is more important than the individual, self-directed learning may include more group activities such as collaborative or cooperative learning. In addition, while the learning contract may work in a variety of cultures, some students may rely on the instructor to be more directive in constructing the learning contract as learners may be more reticent to express their learning needs.

Still, the assumptions of andragogy may be useful to different cultures' curriculum. First, andragogy assumes that the adult learner has a great deal of experience that can be utilized in the learning process. Any andragogically oriented curriculum would tap into that experience by having adults connect their experiences to the material through discussions, personal journal writing, small group work, or individual papers. Teachers would be trained to put the learner's experiences at the center of the class and to draw on them in order to teach the material. Second, andragogy assumes that learners need to know why they are learning something. An andragogy-friendly curriculum would provide concrete reasons to the learner as to why the content was important for their real lives. Course assignments would invite the learners to apply course content to their lives though assignments. Third, moving the learner from dependence to independence would be utilized thoughout the curriculum. Learning contracts would be a staple in an andragogically oriented curriculum. Teachers from all disciplines could modify learning contracts to fit their subject and the level of dependence of their learners. Fourth, addressing learners' psychological and physical comfort would be part of any curriculum. Examining and addressing psychological barriers for learners, learning styles, and learning preferences would be part of any curriculum. Fifth, teaching learners to be self-directed would be part of every class. This could be accomplished through assessing learners' self-direction and slowly going toward more independence using culturally sensitive approaches.

The implementation of andragogical concepts through classroom practices can be culturally modified, if necessary. For example, creating a comfortable climate for learning may differ across cultures. However, the idea of making the classroom a safe place to learn where trust and respect are abundant may transcend cultures. Likewise, the process for creating learning contracts may differ across cultures.

In sum, whether andragogy is a set of assumptions for adult learners or just a different way of learning, learners can benefit from its application to the curriculum and the classroom. Learner-centered instruction benefits the teacher and learner, creates new knowledge, and promotes lifelong learning that benefits the individual and society.

References

Adams, D., & Hamm, M. (1996). *Cooperative learning: Critical thinking and collaboration across the curriculum* (2nd ed.). Springfield, IL: Charles C. Thomas, Publisher.

Alfred, M. (2003). Sociocultural context and learning: Anglophone Caribbean immigrant women in the U.S. post-secondary education. *Adult Education Quarterly, 53*(4), 242-260.

Anderson, G., Boud, D., & Sampson, J. (2004). *Learning contracts: A practical guide.* London: Routledge: Falmer.

Armstrong, T. (2000). *Multiple intelligences in the classroom* (2nd ed.). Alexandria, VA: Association for Supervision and Curriculum Development.

Bangura, A. K. (2005). Ubuntugogy: An African educational paradigm that transcends pedagogy, andragogy, ergonagy and hetagogy. *Journal of Third World Studies, 22*(2), 13-53.

Booth, D. (1999). "By chance and by design: Incidents of Learning." Lecture at St. Olaf

College, Northfield, Minnesota on October 12, 1999. Retrieved July 15, 2007, from http://www.stolaf.edu/people/booth/incident.html.

Clardy, A. (2005, August 1). Andragogy: Adult learning and education at its best?. *Online Submission*, (ERIC Document Reproduction Service No. ED492132) Retrieved June 1, 2007, from ERIC database.

Cranton, P. (2006). Fostering authentic relationships in the transformative class-room. In E. Taylor (Ed.), *Teaching for change: Fostering transformative learn-ing in the classroom* (pp. 5-13). New Directions for Adult and Continuing Education, No. 109, 5-13. San Francisco: Jossey-Bass.

Cranton, P., & Carusetta, E. (2004). Perspectives on authenticity. *Adult Education Quarterly, 55*(1), 5-22.

Davenport, J. (1987, March). *A way out of the andragogy morass.* Paper presented at the Conference of the Georgia Adult Education Association. Savannah, GA.

Draper, J. A. (1998). The metamorphoses of andragogy. *Canadian Journal for the Study of Adult Education, 12*(1), 3-26.

Elias, J. L. (1979). Critique. Andragogy revisited. *Adult Education, 29*, 252-255.

Ellis, E., Worthington, L., & Larkin, M. (n.d.). *Executive summary of the research synthesis on effective teaching principles and the segin of quality tools for educators.* University of Alabama, AL. Retrieved May 28, 2007, from http://idea.uoregon.edu/~ncite/documents/techrep/tech06.html.

Freire, P. (1970). *Pedagogy of the oppressed.* New York: Continuum.

Gardner, H. (1995, November). Reflections on multiple intelligences: Myths and messages. *Phi Delta Kappan, 77*(3), 198-209.

Gardner, H. (2006). *Multiple intelligences: New horizons.* New York: Perseus Books Group.

Grace, A. P. (1996). Striking a critical pose: Andragogy—missing links, missing values. *International Journal of Lifelong Education, 15*(5), 382-392.

Grow, G. (1991). Teaching learners to be self-directed: A stage approach. *Adult Education Quarterly, 41*(3), 125-149.

Guglielmino, L. M. (1977). *Development of the self-directed learning readiness scale. Dissertation Abstracts International, 38*(11), 6467 (University Micro-films No. AAT 7806004).

Guglielmino, L., & Associates (2006). *The Self-Directed Learning Readiness Scale.* Retrieved on May 27, 2007, from http://www.guglielmino734.com/prod01.htm.

Hartree, A. (1984). Malcolm Knowles' theory of andragogy: A critique. *International Journal of Lifelong Education, 3*(3), 203-210.

Kember, D., Kwan, K. P., & Ledesma, J. (2001). Conceptions of good teaching and how they influence the way adults and school leavers are taught. *International Journal of Lifelong Education, 20*(5), 393-404.

Knowles, M. S. (1950). *Informal adult education*. New York: Association Press.

Knowles, M. S. (1970). *The modern practice of adult education*. New York: Association Press.

Knowles, M. S. (1980). *The modern practice of adult education* (Rev. ed.). New York: Cambridge Book Company.

Knowles, M. S. (1989). *The making of an adult educator. An autobiographical journey*. San Francisco: Jossey-Bass.

Lee, M. Y. (1999). The role of cultural values in the interpretation of significant life experiences. In *Proceedings of the 40th Annual Adult Education Research Conference (AERC)* compiled by A. Rose (pp. 193-198). DeKalb, IL: Northern Illinois University. (ERIC Document Reproduction Service No. ED 431 901).

Lee, M. Y. (2003). Andragogy and foreign-born learners. In L. M. Baumgartner, M. Y.

Lee, S. Birden, & D. Flowers (Ed.), Adult l

Lee, S. Birden, & D. Flowers (Eds.), *Adult learning theory: A primer* (pp. 11-16). Information Series No. 392. Columbus, OH: Center on Education and Training for Employment (ERIC Document Reproduction Service No. ED 482 337).

Lin, L. (2006). Cultural dimensions of authenticity in teaching. In P. Cranton (Ed.), *Authenticity in teaching* (pp. 63-72). New Directions for Adult and Continuing Education, No. 111. San Francisco: Jossey-Bass.

Merriam, S. B., Caffarella, R. S., & Baumgartner, L. M. (2007). *Learning in adulthood: A comprehensive guide* (3rd ed.). San Francisco: Jossey-Bass.

Millis, B. J., & Cottell, P. G. (1998). *Cooperative learning for higher education faculty*. Phoenix, AZ: Oryx Press.

Misch, D. A. (2002). Andragogy and medical education: Are medical students internally motivated to learn? *Advances in Health Sciences Education, 7* (2), 153-160.

Oddi, L. F. (1986). Development and validation of an instrument to identify self-directed continuing learners, *Adult Education Quarterly, 36*(2), 97-107.

Pratt, D. D. (1988). Andragogy as a relational construct. *Adult Education Quarterly, 38* (3), 160-172.

Pratt, D. D. (1993). *Andragogy after twenty-five years*. In S. B. Merriam (Ed.), *An update on adult learning theory* (pp. 15-24). New Directions for Adult and Continuing Education, No. 57. San Francisco: Jossey-Bass.

Rachal, J. R. (2002). Andragogy's detectives: A critique of the present and a proposal for the future. *Adult Education Quarterly, 52*(3), 210-227.

Ray, C. W., & Chu, H. (2005). *Does andragogy work in Taiwan? An analysis from eastern cultural perspectives*. Paper presented at the Academy of Human Resource Development International Conference (AHRD) (pp. 101-108). (Estes Park, CO, Feb 24-27, 2005) (Symp. 4-3)

Roberson, D. N. Jr. (2002). *Andragogy in color*. ERIC Clearinghouse on Adult, Career, and Vocational Education Center on Training and Employment, Columbus, OH: Ohio State University. ERIC Document No. 465 047.

Robinson, C. F., & Kakela, P. J. (2006). Creating a space to learn: A classroom of fun, interaction and trust. *College Teaching, 54*(1), 202-206.

Saint Olaf College, N. (1971, January 1). *Paracollege.*. (ERIC Document Reproduction Service No. ED073739) Retrieved July 15, 2007, from ERIC database.

Savicevic, D. (1998). Understanding andragogy in Europe and America: Comparing and contrasting: In J. Reischmann, B. Michal, & J. Zoran (Eds.), *Comparative adult education 1998: The contribution of ISCAE to an emerging field of study* (pp. 97-119). Ljubljan, Slovenia: Slovenian Institute for Adult Education.

Savicevic, D. M. (1991). Modern conceptions of andragogy: A European framework. *Studies in the Education of Adults, 23*(2), 179-202.

Warren, C. (1989). Andragogy and N. F. S. Grundtvig: A critical link. *Adult Education Quarterly, 39*(4), 211-223.

Wilson, L. S. (2005). A test of andragogy in a post-secondary educational setting. Dissertation Abstracts International, 66 (07), 2465A (UMI No. 3184107).

Chapter 3
Learner-Derived Curriculum Development
Vivian W. Mott

Introduction

One strategic approach to curriculum development is to derive programs, courses, and syllabi from adult learners themselves. Whether formal or informal education, for credit or leisure learning, traditional curriculum development models can be readily adapted to support significant learner involvement in a wide variety of learning contexts and environments. Today's learners, in particular, respond positively to having input into their learning opportunities, and embrace assisting in design and development phases as well. This chapter considers not just the models and theories that support stronger learner involvement in the curriculum development process, but more importantly, provides the rationale for doing so, and suggests ways to ensure success in those endeavors.

There are numerous concepts, models, and theories common to the field of adult and continuing education that support the use of learners in developing curriculum. The chapter begins with an overview of three prominent adult learning models—andragogy, self-directed learning, and reflective practice—specifically including the tenets of each models and the rationale provided by these constructs for the inclusion of adult learners in curriculum development. Following this, social learning theory, a learner-centered teaching model, and collaborative learning are reviewed as additional support for learner-derived curriculum development. Case studies are then presented as successful examples of learner-derived curriculum development in formal, nonformal, and informal adult learning venues. The chapter concludes with a summary and implications for more significant learner involvement in curriculum development of adult and continuing education.

Model of Andragogy

Nearly half a century ago, Malcolm Knowles proposed the concept of andragogy to explain how teaching adults could be differentiated from teaching children. While Knowles did not actually coin the term *andragogy*, meaning the "art and science of helping adults learn" (1990, p. 43), he is responsible for the popularization of the concept in North America. Knowles told of first using the term *andragogy* "in an article in *Adult Leadership* in 1968" (p. 42), after learning of the concept from a Yugoslavian adult educator.

Knowles described the concept as a model based on assumptions about adult learners that originally included four distinct adult characteristics or predispositions; a fifth characteristic was later added. These five assumptions follow:

1. Self-directedness. Adults approach their learning in a more independent and self-directed manner as opposed to being dependent on a teacher for one's learning, resources, strategies, and evaluation of outcomes. Knowles went on to explain that self-directedness is always present on a continuum—that all learners, children and adults alike, are more or less self-directed depending on maturity, preexisting knowledge, motivation, and risk involved in the learning experience.

2. Rich reservoir of experience. As adults mature, "they accumulate an increasing reservoir of experience that becomes an increasingly rich resource for learning" (Knowles, 1990, p. 45). According to Knowles, our experience is important not only as a basis for greater and more meaningful learning, but also because such experience provides links and connections that teachers can use in instruction.

3. Readiness to learn. Learning in adulthood is often prompted by some real-life need, such as a life transition, developmental change, personal challenge, crisis, or opportunity. So, adults most frequently pursue their learning on a need to know basis rather than being ready to learn based on age or developmental stage (as with children), or advancement in a standard school curriculum.

4. Problem- or performance-centered orientation. For adults, learning is a means to an end, a process or endeavor aimed at enhanced competencies or skills needed for a job, life stage, or encountered challenge. Therefore, adults want their learning to have immediate application and relevance. Children, on the other hand, more frequently engage in subject-centered learning, sequenced according to some standard curriculum, and some of which will only be applicable at some future time in their lives.

5. Internal motivation. Adults are more often internally or intrinsically motivated to learn. Even though virtually all of formal education includes some external motivation in the form of grades, better jobs, or higher salaries, adults are more likely to focus on the knowledge gained, the experience itself, rather than any extrinsic reward that accrues. That is, even when learning is problem-focused or performance-centered, adults understand that learning is valu-

able and often its own reward, that the learning will add value to their lives, and that it will improve their tomorrows.

In particular, three of these assumptions underlying Knowles's (1990) explanation of andragogy suggest the need for a strong learner role in curriculum development efforts of the learning opportunities adults pursue—the self-directedness with which learners approach their learning, adult learners' rich store of valuable experience, and their problem- or performance-centered orientation to learning. Because the concept of self-directed learning developed as a critical and distinct concept in the field of adult and continuing education, it will be discussed separately in the next section. The rationale for learner involvement in curriculum based on learners' experience and problem-centeredness follows.

Adults possess a rich store of experiences that not only help make relevant their learning, but that should be used by instructors to help anchor and deepen learning. This is because adults have had opportunity for *more* experience by virtue of having lived longer, or simply because we enjoy (or struggle through) *different types* of experience. Adults are also largely defined by our experiences in terms of our very self-identity; as Knowles noted, "adults *are* what they have *done*" (1990, p. 50, original emphasis). Although this occurrence is much more common in the United States than in other countries of the world, almost any communication between two newly introduced people very soon typically turns to where we work, or what we do for a living, for example. Because of our significant investment in our experientially defined self-identity, adults always want to talk about, *to share*, what we've done, where we've lived and worked, what we've learned and accomplished. To dismiss this information, to trivialize it, is to dismiss not just our experiences, but our very selves. This is part of what makes adult learning environments so engaging, so rich, so collaborative. The rich store of adults' experiences not only enables learners to connect new knowledge to earlier experiences, anchoring the learning, making it meaningful and immediately relevant; it also allows adults to contribute more to their own and others' learning. These same advantages can be used as learners assist in the curriculum development process.

Knowles also maintained that adults pursue learning in a problem-centered or performance-centered way, rather than the subject-centered approach that children are exposed to. That is, learning in adulthood is best related to some real-world situation, opportunity, or problem that needs to be addressed through education or training. Consider these examples: Learning to diagram sentences in grammar school or memorizing algebraic theorems in high school. In our childhood thinking and learned compliance, even if we dared question the application value of such knowledge and skill, children accept this need for accumulated knowledge as just part of the schooling experience or something that would some-how show its usefulness at a later date. Adults rarely settle for such explanations and disembodied knowledge; learning must have almost immediate applicability and help us solve some current life situation. In Knowles's words, adults "engage in learning largely in response to pressures they feel from their current life situa-tion . . . education is a process of improving their ability to cope with life problems they face now" (1990, p. 53). So, curriculum development for adult and continu-ing education is best focused on resume writing rather than learning English, improved literacy so as to read a technical manual rather than grammar, computer skills, classroom management skills, conversational Spanish, or any other work-place or life competency needed to function, adapt, and improve. Adults whose lives and jobs depend on those skills are in the very best position to assist with such curriculum development. Finally, Knowles also suggested that "when the principles of andragogy are translated into a process for planning and operating educational programs, that process turns out to be quite different from the curricu-lum planning . . . traditionally employed" (1990, p. 59). The seven phases in-cluded in Knowles' andragogical model of program development—like most models, really—include attention to the learning environment and structure, need for analysis and measurable objectives, plans for effective instructional strategies and activities, and evaluation (also see Caffarella, 2002). Each of these phases, regardless of the model or context, can be enhanced with adult learners' involve-ment.

The distinctions inherent in these foundational assumptions of andragogy are strong indicators that learners can and should play an integral role in such development. Because of these two assumptions of andragogy—learners' rich experiences and problem-centeredness—involving learners in curriculum devel-opment processes promises to result in more relevant, innovative, significant, and immediately applicable educational opportunities.

Self-Directed Learning Model

Self-directed learning (SDL) describes the propensity and ability for adult learners to conceive, orchestrate, and evaluate their own learning. The massive and varied SDL literature differentially characterizes self-directed learning either as an instructional method, a process or approach to learning, or as a learner preference, characteristic, or personality trait. Though the work on the concept began with others many years prior, Hiemstra defined SDL in 1994 as "any study form [of learning] in which individuals have primary responsibility for planning, implementing, and even evaluating the effort" (para. 5).

Before Knowles identified self-directedness as one of the assumptions on which andragogy was based, Houle (1961/1988) and then Tough (1971) were studying and reporting how adults undertook learning projects on their own. Houle's landmark study of 22 adult learners in 1961 demonstrated primarily the reasons that learners engage in SDL. Houle's observations resulted in his now classic *Houle's typology*, a classification scheme that outlines learners' motivation to participate as learning orientation, goal orientation, or activity orientation, based on learning solely for learning's sake, as a means to some end, or merely for the social activity or engagement, respectively. Tough was a doctoral student of Houle's when he continued the stream of SDL research in his dissertation study of 66 people engaged in self-directed learning projects in Canada. Guglielmino (1977) later constructed a Self-Directed Learning Readiness Scale (SDLRS) to determine the degree to which learners could successfully engage in self-directed learning. Her SDLRS is still frequently used to measure self-directedness in adult learners with correlations attempted with learning style, learning outcomes, self-concept, occupation, career advancement, to name only a few. Brockett and Hiemstra (1991) later created a synthesized model they termed the Personal Responsibility Orientation (PRO) model based in learner autonomy and describing the degree to which learners took active control and responsibility for their own learning. And, in 1991 as well, Grow theorized that learners developed self-directed learning abilities in four stages differentiated by their degree of independence and ability. Based on these SDL stages, Grow contended that SDL could be integrated into learning experiences to enhance learning processes and outcomes. These few brief explanations highlight only some of the major contributions to the SDL literature; many other scholars, educators, and practitioners have contributed to the literature as well.

According to the SDL model, then, adults engage in significant learning in which they determine their own learning goals, locate learning partners, determine resources, and monitor the duration and ultimate success of their learning experience. Self-directed learning does not mean learning without a plan; nor does it occur in isolation. SDL can also occur in formal and nonformal, as well as informal settings. Grow's model of SDL is one of several conceptualized as an instructional process model in which teachers take on different roles depending on the SDL maturity or readiness of their learners. Brockett and Hiemstra's PRO model similarly suggested that "an educational agent or resource often plays a facilitating role" (1991, p. 24) in the SDL process depending on the learning context.

Self-directedness on the part of any learner, however, must be considered on a continuum. Adults, as well as children, can be self-directed to a minor or significant degree—depending on the maturity of the learner, depth of desire and motivation toward the learning endeavor, sophistication in locating learning resources and evaluating the merit of web-based and other resources, level of previous experience with the content or skill to be learned, and risk of the learning involved. Two self-directed learning projects from my own experience may help demonstrate how this continuum is dependent on several crucial factors. The first example involves my completely self-directed, though perhaps less than stellar, attempts to learn conversational Spanish. I purchased books and audio tapes that I studied and listened to in a faithful and carefully planned manner. I invested in computer software that would not only allow me to listen to a variety of native Spanish speaking individuals in daily conversation, but actually corrected my attempts at mimicking the phrases as directed. Later, I joined an informal group of others who were trying to learn the language as well. We frequented restaurants and other Latino businesses where we could "practice" our barely recognizable Spanish, and even took a quick weekend trip to Mexico with hopes of becoming more proficient. I was well into Grow's Stage 4 (1991) as a competent self-directed learner and achieved a moderate degree of success. In the other example, years ago I decided I wanted to learn to fly. The requisite meteorology, navigation, and aerodynamics content were easily secured from my local library and my husband's comprehensive, if dated, library; even the flight school sessions of aircraft systems, instrumentation, and aircraft performance were approached with a confident dose of self-directedness on my part. I was thrilled with the flight simulator and successfully completed a preflight instrument check, take-off, right and left banks, and "landing"—albeit, all safe on the ground. Be assured, however, that in the first few minutes of that first actual flight (even with dual controls and an expert flight instructor in the seat beside me), I was a decidedly Stage 1 (Grow, 1991) dependent learner, with no evidence of self-directedness and in grave need of a teacher and authority figure to tell me what to do next.

Regardless of the placement of individual learners on the continuum of self-directedness, adult learners' ability and desire to plan and carry out their own learning and, consequently, the value of their involvement in curriculum development initiatives are without question. Scholars, practitioners, and learners have long challenged the assumption that adult learning requires the guidance or even presence of an instructor; the same can be said of curriculum development whether one considers SDL an instructional method, learning process, or learner characteristic.

Reflective Practice Concept

Though many have written on the concept of reflective practice over the past quarter century, much of the work currently cited on reflection and reflective practice is that of Donald Schön (1983, 1987). Schön maintained that reflective practice is grounded in the necessarily complex intersection of the "high, hard ground of technical rationality" (1983, p. 49) and the metaphorical *swamp* of professional practice—practice often filled with ambiguous, ill-defined, and conflicting situations. Schön maintained that the "artistic, intuitive processes that some practitioners bring to situations of uncertainty, instability, uniqueness, and value conflict" (p. 49) help mediate such unsettling conditions and "account for practical competence in divergent situations" (p. 49).

Reflective practice is a "developmental process in which practitioners first learn a system of rules and procedures, recognize their appropriate application within particular situations, and then develop and verify new forms of knowing in actual practice situations" (Mott, 2000, p. 28). One's capacity to engage in reflective practice is based on experience, tacit and explicit knowing, knowledge of formal theories and theories-in-use, and critical thinking. Mott further described reflective practice as the

> *capacity for thinking about . . . actions while engaged in the midst of practice. This active consideration of one's knowledge and behavior aids in reframing the challenges of practice, and enables the professional to cope more successfully with novelty and uncertainty of practice for a more appropriate response.* (Mott, 1994, p. 12)

Reflective practice involves a deliberate quieting or pause that allows practitioners to consider not only their formal knowledge and espoused theories about any given situation, but also their tacit knowing, theories-in-use, and practical knowledge or intelligence about the issue. Such introspection should also provide for the examination of assumptions, consideration of alternative and multiple perspectives, and the deliberation about one's actions in the circumstance. The outcome of our reflection should be the improvement of practice in terms of more reasoned thought and action.

According to Schön (1983), for most practitioners, such quieting and introspection occurs after the fact, or perhaps in the midst of paused action—when a problem has already occurred and we're thinking about it after the fact. Schön referred to this as *reflection-on-action* and suggested that such reflection carries a past orientation to it, in that it cannot affect the action being reflected upon, but only that which may occur in some future time (1983, 1987). Examples of reflection-on-action are common, not only in our professional practices, but in our personal lives as well. Consider, for instance: our reflection on a troublesome conversation, wishing we had said something other than what was said; reconsideration of a class assignment when students have not performed well; a change in driving habits after a close call on the highway; or even the adjusting of a recipe after a cake fails to rise in the oven.

For some of us, however, some of the time, we engage in reflection in the midst of action—what Schön referred to as *reflection-in-action* (1983, 1987), occurring as it does without pause or before the cessation of our action. In contract to reflection-on-action, reflection-in-action has a future orientation to it, in which "no interruption of action occurs, thinking and doing occur simultaneously while our reflection and reframing can still make a difference" (Mott, 1994, p. 35). According to Schön, reflection-in-action is often unconscious and may occur spontaneously when we sense that some aspect of our actions is no longer working or could be improved. While examples of reflection-in-action are often cited in the arts—such as impromptu jazz sessions or theater scenes, or the painting that emerges differently than planned—examples can also be found in medicine, education, law enforcement, and other contexts of professional practice in which expert practitioners engage (Mott, 1994, 1996, 2000; Schön, 1983, 1987).

If one of the goals of higher education is the development of reflective practice among practitioners, then the involvement of the learner in the development of that learning is crucial. Outside of preparatory education, much of the learning that takes place in one's profession comes about in response to the problems of the practice itself through the processes Schön described as reflection-in-action or reflection-on-action. Hence, the more involvement the learner can have in the curriculum development process, the stronger the learning and resulting link and relevance to practice.

Social Learning Theory

Merriam, Caffarella, and Baumgartner explain that "learning as a process . . . focuses on what happens when the learning takes place. Explanations of what happens are called learning theories" (2007, p. 277). One of major learning theories in adult and continuing education is social learning theory—one learning theory above others that offers support for the involvement of adult learners as members of curriculum development teams.

Even though the origins of social learning theory can be found in both behavioral and cognitive orientations (Merriam et al., 2007), the social and cognitive aspects of the theory soon grew in prominence as an organizing framework for the theory and explanation of how learning may occur. Behaviorism, however, remains important to understand since the interaction of individuals and their environment significantly influence learning and thus the potential for curriculum development. Social learning theory suggests that learning occurs when people observe others' behavior (a cognitive process), all of which takes place in a social setting. According to Schunk, "people acquire knowledge, rules, skills, strategies, beliefs, and attitudes" (1996, p. 102) by observing others, thus learning the rules, adaptations, and resulting consequences of what was observed. Some theorists maintain that imitative behavior must follow as a result in order for learning to occur, while others advocate that learning can occur from observation alone (Bandura, 1976, 1986; Hergenhahn & Olson, 2005; Lefrancois, 1999).

Bandura's (1976, 1986) conceptualization of social learning theory is perhaps the best known and has focused primarily on three factors central to an understanding of how the theory works—the social context, self-regulation, and self-efficacy. That learning through observation must obviously occur in some sort of social environment may be an overstatement, but has given rise to numerous other related constructs about how and where learning occurs. By self-regulation, Bandura proposed that people monitor, control, and adapt their behavior based on the anticipated consequences. And, lastly, adoption and adaptation of observed behavior are assessed and further controlled as a function of their self-efficacy, or people's beliefs about their capacity to produce desired outcomes in their lives based on their behavior. Bandura summarized his understanding of social learning as a three-way interactive model in which the personal, behavioral, and environmental determinants of any learning formed a "triadic reciprocity." More simply stated, "what people think, believe, and feel affects how they behave" (Bandura, 1986, p. 25).

The intersecting factors of cognition, behavior, personal factors such as self-regulation and self-efficacy, and one's social environment account for the nomenclature of social cognitive learning theory ascribed to the theory by some. Social learning theory provides not merely a more comprehensive portrayal of how learning might occur; it can also guide how and why curriculum development efforts should involve learners themselves to promote that learning for adults as well.

Learner-Centered Teaching

Weimer's thought-provoking treatise on learner-centered teaching also offers guidance and rationale for including learners in the creation and development of their own learning experiences. In Weimer's landmark text (2002), *Learner-Centered Teaching: Five Key Changes to Practice*, she discussed five changes to teaching practice necessary to create the learner-centered classroom or experience. The five key changes begin with our consideration of the balance of power in our teaching, classrooms, and relationships with our students. She then suggests we examine our roles as teachers and in whose hands the responsibility for learning lies. The fourth key change to teaching practice focuses on an expanded function of the content we teach. And, Weimer's fifth and final key change involves alternative purposes of evaluation.

In each of the book's chapters, Weimer provides details of and justification for the change toward learner-centered teaching, gives examples and benefits of possible adaptations, and even alerts us to barriers to such change. Many programs, courses, and even classroom activities are often reputed to include active learning or to be student-centered. Weimer makes the distinction, however, that these two concepts are not at all the same as learner-centered teaching. Weimer also warns readers that none of these key changes to teaching practice is easy to implement (even partially) due to restrictive higher educational policies, credentialing agencies, requisite professional competencies, faculty and student resistance, institutional culture, and even time. She promises, however, greater learning outcomes and rewards for both students and teachers will be accrued with even moderate attempts regarding the five changes.

The first three keys to learner-centered teaching are closely related, dealing with roles of teacher and learner and the interaction among them. In her explanation of the balance of power in our teaching, Weimer (2002) cites grading scales, course objectives, assignments, textbook choices, and even seating charts, for example, which are all determined with little if any learner input. She suggests such feasible adaptations as assignment choices, reading choices and supplements, or alternative evaluation measures, all determined in concert with, if not by, the students themselves. She stresses that changes in teacher role is not an abdication of responsibility, but a sharing of control in the learning environment in order to place the responsibility for learning back in the students' hands. Regarding our roles as teachers—integrally related to the issue of balance of power—Weimer urges teachers to relinquish even some of their authority role, urge students toward discovery learning, and help students see their capacity as creators of knowledge rather than merely consumers. In the third closely related key change, Weimer suggests that placing responsibility for learning with students will enhance their learning experience and provide them with the tools they will need to succeed outside of the classroom. She identifies such means of doing so as requiring students to establish class norms, formulate rules for discussion, or decide penalties for academic integrity violations. Learners will often resist taking on such responsibility; to move students forward, teachers must employ both support and challenge, with sufficient encouragement of their progress and recognition of their comfort level in new roles.

The fourth and fifth keys to learner-centered teaching involve looking at content and evaluation from different perspectives. Weimer (2002) suggests that teachers are too focused on covering content instead of using content as a means to learning. Admittedly in many programs and courses, some specific body of knowledge is requisite for advancement in a curriculum or for competency assessment. Where possible, however, Weimer urges teachers to help learners discover how they learn, engage in inquiry-based or discovery learning, and so move toward greater responsibility for their own learning. By doing so, learners are able to continue learning on their own after their formal educational experience ends. Expanding the purposes and value of evaluation can also help develop increased learner responsibility and facilitate learning of course content. Weimer suggests that teachers can lead the way in helping learners avoid placing too much importance on tests, quizzes, and grades. Tests, for instance, should be designed so that learners are motivated and encouraged by their success rather than as a demonstration of how hard the course is to pass. She suggests such adaptations as student submission of test questions, group exams with follow-up reviews, optional test formats, and rubrics to demystify the process, prompt studying and thereby learning.

Learner-centered teaching is "messy" and must evolve; the process will often feel unsettled and ambiguous to both teacher and student. It involves constant reflection, examining of assumptions, and renegotiation by all parties. Inherent in Weimer's (2002) five key changes to teaching are suggestions, justifications, and methods for the increased contribution of learners to curriculum development efforts. The justifications Weimer provides for greater balance of power, shifting authority roles, and increased learner responsibilities are all applicable for curriculum developers as well; just as the outcomes are greater in the learner-centered model, so might they be in curriculum development.

Collaborative Learning

Collaboration is a focused and interactive endeavor, often marked by experimentation, the use of shared rules, and involving work on a common "problem" or situation. The hallmark and central advantage of collaboration are that it frequently leads to innovative outcomes that could not have been achieved otherwise (Peters & Armstrong, 1998; Saltiel, 1998; Wood & Gray, 1991). When collaborators come together, a kind of synergy results in which the outcome "cannot be reduced to what either . . . contributed or knew . . . [and] is more than the individual contributions added together" (Peters & Armstrong, p. 75). Collaborative learning is collaboration with the express goal of knowledge acquisition or creation, often utilized in many contexts, such as higher education, the workplace, nonformal and informal learning initiatives, and grassroots education efforts. Moreover, proponents of collaborative learning, scholars, organizers, and others have maintained that collaborative learning is most valuable in meeting the needs of less advantaged adults. Among the many noted collaborative learning initiatives have been those that facilitated empowerment and social change. Many such efforts have first been in service of a shared vision of social justice and civic participation, transcending race, class, gender, and other dimensions of human difference (Horton & Freire, 1990; Kadel & Keehner, 1994; Knox, 2003).

Two *masters* of collaborative learning were Myles Horton of the Highlander Research and Educational Center in east Tennessee and Paulo Freire of Brazil. Peters and Armstrong (1998) described how Horton and Freire, working as "teachers/facilitators were able to achieve a delicate balance between bringing out the knowledge of people while going beyond the people's knowledge . . . while co-constructing knowledge" (p. 75). Research and practice-based experience as well suggest that collaborative learning groups are "more likely to generate creative solutions to complex problems, . . . [in ways that] actively engage the learner, build community and consensus, and honor the diversity of voices" (Will, 1997, p. 33) of those involved. Effective collaborations require effective communications, understanding of group dynamics, establishment of ground rules, clarification of expectations, and consideration for group size and structure, as well as learning and interaction styles (Cranton, 1996; Kadel & Keehner, 1994; Will, 1997).

Even with careful attention to the above consideration and plans, however, according to Kezar (2005), greater than 50% of all collaborations in higher education settings fail. Kezar stressed that even successful collaborative initiatives are frequently frustrating, and that the building and sustaining of commitment to the process and outcome are critical to their success. Peters and Armstrong suggested that such frustration is due to "habits of expectation—such as the ones that concern the proper role of the teacher as transmitter of knowledge and the role of the student as receiver of knowledge—and the power relationships that traditional role expectations often create" (1998, p. 84). Thus, as Weimer (2002) stressed in her learner-centered teaching model, leaders and facilitators of collaborative curriculum development initiatives should remain mindful of the balance of power in their efforts so that unequal distribution of power and authority are kept from influencing decisions, compromising the process and outcomes, and disenfranchising collaborating partners.

Curriculum development pursued in interdisciplinary and collaborative teams described above can result in stronger educational programs. Collaborative development outcomes are more meaningful because of the relationships and synergy produced by collective efforts; thus, learner involvement is even more crucial. Engagement, or the degree of active involvement in collaborative efforts, has a multitude of beneficial effects on those involved, both affecting the success of the collaboration as well as ensuring buy-in from those participating in the curriculum development efforts.

Summary

That most curriculum development processes fail to actively involve learners may be due to what Mott referred to as a "centuries-old positivist paradigm in which knowledge is thought to be an external commodity, a paradigm in which most of us are not taught to be creators of knowledge used in practice, but merely consumers" (1998, p. 672). Eraut further argued that the "barriers to practice-centered knowledge creation and development . . . are most likely to be overcome if higher education is prepared to extend its role from that of creator and transmitter . . . to that enhancing the knowledge creation capacity of individuals" (1994, p. 57). Scholars and practitioners alike affirm the knowledge generated in practice to be as valuable, if not more so, than that learned in formal preprofessional education. So could be curriculum development efforts created out of real need by those invested in the outcomes and for whom the development occurs. The constructs, models, and theories summarized in the foregoing pages outline both the supporting tenets and rationales for the increased participation of learners in curriculum development. The following section offers further demonstration of that advantage through case studies from formal, nonformal, and informal education and training contexts.

Exemplary Case Studies from Formal, Nonformal, and Informal Education

Case studies are an effective way to demonstrate, as well as clarify and elaborate, how the constructs, models, and theories of adult and continuing education described above reinforce the potential contribution of adult learners in curriculum development initiatives. The following three examples are drawn from formal, nonformal, and informal educational settings. In the first example, a combined Executive Masters of Business Administration and Masters of Public Health degree program involved students admitted to the program as members of a steering committee charged with redesign of the program, course, and syllabi. The second example demonstrates the significant and invested learner involvement of displaced workers enrolled in an outplacement training program for a textile manufacturing facility. And, the third case study details the collaborative curriculum development efforts of several faith communities, human service agencies, and a local technical/community college as they work with adult learners to enhance the reading levels, employability, and quality of life of the residents.

Formal Education

This case study describes an Executive Masters of Business Administration/ Masters of Public Health degree program. In the midwestern United States, a comprehensive state university is home to five colleges and schools; the university offers more than 30 separate undergraduate and graduate degree programs and is the academic home for approximately 1,000 faculty and just under 20,000 students. The university is a major employer and sole higher educational institution in a relatively small, but vibrant, urban area of approximately 100,000 citizens with an extended metropolitan area of nearly 300,000. Within the city and 25 mile radius are a wide variety of businesses and industry, two hospitals, and a full complement of social services and nonprofit agencies, all of which enjoy a healthy economic outlook.

In response to requests from practitioners, critical emerging community health issues, and pressure from credentialing agencies, two of the colleges and schools in the university decided to collaborate on a unique, interdisciplinary preprofessional degree initiative to serve healthcare practitioners and administrators who would ultimately also be required to demonstrate effective business management acumen. Limited university funding to support development and implementation of the new degree was supplemented by funding from three external grant sources, and a coalition of community healthcare partners. The resulting new degree was a 60-semester hour joint Masters of Business Administration (MBA) and Masters of Public Health (MPH). The joint Executive MBA/MPH degree was housed in the College of Business and School of Allied Health, collectively home to 120 faculty. Requirements for admission to the executive degree program included current employment in an administrative capacity in a healthcare practice, hospital, nursing or other community healthcare facility, public health agency, or healthcare-related nonprofit agency. While some of the external funding provided tuition support, much of the cost incurred was covered by the participants' employers.

After completion of two academic semesters of the expensive and specialized joint degree, a formative assessment was initiated by the two academic units – with assistance from the funding agencies, contributing healthcare providers and agencies, and the degree candidates themselves. Through survey, in-depth individual interviews, and focus groups, the evaluation process determined significant dissatisfaction with the program on the part of both those enrolled and their employers. In fact, in only one academic year, the program had lost nearly one-quarter of the original 50 entering candidates. Specifically, the assessment found (a) a lack of awareness and consideration of candidates' competencies upon entering the program, (c) insufficient advising and counseling regarding scheduling, field experiences, and other student concerns, (c) lack of relevance in course content relative to job responsibilities, and (d) ineffective instructional and evaluation strategies.

Following the evaluation, the assessment team (comprised of instructional designers, subject matter experts, contributing employers, and representatives from the degree candidates) began an intensive redesign and development process of the entire joint degree—including admission requirements, course sequence, content and texts, instructional strategies and in-class activities, and the field internship and applied project required for graduation. The most valuable insights provided in the redesign of the degree and related course development came from the remaining 38 candidates who were in the early stages of their degree program and the 12 newly entering participants. Specifically, a competency assessment was designed by one group of degree candidates and shared with the instructors for use in building on participants' knowledge base, thus furthering their learning and developmental opportunities. Core and elective course selections were paired to the requisite competencies in their administrative roles. Suggestions were implemented to assign mentors from partner agencies and organizations, and counseling teams were formed with members from both the university programs and contributing healthcare providers. Expert administrators and practitioners from the contributing healthcare agencies were contracted to teach or co-instruct some of the course sections, thus providing current *real-world* applied relevance in the course content. And, applied projects and field experiences were redesigned to be more developmental, aligned with the employers' strategic plans and community needs, and which would build on the candidates' growing knowledge and career goals.

Following the second academic year of the three-year joint degree, the continuing formative assessment revealed significantly improved satisfaction with the degree program in general, course content and outcomes, and counseling services. Now, entering their third year of the new joint Executive MBA/MPH degree, only 3 additional candidates have withdrawn and the remaining original 35 are beginning their final year of applied projects and internship placements. The third cohort of 20 new candidates is anxiously waiting to begin the redesigned and improved joint degree—made possible in part by the involvement of adult learners in the curriculum development process.

Nonformal Education

This case study concerns out-placement training in textile manufacturing. In a small city in the southeastern United States, a textile manufacturing facility employing approximately 200 workers was recently sold to a larger competitor. During the negotiations, economic developers hoped the sale might mean an expanded facility, new jobs, and a higher tax base for the community with few other industries. Unfortunately, the new owners announced that the facility would be sold and the manufacturing process moved to an offshore location where lower wages could be paid, thus reducing manufacturing costs. While the upper level management team was offered lucrative relocation packages to other facilities, the 200 line employees were told they would receive 6-month severance packages of incrementally reduced wages and health care/insurance benefits, and be eligible for an outplacement training and job-skills assessment program that should help them secure other local employment. The affected employees ranged in age from mid-20s to early 60s, and some had worked for the company for more than 30 years. For many of the men and women, this was the only paid employment they had known. The majority of the displaced workers had either graduated from high school or had completed their general education diploma through an educational assistance program offered through technical/community college system in the state. Approximately 30 percent of the mid-level line managers, foremen, quality assurance personnel, and technicians had either associate degrees or some college.

A consultant was hired by the parent company to coordinate and implement an outplacement training assistance program. In cooperation with the local technical college and career counselor from company headquarters, the consultant was charged with developing and conducting a job skills assessment and interest inventory for all displaced workers who requested it; planning and implementing a training curriculum to prepare workers for available jobs in the region; and evaluation measures that would assess the success of the outplacement initiative. The approach employed by the consultant and career counselor was a collaborative one that included the displaced workers in as many aspects of the initiative as possible.

Although some of the displaced workers were involved in administering the early assessments and inventories to their coworkers, it was in the planning process of the various training curricula that they were most instrumental. The outplacement team embraced an interactive curriculum development approach and involved the workers themselves in virtually every step of the process. The displaced workers certainly assumed a problem-centered approach to the situation. Since what they needed to learn would eventually enable them to find perhaps even more advantageous employment, their interests were not in random content, but in solving the problem of their sudden unemployment. The workers also brought their rich store of experience and knowledge to bear on the curriculum development and even subsequent team-oriented training for one another. Given the short time frame in which the consulting team worked to prepare the displaced workers for new employment, building on what the workers already knew and working with them to develop new competencies were crucial. Following the thorough skills assessment and interest inventories, building curricula that drew on the shared knowledge and experience of the workers enabled the training to be more interactive and dynamic, more relevant, and applicable in their new positions. The involvement of the displaced workers in this example of outplacement training ensured success in the development and implementation of training, enhanced job skills for the workers, and increased potential for success in their new positions.

Informal Education

The focus of this case study is community-based literacy education. In one south-central U.S. state, the literacy rates hovers between 35-50%. Many residents (both immigrants and native-born) struggle with literacy and numeracy in their own language, not to mention the English necessary to engage sufficiently in daily life. This case study explores the curriculum development efforts of several faith communities, social service agencies, and the local community college as they worked with adult learners to enhance the reading levels, employability, and quality of life of the residents.

In the center of this south-central state lies a sparsely populated, but large county of approximately 250,000 residents. The primarily rural county is a mix of numerous small unincorporated communities, three small towns, and one small city of approximately 50,000. The residents work in agriculture, light manufacturing, and service industries throughout the county; the median family income is approximately $30,000 annually. The unemployment rate, by contrast, is more than 7% and nearly twice the state average; additionally, seasonal employment accounts for much of the county residents' employment patterns. While many of the county residents, aged 18-65, have high school diplomas, the high school noncompletion rate for the public school system in the county is nearly 40%. And, according to the literacy council based in the county seat, the illiteracy rate in the county is over 25%, while the national average ranged between 5-10%. In contrast to the working age residents, the county is also home to a growing senior population; many of these older residents have literacy needs as well. Because of the depressed rural economy in the county, some of these seniors are also faced with the need for retraining for continued or new employment.

A state technical and community college system serves the higher and continuing education needs of those residents with education beyond high school, as well as for those in jobs with continuing education benefits or requirements. In concert with several faith communities and the literacy council, the technical/community college system offers a variety of training opportunities to county residents. One model literacy and employment education program is the result of broad interagency collaboration, is supported by a variety of external funding agencies, and enjoys full classes and frequent waiting lists.

The collaboration effort to serve the literacy and employability needs of the county residents was the brainchild of the county's technical/community college system. Following their participation in a county "Workers' Resource Fair," college personnel became aware of the many duplicative but limitedly successful efforts being undertaken by the county's literacy council and several faith communities throughout the county. Leaders discovered multiple literacy initiatives, employability training, computer classes, and career counseling sessions often being conducted in the same locations throughout the county – each with marginal enrollment and nearly prohibitive costs to each small agency or organization in terms of both actual monetary resources and volunteer hours. These technical/community college personnel quickly summoned leaders from various agencies, organizations, and faith communities to examine their respective efforts, compare challenges and successes, and discuss how they could collectively improve services to their county residents. In an innovative and responsive manner, representatives from several faith communities, senior and social service agencies, and the technical/community college began to better coordinate the services offered.

At the insistence of the literacy council, a large steering committee representing consumers of the various programs was convened to assist with the coordination of the new training and education efforts. The invested committee of adult learners gathered comprehensive information about the variety of programs being offered in the county—enrollment numbers, costs, locations, course duration, and completion rates. They helped revise a needs assessment survey, including the translation into three languages that would support outreach to even more residents. Also, with the assistance of an intern from a nearby university campus, these adult learners contributed significantly to the redesign and development of existing programs and the creation of new advantageous programs as well.

Approximately 36 months following the initiation of this collaborative team and redesign of a variety of programs, a team of evaluators from all of the agencies, organizations, faith communities, and the technical/community college reconvened to consider the success of their collaboration. Their report indicated literacy and English as a second language (ESL) classes had served a total 2,700 residents; GED and adult basic education classes had successfully prepared 135 men and women to pass the state high school equivalency test; a streamlined variety of employability classes, including resume-writing, interviewing skills, and business communication classes had resulted in 350 individuals either securing employment or promotion; and more than 200 residents had completed a variety of computer classes. The report also noted the involvement of nearly 50 underemployed residents and participants of former training sessions as one of the key factors in the success of the new programs.

Conclusion and Implications for Education and Practice

This chapter suggests that curriculum development initiatives can and should involve the learners for whom programs are planned. Adult learning constructs and models such as andragogy, self-directed learning, and reflective practice were briefly outlined to provide guiding tenets and rationale for such involvement. Social learning theory and models for learner-centered teaching and collaborative learning were also described as further basis for why and how adult learners can contribute to the development of programs in which they may be participants. These conceptual and theoretical constructs were followed by three case studies that further demonstrated and clarified how others had used the models and theories as they involved adult learners in curriculum development for new program development, program improvement, and redesign.

While it may seem intuitive for learners themselves to be included in curriculum development, this chapter provided support and rationale for doing so. Given the complexity and dynamics of today's world of work, the quickened rate of knowledge obsolescence, technological innovation, interdependent world political and economic contexts, such collaboration just makes *good sense*. More examples, similar to those provided earlier in this chapter, abound describing the use of master teachers as clinical curriculum specialists, expert nurse educators as subject matter experts, and those in areas such as business management, computer sciences, and medical education (to name only a few) serving in a variety of contributing roles in successful curriculum design and improvement initiatives. Adult learners who are not only capable, but who also have a vested interest in the process and product of curriculum development must be at the table with program planners, instructional design specialists, and subject matter experts.

Implications for involving adult learners in curriculum development processes are significant for both education and professional practice. For formal education, actively involving learners in curriculum development initiatives can result in improved programs of study, course availability and focus, and class activities; it also increases buy-in of potential and existing program participants. Programs may also be more innovative, learner-centered, relevant, and immediately applicable. In nonformal and informal educational programming, the same can certainly be true, and additional value accrues in the cost savings from involving volunteer learners. The implications for practice are numerous as well, including increased collaboration and partnerships, enhanced pre-professional education and training, more pragmatic internships and field experiences, among others. From the standpoint of all stakeholders – educational institutions, credentialing and professional agencies, practitioners, and learners themselves, involving learners in curriculum development is not only legitimate and prudent, it is the wise course of action.

References

Bandura, A. (1976). Modeling theory. In W. S. Sahakian (Ed.), *Learning: Systems, models, and theories* (2nd ed.) (pp. 391-409). Skokie, IL; Rand McNally.

Bandura, A. (1986). *Social foundations of thought and action: A social cognitive theory.* Englewood Cliffs, NJ: Prentice Hall.

Brockett, R. G., & Hiemstra, R. (1991). *Self-direction in learning: Perspectives in theory, research, and practice.* London: Routledge.

Caffarella, R. S. (2002). *Planning programs for adult learners* (2nd ed.). San Francisco: Jossey-Bass.

Cranton, P. (1996). Types of group learning. In S. Imel (Ed.), *Learning in groups: Exploring fundamental principles, new uses, and emerging opportunities* (pp. 25-32). New Directions for Adult and Continuing Education, No. 71. San Francisco: Jossey-Bass.

Eraut, M. (1994). *Developing professional knowledge and competence.* Washington, D.C.: Falmer.

Grow, G. (1991). Teaching learners to be self-directed: A stage approach. *Adult Education Quarterly, 41*(3), 125-149.

Guglielmino, L. M. (1977). *Development of the self-directed learning readiness scale.* Unpublished doctoral dissertation, College of Education, University of Georgia.

Hergenhahn, B. R., & Olson, M. H. (2005). *An introduction to theories of learning* (7th ed.). Englewood Cliffs, NJ: Prentice Hall.

Hiemstra, R. (1994). Self-directed learning. In T. Husen, & T. N. Postlethwaite (Eds.), *The International Encyclopedia of Education* (2nd ed.) Oxford: Pergamon. Retrieved July 28, 2007, from http://home.twcny.rr.com/hiemstra/sdlhdbk.html.

Horton, M., & Freire, P. (1990). *We make the road by walking: Conversations on education and social change.* Philadelphia, PA: Temple University Press.

Houle, C. O. (1988). *The inquiring mind* (2nd ed.). Madison: University of Wisconsin Press & Norman, OK: Oklahoma Research Center for Continuing Professional and Higher Education. [Original work published in 1961]

Kadel, S., & Keehner, J. A. (1994). *Collaborative learning: A sourcebook for higher education, Vol. 2.* Washington, DC: National Center on Postsecondary Teaching, Learning, and Assessment.

Kezar, A. (2005). Redesigning for collaboration within higher education institutions: An exploration into the developmental process. *Research in Higher Education, 46*(7), 831-860.

Knowles, M. S. (1990). *The modern practice of adult education: From pedagogy to andragogy.* New York: Cambridge.

Knox, A. B. (2003). Future directions for collaborative strategies. *Adult Learning, 14*(2), 29-30.

Lefrancois, G. R. (1999). *The lifespan* (6th ed.). Belmont, CA: Wadsworth.

Merriam, S. B., Caffarella, R. S., & Baumgartner, L. M. (2007). *Learning in adulthood* (3rd ed.). San Francisco: Jossey-Bass.

Mott, V. W. (1994). *A phenomenological inquiry into the role of intuition in reflective adult education practice.* Unpublished doctoral dissertation, Department of Adult Education, University of Georgia.

Mott, V. W. (1996). Knowledge comes from practice: Reflective theory building in practice. In R. W. Rowden (Ed.), *Workplace learning: Debating five critical questions of theory and practice* (pp. 57-63). New Directions for Adult and Continuing Education, No. 72. San Francisco: Jossey-Bass.

Mott, V. W. (1998, March). *Professionalization and reflective theory building in HRD*. Proceedings of the Academy of Human Resource Development (pp. 671-676). Washington, DC.

Mott, V. W. (2000). The development of professional expertise in the workplace. In V. W. Mott & B. J. Daley (Eds.), *Charting a course for continuing professional education: Reframing professional practice* (pp.23-31). New Directions for Adult and Continuing Education, No. 86. San Francisco: Jossey-Bass.

Peters, J. M., & Armstrong, J. L. (1998). Collaborative learning: People laboring together to construct knowledge. In I. M. Saltiel, A. Sgroi, & R. G. Brockett (Eds.), *The power and potential of collaborative learning partnerships* (pp. 75-85). New Directions for Adult and Continuing Education, No. 79. San Francisco: Jossey-Bass.

Saltiel, I. M. (1998). Defining collaborative partnerships. In I. M. Saltiel, A. Sgroi, & R. G. Brockett (Eds.), *The power and potential of collaborative learning partnerships* (pp. 5-11). New Directions for Adult and Continuing Education, No. 79. San Francisco: Jossey-Bass.

Schön, D. A. (1983). *The reflective practitioner*. San Francisco: Jossey-Bass.

Schön, D. A. (1987). *Educating the reflective practitioners: Toward a new design for teaching and learning in the professions*. San Francisco: Jossey-Bass.

Schunk, D. H. (1996). *Learning theories: An educational perspective*. Englewood Cliffs, NJ: Prentice Hall.

Tough, A. (1971). *The adults' learning projects: A fresh approach to theory and practice in adult learning*. Toronto: Ontario Institute for Studies in Education.

Weimer, M. (2002). *Learner-centered teaching: Five key changes to practice*. San Francisco: Jossey-Bass.

Will, A. M. (1997). Group learning in workshops. In J. A. Fleming (Ed.), *New perspectives on designing and implementing effective workshops* (pp. 33-40). New Directions for Adult and Continuing Education, No. 76. San Francisco: Jossey-Bass.

Wood, D. J., & Gray, B. (1991). Toward a comprehensive theory of collaboration. *Journal of Applied Behavioral Science, 27*(2), 139-162.

Chapter 4
Designing Meaningful Curriculum for Disadvantaged Learners

Claretha H. Banks and Fredrick M. Nafukho

Abstract

Disadvantaged adult learners can be characterized based upon their diversity from mainstream adult learners. They may be defined as individuals and such groups of individuals comprising that population of adult learners with special educational needs relating to their various physical, mental, social, cultural, linguistic, and economic differences. Examples of special needs may include adult learners with culturally and linguistically diverse learning needs. To some extent, these adult learners are "disadvantaged learners" compared with mainstream American adult learners. When developing meaningful curriculum for this population of adult learners, insights into specific human conditions may broaden the designers' understanding of andragogical applications that may best be used to respond to their educational and social needs.

This chapter seeks to demonstrate how curriculum should be developed to distinguish among the various conditions that singularly or in combination attribute to the adult learners with diverse background needing special assistance. In addition, the chapter will analyze and synthesize the place and function of the practice of education for adults with special needs in the global community; allow for discussion of the ethical, legal, social, and economic justifications for providing services for adults with special needs; identify sources of networking for services provided for adult learners with special needs; and discuss the development of technologies and methodologies that have proven to be effective with the disadvantaged adult learning population.

Introduction

Within the world community, strategic approaches are needed to enhance the curriculum for disadvantaged adult learners. Disadvantaged learners can be characterized based upon their diversity from mainstream learners. They may be defined as individuals and such groups of individuals comprising a population of learners with special educational and learning needs relating to their socio-economic disadvantage based on: (1) cultural, ethnic, linguistic differences; (2) gender/role; (3) homelessness; and (4) incarceration. They may be blind/visually impaired, deaf/hearing impaired, physically exceptional, or mentally exceptional. They may need physical facilities/technological accommodations and/or networking with special providers. Without the curriculum being modified and developed to meet their needs, uneducated, disadvantaged adults can become more of a burden upon the world community. This chapter seeks to demonstrate how curriculum should be developed to distinguish among the various conditions that singularly or in combination attribute to the learners with diverse backgrounds needing special assistance. The chapter also analyzes and synthesizes the place and function of the practice of education for learners with special needs in the global community.

Global Adult Education

It is a truism that we now live in a globalized world that requires global curricula with the aim of promoting global learning partnerships. When developing meaningful curriculum for disadvantaged learners, insights into specific human conditions may broaden the designers' understanding of applications that may best be used to respond to their educational, economic, environmental, and social needs. Thus, the ethical, legal, social, and economic justifications for providing services for learners with special needs must be considered from a global perspective; sources of networking for services provided for learners with special needs must be identified; and development of technologies and methodologies which have proven to be effective with the disadvantaged learning population should be integrated into the curriculum.

Understanding the history of adult education can provide a foundation upon which one can build a curriculum for disadvantaged adults. This is not a new phenomenon. For many years the disadvantaged adult has been overlooked or intentionally left out of mainstream culture and education. As paraphrased from Merriam and Brockett (1997), international or global adult education can be traced back to *The 1919 Report* in Great Britain, the World Association of Adult Education which published an international handbook in 1929, and Laubach Literacy International. Knowing that the history of adult education is a long one provides one with the opportunity to explore effective curriculum methods that have been used worldwide to successfully educate adults. However, one does not find much that refers to the success of dealing with disadvantaged adults.

When referring to the global disadvantaged adult population, the people of Third World nations often come to mind. Third World nations are often "characterized by low per capita income, a low gross domestic product, poor health and nutrition, a high birthrate, and a primarily agricultural economy" (Merriam &

Brockett, 1997, p. 164). Based on this characterization, adults in these low and middle income countries could all be classified as disadvantaged and would represent a large extent of the world's disadvantaged adult education population since "70 percent of the world's people live in Third World countries" (Merriam & Brockett, 1997, p. 164). In today's globalized economy Third World countries are receiving more attention because of technological advances and the availability of natural resources such as oil, gold, and diamonds. They are also sought after due to cheap labor sources, yet there is still a need for basic education and lifestyle advances for laborers who are provided new opportunities through job creation and economic development.

There are many reasons for education of adults worldwide; yet, two of the most important reasons for education of adults has been the global economy and advanced technologies (Merriam & Brockett, 1997). Titmus (1989) also defined "four major categories of purpose of adult education worldwide" (Merriam & Brockett, 1997, p. 167):

1. [S]econd-chance education, which offers adults who missed it the kind of education obtainable in the initial education system. This may range from basic literacy to mature entrance to university.
2. role education, which is education for social function (outside employment) and includes social role education (e. g., as citizen, member of an association) and personal role education (e.g., as parent, spouse, retired person);
3. vocational education, that is, education in the skills and knowledge required in employment;
4. personal enrichment education, or education intended to develop the individual without regard to his or her social or economic function which includes, in effect, anything not covered by the other headings. (p. 384)

These categories appear to encompass the broad needs of adult education worldwide, but the implementation process is vastly different depending on the country and individuals involved. Disadvantaged adults can fall into all four categories. The delivery of the category(ies) of education needed vary across countries; however, "developing nations . . . have found formal education to be inadequate in raising the socioeconomic status of the underclass and in preparing people for work in a competitive world economy" (Merriam & Brockett, 1997, p. 170). Nonformal education has also been limited in its success, due to its "failure to reach the very poor and illiterate; uneven local leadership; resources that are spread too thinly, resulting in weak impacts and a lack of follow-up in skills development and/or a lack of methods for implementing newly learned skills" (Merriam & Brockett, 1997, p. 170).

Developing curriculum for disadvantaged adults requires a unique perspective with regards to the adults and their needs. From a global perspective there are disadvantaged adults in higher proportion to the non-disadvantaged adult population, and they suffer due to a lack of access to education for a sustained period of time.

Curriculum Needs

The sheer number of functionally illiterate and semiliterate adults throughout the world begs for a curriculum that will address their needs. The keen awareness of the importance of educated adults is profound. Immigration of adults throughout the world has also increased the need for adult education. Many adults are migrating from their native homelands in search of a better life, yet that life cannot be obtained without adequate education. Adults have basic educational needs beyond reading, spelling, writing, and arithmetic including "law for the layman, good health practices, practical economics, occupational orientation, and the fundamental concepts of science and social studies" (Smith, 1970, p. 6) regardless of their being identified as disadvantaged. Communication skills have consistently been an important skill for adult education (Puder & Hand, 1966; Smith, 1970); however, it is of paramount importance for globalization and disadvantaged adult success.

Historically, adult education curriculum has been hindered by two problems: "the great variety of settings considered adult education and the reluctance of many adult educators to discuss curriculum as a legitimate topic" (Langenbach, 1988, p. 1). Curriculums are developed to provide access to knowledge (Apple, 1979), yet there is much debate regarding what should be included within the curriculum for adults. Curriculum for disadvantaged adults has received very limited attention, but in the global economy, the education of the adult workforce is of preeminent importance. Nations throughout the world are competing for educated workers and those who are disadvantaged must be developed if countries are to become competitive. Curriculum for the general adult population is often rigorous and does not consider the specific needs of adults who fall into the disadvantaged category. Curriculum, however, can be modified to meet those needs; thus, the purpose of this chapter.

Disadvantaged Adult Students

Disadvantaged adult students present a significant challenge to the adult education community. They make up a large proportion of the adult learner population, yet there is very little if any empirical research that addresses their needs from a global perspective. The characteristics of these types of learners are varied and each has its own challenges and successes. Identifying successes that can be duplicated worldwide may produce elements that can significantly influence curriculum as we learn more about this population of learners.

Characteristics

All countries face challenges to developing disadvantaged adult students. Determination of who is a disadvantaged encompasses "[t]he rural poor, women, illiterate adults, ethnic minorities, immigrants, and people with disabilities" who are "commonly underserved in both industrialized and Third World nations" (Merriam & Brockett, 1997, p. 179).

The Rural Poor

Much of the world's population lives in rural communities but there is also a significant portion of those individuals who represent the rural poor who do not have access to the fundamental life resources such as electricity and indoor plumbing. Many do not have access to education as children and often grow up to become the illiterate adult population.

> *Though poor neighborhoods and families face daunting challenges, technology deployed in education can help remove inequities between the schools of the inner city and the suburbs, between cities and rural districts, and inequities faced by people with physical disabilities and by Native Americans. Technology can become the force that equalizes the educational opportunities of all...regardless of location and social and economic circumstance.* (Banks, Parker, & Thomson, 2006, p. 1102)

This should not only be a national goal in the United States but also worldwide (Reinventing Schools, p. 4). Resolving poverty issues may significantly raise the socio-economic status of the rural poor and providing access to education would reduce the number of illiterate adults in the global community (Muiru & Mukuria, 2005).

Women

Women have traditionally been excluded from educational systems worldwide and there are many programs throughout the world that seek to end domestic violence, teach human rights, and facilitate gender equality (Kollins & Hansman, 2005). Yet, there are not many that allowed women to be educated on an equal basis with men. They were taught domestic skills or encouraged to pursue traditional female careers such as nursing or teaching. In Kollins and Hansman's study in Bolivia, they found that "gender dynamics played an important role in the development [of the adult education] program" for women (p. 12). They also noted that:

> *When focused upon women, the ideal [adult education] program should not focus solely on household issues, but should address social, economic, and legal constraints present in the lives of women. Finally, the women should play the role of decision-makers in the program, not beneficiaries, thereby developing leadership abilities that they can translate into community and societal leadership roles.* (p.17)

These findings led them to reach the conclusion that:

> *The process utilized by the program is strengthened when women are not held in the domestic sphere, but instead in a space in which men and women can work together and in which there is a balance of power between teacher and student. Through this process, the balance of power in society can be challenged and shift as people become critically aware of the societal forces that shape their personal and political experience, and further, realize that they themselves are creating constantly changing "knowledge."* (p.18)

Women are vital to the success of the global economy. They make up almost half the world's population and must be included in the educational process for a society to be functionally effective. During World War II in the United States, women were asked to work in factories and teach more in the school system when the men went off to war. In Mexico many women were left to maintain their communities while the males immigrated to the United States in search of a better life. The experiences and differences among women are vast, yet their struggles are not their own. Their struggles become society's struggles when the systems of government have to support them because of their lack of an education and inability to support their families. Many women in the United States make up the working poor and the majority of welfare recipients (Ziegler, Ebert, & Cope, 2004).

Ethnic Minorities and Immigrants
Ethnic minorities and immigrants throughout the world have faced many struggles. Particularly "[i]n U.S. society, the myths that undergrid [welfare] programs stereotype and stigmatize the poor, particularly poor African American women, leading to a deficit-driven and judgmental view of welfare recipients highly infused with racism and sexism" (Sandlin, 2003, p. 164). The racist and sexist myths that were found in Sandlin's study have major implications for adult

educators. "Because these myths are providing context for these programs and guiding the beliefs held by teachers and promoted in curriculum materials, it is crucial that critical educations continue to deconstruct and problematize these myths" (p. 166). In most cases educators try to be objective in their assessment of students; yet, the disadvantaged, particularly ethnic minorities and immigrants, face many stereotypes and discrimination that are beyond their ability to control. Educators assume that because students may have a different dialect or speak a different language, they are illiterate and limited in their ability to obtain knowledge. Educators may "dumb" down the curriculum which limits students' ability to be challenged in the classroom. This can be very demotivating for adult students.

When immigrants leave their native, cultural environment to enter another country, they face many challenges beyond culture and language; however, these are two of the most essential barriers to their educational success. They are often asked to learn the language of the community into which they have entered, yet they struggle with adapting. In one case of older Russian immigrants, they faced barriers including: "perceived memory problems, shame, poor health, lack of accessible ESL classes, and Russian social context" (Hubenthal, 2004, p.104).

In 2000, Johnson-Bailey and Cervero reviewed eight handbooks that defined the field of adult education (Ribeiro, 2005). They found that "although race is a central location for the negotiation of power and privilege in education and in society, this topic has never formed the focal point of a single chapter in the entire corpus of eight previous handbooks" (Johnson-Bailey & Cervero, 2000, p. 151). Without consideration for racial and cultural differences within segments of adult education history, one must be concerned the curriculum within the field also lacks enough emphasis upon the differences of disadvantaged learners who are identified as such based upon their race or culture. Within the global educational environment, this issue must be addressed to achieve better opportunities for success.

Learners with Disabilities

Learners with disabilities have long been minimized in the educational process. "Physical disability can be defined as the restriction of activity caused by impairments, for example, the loss of a limb, involuntary movements, loss of speech or sight" (Carpenter & Readman, 2006, p. 131). However,

[P]eople with complex physical disabilities frequently benefit from one-to-one learning situations, a specially designed environment, and specialized equipment. By providing instructors with effective training in these areas, the potential for some physically disabled individuals to pursue further educa-

tional and career development activities can be facilitated. This would in-crease opportunities for community participation by those who are most marginalized. (Carpenter & Readman, 2006, p. 145)

By incorporating successful strategies in meeting the needs of the physically disabled into the adult education curriculum, educators may provide improvements in the social and economic status of physically disabled people (Carpenter & Readman, 2006; Jurkowski, Jovanovic, & Rowitz, 2002; Macht, 2000). Although individuals are protected under the Americans with Disabilities Act in the United States from discrimination due to their disability, educators must still remain cognizant of the need to remain objective when instructing individuals who are disabled. Covington (2004) noted that,

The presence or absence of a learning disability is secondary to instructors' attempts to create a humane and supportive relationship with learners, and to provide multiple opportunities for success using a curriculum based on the needs and interests of each adult. By creating such experiences, adult educators empower those they serve to move beyond the limits of learning. (p.101)

Disabled individuals are capable of being successful in the adult education class-room. Many tools and resources can improve the learning experience of the disabled student. With the introduction of the Internet, computers, and other techno-logical innovations, the abilities of the physically disadvantaged have been enhanced worldwide.

The Elderly

The aging of the population is of major consideration to adult educators throughout the world. Health care concerns of this population of adult learners are of paramount concern as their development is often contingent upon their ability to comprehend and analyze information (Hubenthal, 2004; Pennequin & Fontaine, 2000). The research regarding the educational function ability of the elderly is a part of continuous research (Denny, 1982; Willis, 1987, 1991; Yesavage, Lapp, & Sheikh, 1989) but the regression hypothesis is of note because it is "based on the assumption that with aging, cognitive functions undergo a destructuring process that reappears as childlike reasoning [and] the regression is considered irrevers-ible because the structures supporting reasoning mechanisms are believed to have been 'destroyed' " (Pennequin & Fontaine, 2000, p. 70).

Pennequin and Fontaine (2000) "found that elderly individuals will benefit most from remedial training if it is maintained over an extended period and if the previously reacquired skills are regularly reinstated" (p. 85) and that "training in categorization can help elderly persons regain some of the skills that they no longer seem able to use" (p. 85). Understanding the issues faced by older adults is very important to the future of adult education. As they retire from one career, they may be interested in pursuing other less strenuous forms of work that require learning a new skill. Their participation in the adult education classroom is not necessarily new; however, the numbers within this category of learners (60 years and above) is expected to increase significantly within the next 10 years.

Educational Access and Opportunity

Access and opportunity for disadvantaged adults to obtain an education have been an issue for centuries (Merriam & Brockett, 1997). In many countries, disadvantaged adults are often discriminated against with regards to equal access and opportunity for an education. Prosser (1967) identified four main elements through which adult learners have opportunities to learn: formal adult education, fundamental (basic) adult education, liberal adult education, and technical and in-training adult education.

Using Technology in Adult Education

In today's competitive environment, the access to technology is a major challenge for the rural poor. Although "the computer and Internet make global markets possible" (Berger, 2001, p. 162), it is ineffective if the rural poor and other disadvantaged adults do not have access to or know how to use the technology. Technology is being used to provide basic skills training, curriculum development, and teacher training (Merriam & Brockett, 1997), yet the access to computers is very limited in many low income countries due to lack of affordability. According to Banks, Parker and Thomson (2006),

> When integrating technology into the curriculum, it is very important to create plans and policies to ensure equitable access and use for all members of the learning community. Funding and professional development characterize the key means of supporting equitable access and use of technology to ensure technology literacy and to support meaningful learning for all students. (p. 1102)

Despite the limitations, technology combined with distance education can be a key to improving the educational opportunities of the disadvantaged. In the United States, "[t]he Bush administration . . . presented a blueprint for changes to federal adult basic education. The blueprint emphasize[d] improving program accountability, research to practice applications, expanding program choices, and increasing program flexibility" (Porter, 2004, p. 135). "The program flexibility identifies technology facilitated learning and distance learning to 'accelerate student achievement and expand access to adult basic and literacy education' (U.S. Department of Education [USDOE], 2003). These emphases … encourage[s] states to explore distance learning interventions in their instructional strategies" (Porter, 2004, p. 135).

When integrating technology into adult education programs, Gopalakrishnan (2006) found after evaluating eight different programs, the following list of items are critical to successful implementation:

1. This support must be available on demand.
2. It must provide personal encouragement, instructional mentoring, and technical support of a routine nature. Administrative level technical support can be procured in partnership with others.
3. Individuals from both educational and technical orientations can support teachers with technology integration as long as they are able to "translate" between the two domains and work with users of varying technical abilities. Administrative level technical proficiency is not required of the persons involved in supporting teachers to integrate technology.
4. The factors influencing an administrator's choice of the technology support model include the size of the program, its geographic span, and the leader's preferred connections to the technology support infrastructure of the parent organization.
5. Program leaders need to be aware that they may be creating within their organizations support roles that did not exist before. They also need to be sensitive to the fact that since these support persons are charged with changing classroom practice, they may be functioning in a leadership role without formal positional authority. As a result, program leaders must publicly legitimize the roles of these support persons. They must encourage teachers to cooperate with and be receptive to the ideas suggested by the technology support persons. (pp. 54-55)

Lack of Funding

According to Merriam and Brockett (1997), "[r]esearch has demonstrated that removing perceived barriers to participation in adult education, such as making a program cost-free or offering an on-site class, has little overall effect on increasing participation" (p. 189). They, instead, suggest that where people live, their color or sex, occupation, and ethnicity "all contribute to explaining the skewed participation patterns in adult education worldwide" (p. 189). The lack of funding for adult literacy programs continues to be a major barrier to access and opportunity for disadvantaged adults worldwide as noted by Muiru and Mukuria (2005) and Jaffee (2001), but as noted above, providing cost-free programs alone does not solve some of the problems associated with adult education programs for the disadvantaged.

All programs want to have funding sufficient for operations; yet, there never seems to be enough funding to meet the needs of the programs for the disadvantaged due to the magnitude of issues that they face. The needs appear insurmountable. From a global perspective, it is magnified much more; yet in Shanghai, they have introduced programs and are making concerted efforts to solve the most pressing problems first. "[A]dult educators face learners with a diverse array of needs. Some [needs] stem from the Cultural Revolution, others from living in a throbbing metropolis and the spatial geographies of a new individualism" (Boshier, Huang, Song, & Song, 2006, p. 202). Beijing has chosen to make investment in adult education a priority for citizens throughout China (Boshier, Huang, Song, & Song, 2006).

Funding issues are prevalent within the adult learning community as governments try to prioritize issues they believe to be most essential to the success of their nations. There are issues of poverty, war and defense, human rights, national security, import and export issues, technology infrastructure, agricultural, health care, the environment, and education. All of these issues and many others are important to the well-being of a nation's citizens and they are all in competition for the limited funds that a country has in its possession. As each nation determines what is most vital to its success, one would hope that educating its disadvantaged adult citizens would become a top priority. Basic education is essential, but continuous learning is a key to survival in the global economy. This will not occur without consistent funding.

Political Influence

Governments throughout the world have been involved in the education of their citizens for centuries. The opportunity for all citizens has not been of preeminent importance in most countries unless there was some type of crisis. In the United States, it was illegal for slaves to be taught to read until the Civil War (Smith, 1970). Apps (1979) noted that the purpose of continuing education is "to enhance the quality of human life in all its personal and social dimensions" (p. 91). As paraphrased from Blunt (2000) adult literacy only became a priority because of economic, workplace, and technological changes related to the global economy as opposed to community social welfare, justice, and equality. Based on this assessment, society appears to be of more importance than the individual.

As noted by Merriam and Brockett, there is "an ongoing debate about whether the individual or society should be the focus of adult education . . . with the individual at one end and the mission of changing society at the other" (p. 99) end of the continuum. This debate is true not only in North America but around the world. Many Third World governments focus adult education efforts on the skills that are needed to enhance their country as opposed to the skills that would enhance the individual. In some cases the individual may benefit as well; however, the achievement of knowledge and skills may not be the first priority. Apps (1989) identified four types of learning opportunities for adult learners: tax-supported, nonprofit, for-profit, and nonorganized. These opportunities can be found in other countries as well; tax-supported may be referred to as government-supported.

A number of factors and conditions limit adult learners' accessibility to adult education programs. Nafukho, Amutabi, and Otunga (2005) identified the following three factors that limit adult learners' accessibility to adult learning programs in Africa:

1. Program-based factors—The main issues of concern will include the nature of the adult program. Thus, is the program formal, or nonformal? Who is the target audience? "If the right groups of adult learners are in the right program, then there will be interest in the program as well as sustained attendance." (p. 78).
2. Community-based factors—These are factors relating to the general perception of the adult learning program by the community involved. As noted, "The adult community appreciation for education motivates adult learners to seek education places. However, if the reverse is true then, the adults' motivation to study falls very low and it does not matter how many adult education programs exist in a country, the attendance level will be very low." (p. 79).
3. Learner-based factors—As discussed earlier in this chapter, disadvantaged adult learners have unique characteristics that curriculum developers must recognize in order for them to enroll and complete their programs successfully. Factors such as the nature of the adult learners and their objectives for attending adult education programs will determine their motivation. In many cases if the adult learners do not see the connection between participation in adult education programs and improvement of life, then they are not likely to seek enrollment in adult education programs. The other personal factors that limit access to adult education may include work conditions, unemployment, marital status, stage in life span, size of the family, and family problems.

Muiru and Mukuria (2005) discussed in detail six of the main barriers to adult literacy program success in Kenya. They included: "lack of adequate resources, poverty, the HIV/AIDS pandemic, gender disparities, traditionalism, and lack of a literacy environment" (p. 90). They suggested that:

> *To raise levels of literacy, governments must be prepared to give high priority to literacy and integrate it with the country's political, economic, and social planning. Second, governments must adopt a multi-sectoral approach in order to promote literacy. All government ministries and departments must be mobilized in this endeavor. Third, there must also be a desire to eliminate poverty. In Kenya, poverty has been identified as the single underlying cause of low levels of literacy. A clearly demonstrated way must exist for neo-literates to begin a path to financial security. Finally, the negative attitude towards adult education among some individuals and communities has to change. It is important for individuals and communities to recognize the importance of literacy. (p. 99)*

The factors discussed above may not be unique to adult students in Africa but could be relevant to all adult learners the world over. It is of interest to learners in China (Boshier, Huang, Song, & Song, 2006), Israel (Oplatka & Tevel, 2006), Bolivia (Kollins & Hansman, 2005), Canada (Blunt, 2004), and many other countries.

Program Development

The success of the disadvantaged adult curriculum will be influenced by the program that is developed to implement the curriculum. Studies (Crandall & Peyton, 1993; Guerra, 1998; Shank & Terrill, 1995) have shown that there are needs exclusive of the educational needs of the participants that will need to be addressed. Kilgos and Valentine (2006) noted that "[p]rogram decisions have historically been made in the face of competing expectations from society and its various agencies, from the literacy profession and its institutions, and from the needs of individual students" (p. 152). The development of adult education programs has been a topic in the literature for many years (Sork & Buskey, 1986); yet, recently an emphasis on quality and accountability has led to more studies related to the assessment and evaluation of adult education programs. Ziegler (2005) evaluated the prospect of using the Malcolm Baldrige process as a possibility for evaluating the quality of adult education programs. The quality of the program is essential to its success; however, the right questions must be asked and the correct assessment and measurement tools must be employed. Understanding the effectiveness of programs has the potential to strengthen education of the disadvantaged worldwide. Quality programs such as the International Organization for Standardization (ISO) and Malcolm Baldrige have been effectively used in the business communities both domestically and internationally. It is feasible that using techniques from these types of systems may provide some useful ideas within educational systems throughout the world.

Community Development

Community support of adult education programs can provide a foundation upon which learners and educators can continuously build. Maruatona (2002) in Botswana and Cervero and Wilson (2001) noted that society plays a role in the development of programs for adult learning. The differences of interests that exist between society and the individual can influence participant involvement in their own success. If the society or community is not seen as a support system for the educator and the learners, success may be limited. Kollins and Hansman (2005) also found community to be essential to the success of a program in Bolivia. They found that:

> Although program facilitators and participants face economic, organizational, and societal challenges in sustaining the program, demand for the program among community members kept the program alive and continuing efforts among graduated participants disseminates the internal workings of the program to the larger community. (pp. 12-13)

Learner Development

Learner development can become a problem due to high drop out rates and erratic schedules of participants who do not attend the programs consistently (Berger, 2001). Maruatona (2002) in the analysis of literacy in Botswana suggests that students be involved along with the teacher in the "selection of language for instruction, texts and other materials in order to make learning transformative" (p. 95). Learning that is student-centered has been shown to be effective and may be an asset in the development of curriculum for disadvantaged adults (Freire, 1970; Knowles, 1975; Nafukho, Kang'ethe, & Mutema, 2000; Tough, 1979;). Banks (2002) noted that "When facing barriers, individuals often decide to participate in activities that are worthy of their effort or offer valuable return as a result of their effort. They seek a payoff that will enhance skills they already possess" (p.4). Disadvantaged adults possess skills that are often not utilized during traditional educational processes. Incorporating some of their current skills may inspire them to further develop those skills and possibly provide an opportunity for the instructor to introduce new skills.

Learning Theories

The primary learning theories in adult education include the behaviorist, cognitivist, humanist, social learning, and constructivist perspectives (Merriam & Caffarella, 1999). Individuals who employ the behaviorist perspective refuse to speculate on what goes on internally when learning takes place and typically relies solely on observable behaviors (Skinner, 1971, 1974; Smaldino, Lowther, & Russell, 2008). Cognitivists typically focus on how people think, solve problems, and make decisions. The instruction is designed to inspire students to rely on their own cognitive strategies while using available learning resources (Smaldino et al., 2008). Humanists depend upon personal action to fulfill potential (Merriam & Caffarella, 1999) and social learning theory explores "interaction with and observation of others in a social context" (Merriam & Caffarella, 1999, p. 264). The constructivist perspective considers the engagement of students in meaningful experiences as the essence of experiential learning; introduces active problem solving and discoveries; motivates learners to create their own interpretations of the world of information; and uses instruction to provide students with ways to assemble knowledge, not to dispense facts—students learn by doing (Smaldino et al., 2008).

All of the above mentioned theories have been used within the context of curriculum design for adult learners; however, the use of constructivist theory in the curriculum design for disadvantaged students may allow students to use personal experiences and knowledge to facilitate learning in real life (Merriam & Caffarella, 1999; Smaldino et al., 2008; Steffe & Gale, 1995). It may motivate them to become more active throughout the learning process.

Adult Education Curriculum Models

Langenbach (1988) identified 14 adult education curriculum models designated within seven areas or categories. They have been summarized within this chapter and into Table 4.1 along with other models that may be useful in developing a curriculum for disadvantaged adults.

Langenbach's (1998) text provides extensive coverage of curriculum models from some of the most prominent adult educators; therefore, duplication of that work cannot be found in this chapter but would suggest that readers use this resource when considering the development of a curriculum for disadvantaged adults worldwide.

Organizational Effectiveness

Increasing employee effectiveness directly impacts the effectiveness of the organization. Often training is used to enhance employee effectiveness within the workplace. Organizational effectiveness also addresses job preparation prior to obtaining employment. Many companies work with vocational and technical schools to develop and prepare workers for specific types of jobs. Disadvantaged adults may benefit from this type of training since its competency development goals are task-based and student-centered.

Table 4.1

Summary of Adult Education Curriculum Models

Area	Model	Source	Purpose
Organizational Effectiveness	1. The Critical Events Model.	Nadler, 1982, p. 12.	Within noneducational organization.
	2. Twelve Tasks to Develop a Competency-Based Training Method.	Blank, 1982, p. 26.	Occupation or job specific within any organization.
Liberal Education	1. The Paideia Proposal.	Adler, 1982, p. 23.	Basic education, K-12 and lifelong education for adults.
	2. The Bachelor of Liberal Studies Program.	College of Liberal Studies Bulletin, 1985-86, p. 9.	Nontraditional undergraduate.
Adult Basic Education	1. A Literacy Curriculum Model.	Newman, 1980, p 46.	Basic literacy.
	2. Freire's Literacy Model.	Freire, 1970.	Basic education based on student-teacher relationship.
Continuing Professional Education	1. An Emerging Model of Professional Education.	Houle, 1980, p. 106.	Continuing education.
	2. Relation between Continuing Education and Staff Development.	ANA, 1984, p. 6.	Continuing education.
	3. Steps in Program Development.	ANA, 1978, p.13.	Continuing education.
A Multipurpose Model	1. A Social Action Model.	Beal et al., 1966, p. 98a.	Social action dependent upon individual action.
Self-Directed Learning	1. Outline of Essential Elements in Self-Directed Learning	Tough, 1979.	Individual needs.
	2. Knowles's Model of Self-Directed Learning.	Knowles, 1975.	Individual and instructor needs.

Area	Model	Source	Purpose
Generic Models	1. A Generic Curriculum Model.	Houle, 1972, p. 47.	All categories of adult education.
	2. A Conceptual Programming Model.	Boone, 1985, p. 61.	Formal and non-formal context based on adult educators' experiences.
	3. Banks's Instructional Design Model.	Banks, 2002, p. 99.	Instructot focus within eductional and noneducttional organ-izations.
	4. SPICES Model.	Nafukho, Kang'ethe and Mutema, 2000.	Problem-based and student-centered learning for adults.
Book Model	1. Tools and Resources to Teach Adults.	Apps, 1991.	Instructor-based resources and tools.

The Critical Events Model

Nadler's (1982) critical events model provides information on all the critical events that should occur when planning training that is intended to impact organizational effectiveness within a specific organization. The model identifies nine critical events including: 1. Identify needs of the organization. 2. Specify job performance. 3. Identify learner needs. 4. Determine objectives. 5. Build curriculum. 6. Select instructional strategies. 7. Obtain instructional resources. 8. Conduct training. 9. Obtain evaluation and feedback. This model is primarily designed for use within a noneducational organization. It is an open model that allows for changes as needed based upon evaluation and feedback obtained during its use.

Twelve Tasks to Develop a Competency-Based Training Model

Blank's (1982) competency-based training program model is designed to address organizational needs and is broad enough to meet the needs of different types of organizations. This model is designed for "educational and training organizations that prepare students for employment" (Langenbach, 1988, p. 37). The 12 steps in this model are:

1. Identify and describe specific occupations.
2. Identify specific student prerequisites.

3. Identify and verify job tasks.
4. Analyze job tasks and add necessary knowledge tasks.
5. Write terminal performance objectives.
6. Sequence tasks and terminal performance objectives.
7. Develop performance tests.
8. Develop written tests.
9. Develop draft of learning guides.
10. Try out, field test, and revise learning guides.
11. Develop system to manage learning.
12. Implement and evaluate training programs. (p. 39)

Competency-based models allow the learner to self-pace and self-check their progress. The ultimate success of the program is relative to student and instructor motivation.

Liberal Education

Liberal education is considered to be voluntary, lifelong, and the teacher is beyond competent while the student is striving for competency. However, both the student and teacher are open to continuous learning and are generally well-rounded with regards to educational topics including mathematics, science, history, philosophy, the social sciences, and the fine arts (Langenbach, 1988).

The Paideia Proposal

Adler's (1982) Paideia model focuses upon adult education as a lifelong educational process with emphasis upon basic education which is preparatory to liberal education. The model emphasizes learning that prepares adults for further learning. In the global community a broad or liberal education can only be advantageous to disadvantaged adults as they may interact with many others who are different than they. The Paideia model addresses goals, means and areas, operations, and activities through didactic instruction, coaching, and Socratic questioning. The emphasis during didactic instruction is upon the instructor, the student during coaching, and the teacher and student during Socratic questioning. The three goals of liberal education addressed within the model are: "knowledge—knowing that or what; skills—knowing how; and understanding—knowing why or wherefore" (Langenbach, 1988, p. 61). Adlers' (1984) proposal proclaims to address three essential goals for the learner: (1) earning a living; (2) being a good citizen; and (3) living a full life.

The Bachelor of Liberal Studies Program

The Bachelor of Liberal Studies Program curriculum is a model of the steps and learning process students undertake to obtain a bachelor of liberal studies degree. The uniqueness of this program is that it is essentially self-paced with two area seminars a year. The student learns primarily through reading and independent study. Disadvantaged adults who may be in isolated areas with limited access to technology may benefit from this type of curriculum.

Adult Basic Education

Literacy models are typically used within adult basic education (ABE). In the United States, ABE began in the 1960s to enhance education and reduce poverty (Langenbach, 1988). Yet, there is still a continuous need for literacy programs in the United States and worldwide. Poverty is a huge problem for disadvantaged adults and is a primary reason for the lack of education.

A Literacy Curriculum Model

Newman's (1980) model focuses first upon instructors getting to know who their students are so that they can provide the most effective education possible to the students. Cultural influences such as dialect, values, and living patterns should be considered because they can impact an adult's learning experiences (Langenbach, 1988). Fear, lack of hope, and indifference are also issues of concern when addressing the educational needs of disadvantaged adults. Without an awareness of these issues, global educators may struggle to meet the needs of their students. Other aspects of the model include: diagnosing learner characteristics, setting objectives, planning assessment, planning strategies, planning organization, planning use of resources, integrating learner environment, implementing, evaluating, and revising (Langenbach, 1988).

Freire's Literacy Model

Friere's model focuses upon the use of words that the learner is familiar with to influence their participation within the educational process. He was critical of education in Third World countries and in the United States with regards to how basic adult education literacy was implemented. Friere was most concerned with cultural action (Langenbach, 1988) when trying to resolve issues of illiteracy within the global community. His goal was to reduce the impact of oppression through education. Most of his work was in Brazil, Chile, Africa, and other Third World countries; however, "his concept of the Third World is ideological and political rather than merely geographical" (Giroux, 1983, p. xviii). His goal was to liberate individuals through education so that they could be productive within their respective communities.

Continuing Professional Education

Continuing professional education is a critical aspect for disadvantaged adults within the global community. Typically, continuing education may not come to mind when considering disadvantaged adults, but it must be a part of the solution for the future of disadvantaged adults as the global economy evolves. After the initial success of disadvantaged adults, there should be continuous educational opportunities available to continue to inspire their motivation for educational attainment. Also, as the community grows, the adults' educational levels should also continue to grow.

An Emerging Model of Professional Education

Houle's (1980) model considers continuing education within the professional environment. One may not consider this concept for disadvantaged adults because most of them may not have jobs or be employed in professions that are progressively expanding within the global community. However, there is a need for progressive adults within disadvantaged communities who can be examples for those who are not yet educated. Seeing these individuals continue to expand their knowledge and share that knowledge within the community may inspire others who are less fortunate to do the same. Houle (1980) model considers: (1) General Education, often with some emphasis on the basic content required for specialization, (2) Selection, (3) Pre-Service Specialized Education, (4) Certification of Competence, and (5) Continuing Education with steps of maintenance and modernization, preparatory to change, induction into new responsibilities, and refresher. Through his model, Houle (1980) expanded learning from one mode to three: (1) inquiry—"the creation of some new synthesis, idea, technique, policy or strategy of action" (p. 31), (2) instruction—using objectives to transfer knowledge to the learner, and (3) performance—" the process of internalizing an idea or using a practice habitually, so that it becomes a fundamental part of the way in which a learner thinks about and undertakes his or her work" (p. 32).

One key aspect from Houle's model that may be most beneficial for disadvantaged adults is the entrepreneurial setting. In disadvantaged communities the creation of jobs may only come through entrepreneurial efforts via education related to specific needs within their communities. Often these are small businesses, yet they provide numerous benefits to individuals, their families, and their communities. Continuing education related to new business development and maintaining those businesses can only be an asset to disadvantaged adults.

Relation between Continuing Education and Staff Development

The American Nurses Association's (ANA) (1984) model that looks at the relationship between continuing education and staff development is essential for the continuous development of disadvantaged adults in communities that are struggling to overcome their lack of educated citizens. Once a company or organization locates within these communities, there needs to be a process in place that will allow for continuous development especially in fields such as the medical professions where new techniques and medicines are always being introduced.

Many of the countries in the global community are facing health care issues that prevent them from educating disadvantaged adults. Those individuals who are educated must be trained to maintain and enhance their knowledge so that they can be a benefit to themselves, their organization, and the community. This model looks at the overlap of orientation, in-service education, and continuing education within the profession. It also addresses the standards that must be maintained as a priority within the curriculum.

Steps in Program Development

The steps in program development can be used by educators to develop a curriculum for staff development. The steps of this model are as follows:

1. Develop a philosophy.
   a. Define staff development.
   b. Determine purpose of staff development.
2. Develop and determine program goals, including short- and long-range objectives.
3. Determine and define components.
4. Determine policies.
5. Determine organizational structure.
   a. Determine human resources needed.
   b. Identify roles, responsibilities, and accountability of department personnel.
   c. Establish communication system.
6. Identify needs.
   a. Assess organizational needs.
   b. Assess group needs.
   c. Assess individual needs.
   d. Establish priorities.
7. Formulate objectives.
   a. Write general educational objectives.
   b. Write general learner objectives.
8. Determine program evaluation.
   a. Establish system of collecting, organizing, and reporting data.
   b. Develop evaluation tools.
9. Determine physical and material resources needed.
   a. Identify hardware and software needed.
   b. Determine class and conference room space needed.

    c.   Determine needed office space.

    d.   Identify library needs.

10. Develop record keeping system.

11. Prepare budget.

12. Determine schedule of activities.

    a.   Identify dates of employment by category of employee (registered nurse, licensed practical nurse, nurse's aide, etc.).

    b.   Identify specific courses, conferences, etc., based on priorities of need.

13. Communicate plan to significant others.

14. Implement program.

15. Evaluate program.

    a.   Collective evaluative data.

    b.   Organize evaluative data.

    c.   Report evaluative data.

16. Revise program as indicated. (American Nurses Association, 1978, p. 13)

A Multipurpose Model.

    An example of a multipurpose model is the cooperative education programs that are a part of the U.S. Department of Agriculture. They have been used effectively across the United States for years. The course offerings from nutrition to budgeting have been beneficial to the disadvantaged and are offered at no cost. These programs may be a great model for consideration by global educators when developing a curriculum.

A Social Action Model

    Beal's (1966) social action model is designed from the perspective of a "change-agent working within a social system" and is dependent upon key leaders being effective within the system (Langenbach, 1988, p. 145). This is a very comprehensive model that is encompassed within a social system boundary. There are 34 steps within this model which are undergirded by four assumptions:

1.   A complex set of interrelated functions are performed in the social action program.

2.   The functions can be logically integrated to show a flow of action from beginning to end.

3.   The functions can be separated into stages.

4.   Methods can be devised to observe and analyze the functions at each stage. (Langenbach, 1988, pp. 138-139)

This model needs to be considered within the context of the system that it is to be used; therefore, global educators should be careful when attempting to generalize its functions.

Self-Directed Learning

Self-directed learning has become very important with the technological innovations that have occurred throughout the past few years within the global community. With access to the Internet and the World Wide Web (www), the opportunity to learn at one's own pace and within one's selected environment has become a benefit, yet for disadvantaged adults it may be a hindrance. With the lack of access to technology, they may miss out on this opportunity. However, print materials can still be used to enhance opportunities to learn independently. Regardless of the type of learning materials used, essential elements in self-directed learning must be considered. Allen Tough and Malcolm Knowles are considered to be the pioneers of self-directed learning (Langenbach, 1988) and their models are described below.

Outline of Essential Elements in Self-Directed Learning

Tough's (1979) essential elements of self-directed learning include: the overview, definitions, frequency, purpose of learning, what is learned (six categories), why learning occurs (six reasons), deciding to begin, preparatory steps, assistance, choosing a planner, self as planner, group or leader, one-to-one, nonhuman resource, and advantages and disadvantages. All of these elements should be considered when deciding to embark upon a self-directed learning experience. Tough describes "six categories of content that serve different purposes for the learner" (Langenbach, 1988, p. 152) including "preparing for an occupation, and then keeping up" (p. 35), "specific tasks and problems on the job" (p. 36), "learning for home and personal responsibilities" (p. 37), "improving some broad area of competence" (p. 38), "learning for interest or leisure" (p. 38), and "curiosity or a question about certain subject matter (p. 39). All of these categories may apply to disadvantaged adults within the global environment and should be considered as educators develop curriculum and provide the resources to meet their needs.

Knowles's Model of Self-Directed Learning

Self-directed learning involves the teacher and the learner understanding their specific roles prior to starting a self-directed learning project. Knowles's (1975) model outlined self-directed learning. Teacher and learner develop a learning contract. Throughout the model, competencies are used to address the concerns of both the teacher and the learning. Understanding these competencies will assist global educators should they choose to use this model to develop disadvantaged adults. Teacher competencies include setting an appropriate climate, planning, diagnosing needs, setting goals, designing a learning plan, engaging in learning activities, consulting, and evaluating learning outcomes. Learner competencies include building relationships with others, practicing self-assessment, translating learning needs into objectives, selecting effective strategies, and collecting and evaluating evidence of accomplishment.

Generic Models

The ability to generalize models would be the ideal solution to global education efforts for disadvantaged adults. This is not realistic due to the diversity of problems and issues faced by the learners. However, several models described below may be evaluated and modified as applicable to meet the needs of this population of learners.

A Generic Curriculum Model

Houle developed a continuous cycle model that circulates through seven steps to address generic curriculum needs for adults. The model steps are as follows:

1. A possible educational activity is identified.
2. A decision is made to proceed.
3. Objectives are identified and refined.
4. A suitable format is designed.
    a. Resources
    b. Leaders
    c. Methods
    d. Schedule
    e. Sequence
    f. Social reinforcement
    g. Individualization
    h. Roles and relationships
    i. Criteria for evaluation
    j. Clarity of design
5. The format is fitted into larger patterns of life.
    a. Guidance
    b. Lifestyle
    c. Finance
    d. Interpretation
6. The plan is put into effect.
7. The results are measured and appraised. (Houle, 1972, p. 47)

This model is designed for use within any community or organization to design curriculum for adult learners. It is based on 11 categories that encompass the individual, group, institution, and a mass audience (Langenbach, 1988). It allows the adult educator to look at the many forms and purposes for adult education.

A Conceptual Programming Model

Boone's (1985) model involves planning, design and implementation, evaluation and accountability. It is a broad model that attempts the following:

1. Linking the organization and its renewal process —" focus of each element is the quality of relationship of the adult educator to his or her organization" (Langenbach, 1988, p. 196).
2. Tying the organization to its publics—"programs for adults should have their origin in the needs of the publics being served" (Langenbach, 1988, p. 198).
3. Designing the planned program.
4. Implementing the planned program.

All of the elements of this model provide an opportunity for adult educators to develop a comprehensive curriculum to meet the needs of the educator and the students. It is an action-oriented model that allows for practical application.

Because this is a needs-based curriculum model, it may be very suitable for global educators of disadvantaged adults. It can be tailored to specific needs and implemented quickly with active participation of the students. Students and educators can be involved in the action plans that are developed so that they can work together to meet educational goals.

Banks's Instructional Design Model

Banks's (2002) model may be very useful for global adult educators from a program and curriculum perspective. It suggests that instructors consider the constraints of politics, culture of organization, budget/costs , mission/goals, and the organization, division, department, and/or shift prior to developing the curriculum or instruction. Once the curriculum or instruction is determined, the focus is on the instructors to consider feedback throughout the development and during instruction via their own thoughts and input from students. This model also has a return on investment (ROI) component that is of utmost importance in the global economy for both for-profit and not-for-profit organizations. Other steps in the model after a strategic decision has been made include: determine task/objective, determine content through analysis techniques, design instruction based on need to know info that will provide desired knowledge and skills, develop materials, determine methodology, design a formative evaluation (pilot test), deliver in-

Table 4.2

SPICES vs. Traditional Methods of Curriculum Development

SPICES		TRADITIONAL
S	Student-centered	Teacher-centered
P	Problem-based	Information gathering
I	Integrated	Discipline based
C	Community-oriented	Institution-based
E	Electives	Standard program
S	Systematic	Apprentice-based/ Opportunistic

struction (feedback), do a summative evaluation, and include a return on invest-ment.

This model focuses on the broader picture of how instruction impacts that entire culture of an organization or institution and attempts to address the needs up-front. A lot of disadvantaged communities must address issues beyond just the need of the learner when developing a curriculum. If the constraints are addressed prior to implementing the instructional design, many issues of concerns may be averted and more time and effort may be devoted to course content and not com-munity or organizational issues.

The SPICES Model of Curriculum Development for Adult Learners

The SPICES methods are more than a teaching/learning method. It is also a curriculum development approach (Kang'ethe, Nafukho, & Mutema, 2000). The SPICES model is a curriculum development approach that has been found ex-tremely useful in developing curricula in health professions and especially those educational programs that put emphasis on student-centered learning, problem-based learning, integrated, community-oriented, electives, and systematic as the acronym "SPICES" shows. The SPICES model has been found appropriate in plan-ning, reviewing, and tackling problems related to the curriculum and student learning outcomes. In planning the curriculum and especially in adult learners with unique learning needs, innovative approaches such as SPICES should be considered. The SPICES methods are shown in Table 4.2 and are compared with traditional teaching/learning methods.

In planning and developing a curriculum, the use of SPICES has to be consid-ered in order to assist the teachers to understand the particular educational strate-gies they will use in implementing their programs. Also, examining each of the SPICES issues gives teachers and curriculum developers a better understanding and insight into the holistic view of curriculum development. The SPICES model of curriculum development is a useful education strategy that can be used to develop relevant curricula that are responsive to the learner and community needs. The application of this model can also assist in making rational decisions during the information gathering, planning stages, developing, designing, integrating, implementation, and evaluating the curricula.

Book Model
Tools and Resources to Teach Adults

Apps (1991a) provides sage advice for adult educators along with valuable tools and resources within his work. The book

> . . . discusses the demand for continual learning, information paralysis, and information technology[;] . . . [provides] two exercises designed to show adult educators that they know more about teaching adults than they think; [s]trategies for taking charge of teaching (including assuming responsibility for personal improvement, unlearning, and journal writing) . . . ; . . . addresses myths about teaching adults; . . . [and] present[s] specific suggestions regarding the following aspects of teaching adults: thinking as a teacher, developing a basis (belief system) for teaching, understanding adult learners, using teaching tools for providing information and skill training, using teaching tools for developing in-depth understanding, using teaching tools for creating a good learning environment, selecting the right tool, teaching critical thinking, organizing content, making ethical decisions, and assessing quality. Five evaluation forms, a list of 15 references, a partially annotated list of 113 suggested readings, and an index are also included. (Apps, 1991b, Abstract)

Apps suggests that adult educators complete a self-assessment prior to designing courses and/or curriculum for disadvantaged learners. The book also provides valuable tools that encompass the concept of teaching in a diverse, global community related to ethics, quality, and critical thinking. New and seasoned adult educators can benefit from using its resources to continuously update and enhance their curriculum development and teaching skills.

The models are comprehensive enough to meet the needs of K-12 through advanced education of adults. This comprehensive approach is also needed for disadvantaged adults. Most often adults do not become disadvantaged after they become adults. They are often disadvantaged throughout their entire life. One cannot address the needs of a disadvantaged adult without exploring and or acknowledging who they were as children. As noted in several of the literature studies in this chapter, adults bring experiences with them into the classroom. Some of these experiences will most assuredly be childhood experiences related to poverty, disabilities, illiterate parents, unsupportive communities, language barriers, and many other barriers associated with their status as disadvantaged adults.

The various purposes for the different models provide an ample foundation from which to begin the development of a model of learning for disadvantaged adult learners. However, they do not represent all of the models that may be available. They also do not represent the programs within which the curriculums are found. There are numerous programs that can serve as examples for educators within the global community who are looking to develop curriculums for the disadvantaged adult. One such study would be Sork and Buskey (1986) whose analysis included 93 publications consisting of book-length and shorter articles containing explicit or implicit planning models.

Teacher Involvement in Curriculum Development

Teacher involvement in curriculum development for disadvantaged adults is a very critical component. Teachers' ability to implement the curriculum will be enhanced if they are actively involved with the development of the curriculum. Their ability to select the appropriate books and learning materials was found to be effective in the development of disadvantaged students (Buttaro, 2001). Buttaro (2001) found that teachers' ability to foster self-esteem and an interest in learning within the classroom environment played a positive role in the success of disadvantaged Hispanic women who were ESL learners.

Rogers (1969) defines the role of the teacher as that of a facilitator of learning. There is no way teachers can facilitate the learning of any specific curriculum that they are not familiar with. While several sources of curriculum development exist—such as the learners, community, education experts, education administrators, politicians, industry, religious groups, and civil rights groups—it is believed that teachers as implementers of the curriculum have an important role to play in its development. Teachers are important in the curriculum development process of adult learners in the following ways:

1. *Teachers as experienced adult learners and facilitators.* When it comes to the teaching of adult learners, especially those with special needs, the majority of the teachers are themselves adults. This means that they can provide invaluable input on the strengths and limitations of the curriculum being developed for adults in an objective way based on their own experiences as both adults learners and educators. The interaction with disadvantaged adults provides the teachers with a great opportunity to help design a curriculum focused on teaching such adults how to learn and not how to memorize facts.

2. ***The teachers' philosophy of learning and its importance to curriculum development process.*** A conceptual framework founded on a teaching philosophy must guide every curriculum development process for adult learners. Such a framework specifies the knowledge and skills that the disadvantaged adult learners are expected to acquire after successfully completing the program and what they should be able to do differently. As noted, a conceptual framework " . . . provides direction for programs, courses, teaching and candidate performance . . ." (NCATE, 2002, p. 52). While developing a philosophy that should guide the learning of adult learners, teachers should be able to provide input with regard to such a philosophy. Teachers as adult educators believe that adults prefer a learner-centered philosophy of learning as opposed to a teacher-centered philosophy of learning. Teachers are also open-minded and will employ andragogical approaches of teaching adults, hence their importance in the curriculum development process.

3. ***Teachers' role in the identification of resources needed for curriculum implementation.*** Curriculum development involves gathering information, designing curriculum, implementation, and evaluation to determine success. The success of any curriculum for adults will depend on the teaching and learning resources provided for learners and teachers. Teachers as curriculum implementers can provide information on the resources needed, including resource persons, equipment, learning materials, trips, audio-visual teaching aids, internships required, financial resources, and time resources.

4. ***Teachers as resources for the curriculum development process.*** The wealth of knowledge and information possessed by teachers is an invaluable resource for the curriculum developers. For example, teachers know under what circumstances the adult learners learn best, what learning needs they have, what challenges and opportunities the learners are faced with, and what the community and industry are looking for among the learners. As correctly noted, teachers as facilitators of the learning process regard themselves as resources to be utilized by both the learners and the curriculum developers (Knowles, 1990). Since the teachers of adults know that learners have varied intelligences, they should guide the curriculum development by ensuring that the content pays attention to the cognitive, affective and psychomotor learning domains.

5. ***Teachers as facilitators of learning who recognize and accept their own limitations.*** Curriculum developers in most cases are overambitious and expect the curriculum to achieve the intended objectives in a timely manner. But, since teachers are the people on the ground, they should assist the curriculum developers by providing information on what they themselves can achieve within the set time frame and what they cannot. This should also

apply to students. Since teachers interact with the students on a daily basis, they have an idea of the adult learners' self-concept and should guide the curriculum development process in terms of the diagnosing educational needs, planning the learning experiences, and developing a curriculum that provides for a suitable learning climate for all adults regardless of the limitations they may have. (Kabuga, 1977)

Student Motivation

Regardless of the curriculum that is developed for the adult disadvantaged students, their motivation, both internal and external, will play a role in their educational development. With adults, expectancy theory of motivation is of utmost importance. Expectancy theory looks at the future anticipation of the learner. In this situation, it would allow the instructor to determine from the students what they expect from the course or program and how they expect to use the knowledge and/or skill within their future activities. According to Buttaro (2001) "[a]dult learners are both embedded in their lifelong cultures and bring a wealth of information and experience with them to the classroom" (p. 40). Through development of an understanding of this information and experience, instructors may be able to inspire the educational development of the learners beyond what they would typically imagine. Expectancy theory addresses the internal motivational needs of the students but their external motivational needs must also be met.

One can use Maslow's (1943) hierarchy of needs as a resource when addressing the external motivational needs of the disadvantaged adult. Maslow addresses deficiency needs of the individual that lead to physiological, safety, love/belonging/social, esteem, cognitive, and aesthetic needs and growth needs which includes self-actualization and self-transcendence.

Most of the learners who are characterized as disadvantaged are at or near the bottom with regards to Maslow's theory. Their basic or deficiency needs must be met prior to their reaching the ultimate goal of self-actualization and/or self-transcendence. Adult educators in the global community may achieve higher success rates and less dropout if they would consider ways to measure where the learners are with regards to Maslow's hierarchy and introduce methods within the program and/or curriculum to assist the learners in meeting those needs.

External incentives have been shown to be effective in adult learning programs. Ziegler, Ebert, and Cope (2004) noted that although many participants dropped out of the adult basic education program they studied, the use of a cash incentive encouraged those who remained to achieve the academic outcomes of the program. They also found that although cash incentives were important to the participants, "program factors were equally or more important. The incentive may not have been as effective in encouraging persistence, if other program factors important to the welfare recipients were not in place" (p. 29).

Conclusion

In this chapter it has been demonstrated that designing meaningful curriculum for disadvantaged learners has taken a global dimension. Designing curriculum for disadvantaged learners should recognize the need for global partnerships in learning. First the global nature of adult education is discussed. This is followed by a discussion on the curriculum needs of disadvantaged learners. The chapter further discusses 17 different curriculum models/methods of teaching and curriculum development as a strategy to meet the changing needs of learners (Apps, 1991a; Banks, 2002; Langenbach, 1998; Nafukho, Kang'ethe, & Mutema, 2000). There was no specific curriculum model or method identified to teach disadvantaged adults. The characteristics and needs of disadvantaged adults are so varied that there is no specific model to meet all the needs. However, the information found in this chapter could be used to assist researchers who may be interested in developing curriculum models/methods to meet the needs of disadvantaged learners throughout the world.

In addition, the chapter has examined who disadvantaged adult learners are including their characteristics, educational access and opportunity, and the role of politics in the process of curriculum development. Also examined in the chapter are the learning theories that should guide the teaching of adults, adult education curriculum models, the critical role of the teacher as a facilitator of learning in the curriculum development process, and the role of disadvantaged student motivation in their ultimate success which will also enhance our global society.

Future Research

This chapter provides an opportunity for future research into the development of the disadvantaged adult in the worldwide community. There are many single case studies that have been conducted in countries such Kenya, Botswana, Canada, Israel, and many others; yet, there is very little in the way of definitive solutions to the problem of the disadvantaged adult learner. Many societies are impoverished due to the lack of educated adults within their communities. Many companies will not locate in areas where it is difficult to find educated adults and the global economy is leaving these communities behind as the "world becomes flatter" (Friedman, 2005).

The challenge as researchers look at this area of adult education is to provide objective solutions to century-old concerns without becoming discouraged due to the extensiveness of the problem. Longitudinal research studies may be needed to address the issue of dropouts among program participants. The opportunities for research appear endless as opportunities to study the successes and constraints as curriculums are modified and developed to meet the needs of disadvantaged learners throughout our world.

References

Adler, M. J. (1982). *The Paideia proposal.* New York: Macmillan.

Adler, M. J. (1984). *The Paideia program: An educational syllabus.* New York: eMacmillan.

American Nurses' Association. (1978). *Continuing education in nursing: Guidelines for staff development.* Kansas City: American Nurses'Association.

American Nurses' Association. (1984). *Standards for continuing education in nursing.* Kansas City: American Nurses' Association.

Apple, M. (1979). *Ideology and curriculum.* London: Routledge and Kegan Paul.

Apps, J. (1979). *Problems in continuing education.* New York: McGraw-Hill.

Apps, J. (1989). Providers of adult and continuing education: A framework. In S. B. Merriam, & P. M. Cunningham (Eds.), *Handbook of adult and continuing education* (pp. 275-286). San Francisco: Jossey-Bass.

Apps, J. (1991a). *Mastering the teaching of adults.* Malabar, FL: Krieger.

Apps, J. (1991b). *Mastering the teaching of adults.* [Abstract]. (ERIC Document Reproduction Service No. ED362671).

Banks, C. H. (2002). *A descriptive analysis of the perceived effectiveness of Virginia Tech's faculty development institute.* Dissertation Abstracts International, 64 (08). (UMI No. 3102585)

Banks, C. H., Parker, J., & Thomson, M.A. (2006).The role of social setting in adult information technology (IT). In F. M. Nafukho (Ed.), *2006 Academy of Human Resource Development annual research conference proceedings* (pp. 1097-1103). Bowling Green, OH: Academy of Human Resource Development.

Beal, G. M., Blount, R. C., Powers, R. C., & Johnson, W. J. (1966). *Social action and interaction in program planning.* Ames: Iowa State University Press.

Berger, J. I. (2001). Effectiveness of computers in ALBE classrooms: An analytical review of literature. *Adult Basic Education, 11*(3), 162-183.

Blank, W. E. (1982). *Handbook for developing competency-based training programs.* Englewood Cliffs, NJ: Prentice-Hall.

Blunt, A. (2000). Workplace literacy: The contested terrains of policy and practice. In M. C. Taylor (Ed.), *Adult literacy in Canada: Coming of age* (pp. 89-108). Toronto: Lorimer.

Blunt, A. 2004). Literacy discourse analysis: Making space at the policy table.

Adult Basic Education, 14(1), 3-17.

Boone, E. J. (1985). *Developing programs in adult education*. Englewood Cliffs, NJ: Prentice-Hall.

Boshier, R., Huang, Y., Song, Q., & Song, L. (2006). Market socialism meets the lost generation: Motivational orientations of adult learners in Shanghai. *Adult Education Quarterly, 56*(3), 201-222.

Buttaro, L. (2001). Understanding adult ESL learners: Multiple dimensions of learning and adjustments among Hispanic women. *Adult Basic Education 11*(1), 40-61.

Carpenter, C., & Readman, T., (2006). Exploring the literacy difficulties of physically disabled people. *Adult Basic Education 16*(3), 131-150.

College of Liberal Studies. (1985). *Bulletin, 1985-86*. Norman: University of Oklahoma.

Covington, L. E. (2004). Moving beyond the limits of learning: Implications of learning disabilities for adult education. *Adult Basic Education, 14*(2), 90-103.

Crandall, J. A., & Peyton, J. K. (1993). *Approaches to adult ESL literacy instruction. Washington, DC: Center for Applied Linguistics and Delta Systems.* (ERIC Document Reproduction Service No. ED 364127).

Denny, N. W. (1982). Aging and cognitive changes. In B. B. Wolman (Ed.), *Handbook of developmental psychology* (pp. 807-827). Englewood Cliffs, NJ: Prentice Hall.

Department of Adult Education, University of Nottingham. (1980). *The 1919 report: The final and interim reports of the adult education committee of the Ministry of Reconstruction, 1918-1919*. Nottingham, UK: (Original work published in 1919).

Freidman, T. (2005). *The world is flat*. New York: Farrar, Straus & Giroux.

Freire, P. (1970). *Pedagogy of the oppressed*. New York: Herder and Herder.

Giroux, H. A. (1983). Theory and resistance in education: A pedagogy for opposition. South Hadley, MA: Bergin & Garvey.

Guerra, J. C. (1998). *Close to home: Oral and literate practices in a transnational Mexicano community*. New York: Teachers College Press.

Houle, C. O. (1972). *The design of education*. San Francisco: Jossey-Bass.

Houle, C. O. (1980). *Continuing learning in the professions*. San Francisco: Jossey-Bass.

Hubenthal, W. (2004). Older Russian immigrants' experiences in learning English: Motivation, methods, and barriers. *Adult Basic Education, 14*(2), 104-126.

Jaffee, L. L. (2001). Adult literacy programs and the use of technology. *Adult Basic Education 11*(2), 109-124.

Johnson-Bailey, J., & Cervero, R. M. (2000). The invisible politics of race in adult education. In A. L. Wilson & E. R. Hayes (Eds.), *Handbook of adult and continuing education* (pp. 147-160). San Francisco: Jossey-Bass.

Kang'ethe, S., Nafukho, F. M., & Mutema, A. M. (2000). Innovative techniques in the training of health professionals: The case of Moi University, faculty of health sciences. In K. P. Kuchinke (Ed.), *Proceedings of the Academy of Human Resource Development* (pp. 3-9). Raleigh-Durham, NC: Academy of Human Resource Development.

Kilgos, E., & Valentine, T. (2006). Three perspectives on welfare-to-work curriculum. *Adult Basic Education, 16*(3), 151-170.

Knowles, M. S. (1975). *Self-directed learning: A guide for learners and teachers.* Chicago:Follett.

Kollins, J. M., & Hansman, C. A. (2005). The role of women in popular education in bolivia: A case study of the Oficina juridica para la mujer. *Adult Basic Education, 15*(1), 3-20.

Langenbach, M. (1988). *Curriculum models in adult education.* Malabar, FL: Kreiger.

Maruatona, T. (2002). A critical analysis of literacy practice in Botswana. *Adult Basic Education, 12*(2), 82-99.

Maslow, A. (1943). A theory of human motivation. *Psychological Review, 50,* 370-396. Retrieved August 1, 2007, from http://psychclassics.yorku.ca/Maslow/motivation.htm.

Merriam, S. B., & Brockett, R. G. (1997). *The profession and practice of adult education: An introduction.* San Francisco: Jossey-Bass.

Merriam, S. B., & Caffarella, R. S. (1999). *Learning in adulthood.* San Francisco: Jossey-Bass.

Muiru, J., & Mukuria, G. (2005). Barriers to participation in adult literacy programs in Kenya. *Adult Basic Education, 15*(2), 85- 102.

Nadler, L. (1982). *Designing training programs.* Reading: Addison-Wesley.

Nafukho, F. M., Amutabi, N. M., & Otunga, R. N. (2005). *Foundations of adult education in Africa.* Cape Town: UNESCO/Pearson.

National Council for Accreditation of Teacher Edication (NCATE). (2002). *Professional standards for the accreditation of schools, colleges, and departments of education.* Washington, DC: Author.

Newman, A. P. (1980). *Adult basic education: Reading.* Boston: Allyn and Bacon.

Oplatka, I., & Tevel, T. (2006). Liberation and revitalization: The choice and meaning of higher education among Israeli female students in midlife. *Adult Education Quarterly, 57*(1), 62-84.

Pennequin, V., & Fontaine, R. (2000). Training the elderly: The example of class inclusion. *ADULTSPAN Journal, 2*(2), 68-88.

Porter, D. (2004). California's experience with distance education for adult basic learners. *Adult Basic Education, 14*(3), 135-152.

Prosser, R. (1967). Adult education for developing countries. East African Publishing House: Nairobi.

Puder, W. H., & Hand, S. E. (Eds.). (1966). Frontiers in adult basic education. Tallahassee, FL: Florida State University, Office of Continuing Education.

Ribeiro, M. D. (2005). Fostering multicultural and identity development in adult learners through study tours. *ADULTSPAN Journal, 4*(2), 92-104.

Rogers, C. R. (1969). *Freedom to learn.* Columbus, OH: Merrill.

Sandlin, J. A. (2003). Sympathy and scorn: Negotiating popular rhetoric about welfare recipients in welfare-to-work educational programs. *Adult Basic Education, 13*(3), 146-167.

Shank, C., & Terrill, L. (1995). Teaching multilevel adult ESL classes. Washington, DC: National Clearinghouse for ESL Literacy Education.

Skinner, B. F. (1974). *Beyond freedom and dignity.* New York: Knopf.

Skinner, B. F. (1974). *About behaviorism.* New York: Knopf.

Smaldino, S. E., Lowther, D. L., & Russell, J. D. (2008). *Instructional technology and media for learning* (9th ed.). Upper Saddle River, NJ: Pearson Education, Inc.

Smith, E. H. (1970). *Literacy education for adolescents and adults.* San Francisco: Boyd & Fraser.

Sork, T. J., & Buskey, J. H. (1986). A descriptive and evaluative analysis of program planning literature, 1950-1983. *Adult Education Quarterly, 32*(2), 86-96.

Steffe, L. P., & Gale, J. (Eds.). (1995). *Constructivism in education.* Hillsdale, NJ: Erlbaum.

Titmus, C. J. (Ed.) 1989. *Lifelong education for adults: An international hand book.* Elmsford, NY: Pergamon Press.

Tough, A. (1979*). The adult's learning projects: A fresh approach to theory and practice in adult learning.* Toronto: Ontario Institute for Studies in Education.

U.S. Department of Education. (2003). *A blueprint for preparing America's future – The adult Basic and Literacy Education Act of 2003: Summary of major provisions, Office of Vocational and Adult Education.* Retrieved August 6, 2007, from http://www.ed.gov/policy/adulted/leg/aeblueprint2.doc.

Willis, S. L. (1987). Cognition and everyday competence. In K.W. Schaie (Ed.), *Annual review of gerontology and geriatrics* (pp. 159-188). New York: Springer.

Willis, S. L. (1991). Cognition and everyday competence. In K.W. Schaie & M. T. Lawton (Eds.), *Annual review of gerontology and geriatrics* (pp. 80-129). New York: Springer.

Yesavage, J. A., Lapp, D., & Sheikh, J. I. (1989). Mnemonics as modified for use by the elderly. In L. W. Poon, D. C. Rubin, & B. A. Wilson (Eds.), *Everyday cognition in adulthood and late life* (pp. 598-611). New York: Cambridge University Press.

Ziegler, M. (2005). It opens your eyes: Transforming management of adult education programs using the Baldrige education criteria for performance excellence. *Adult Basic Education, 15*(3), 169-186.

Ziegler, M., Ebert, O., & Cope, G. (2004). Using cash incentives to encourage progress of welfare recipients in adult basic education. *Adult Basic Education, 14*(1), 18-31.

Chapter 5
Sequencing Instruction in Global Learning Communities
Renée L. Cambiano

All students can attain a high level of learning capability
if instruction is approached sensitively and systematically,
if students are helped when and where they have learning difficulties,
if they are given sufficient time to achieve mastery,
and if there is some clear criterion of what constitutes mastery.

Bloom (1976, p. 4)

Introduction

Even though there are numerous articles and books about sequencing instruction, there is not experiential evidence that one way of sequencing is better than another. In fact, one might say that students will learn despite the fact of the sequence. This is probably true for 10% of the students, but the rest of them need instructors to sequence the instruction so they can assemble the information before they take it in and absorb it. First year teachers are usually more concerned with the content than the sequence; in fact, it is rarely even thought of by educators until they have already taught a lesson and they say, "That did not go well." Being aware of sequencing is akin to saying "Wait until the water is boiling before putting the pasta into the pot."

Van Patten, Chao, and Reigeluth (1986) affirm that there are two important questions facing curriculum developers when developing any piece of instruction:

(a) How should the instructional events be sequenced over time? (e.g., In what order should the ideas be taught? When should definitions be given? Where should the practice be placed?); and (b) How should the interrelationships among these ideas be taught to the students? (e.g., How is idea A related to idea B? Where does idea C stand in relation to ideas A and B?). Therefore, strategies for sequencing and synthesizing aim to help instructional designers break the subject matter into small pieces, order the pieces, teach one at a time, and then pull them together based on their relationships. (pp. 437-438)

The purpose of this chapter is to explore the theory, types, and implications concerned with sequencing instruction for adult learners. In other words, the chapter deals with "preparing an instructional plan that involves preparing instructional objectives, selecting and ordering content, designing the instructional process, selecting appropriate resources, and determining the evaluation procedures" (Sork & Caffarella, 1989, p. 233). In addition, the following principles will be addressed:

1. What is the educator's role in the teaching and learning process?
2. How do educators select content appropriate for adult learners?
3. What is sequencing instruction, and how does it relate to adult learning and education?
4. How should facilitators sequence instruction to promote learning and create effective learning environments for adult learners?

One might be thinking that sequencing instruction goes against every principle of adult education. On the contrary, it is imperative to plan, select, sequence, instruct, and evaluate content. Following these guidelines will "(1) ensure that instructional objectives are met; (2) keep you organized and on topic; (3) cue yourself on methodology, references, media and/or activities, etc., which are to be used at various points in the lesson; and (4) keep within your scheduled time" (Cantor, 2001, p. 117). Hopefully, at the conclusion of this chapter, you will have a better sense of how important sequencing instruction is to an effective learning environment.

Teaching and Learning Process

Before sequencing of instruction is addressed, whom we are teaching needs to be examined. Adults are very different than children; therefore, the theory of pedagogy is not appropriate for adults. Knowles (1980) is known in the United States for popularizing the term *andragogy*, "the art and science of helping adults learn" (p. 43). The assumptions of his theory, the andragogical model, also need to be mentioned:

1. Adults need to understand why they are learning something, before they will attain ownership in the learning process.
2. Adults have a sense of responsibility for their learning.
3. Adults' experiences should be valued.
4. Adults have a readiness to learn.

5.   Adults are life-centered learners.
6.   Adults are internally motivated. (pp. 57-63)

When developing instruction, if these assumptions are addressed, learning will be more successful for the adult. If educators create instruction for adults and do not take these assumptions into account, the learner may flee from the learning situation. Remember that adults bring more to the learning experience than their books and pencils. As an adult educator, it is imperative to create successful curriculum and, in turn, a successful learning environment.

According to Birkenholz (1999), there are eight principles that support planning, conducting, and evaluating adult education activities:

Principle 1:   Learning is change.
Principle 2:   Adults must want to learn.
Principle 3:   Adults learn best by doing.
Principle 4:   Learning should focus on realistic problems.
Principle 5:   Experience affects adult learning.
Principle 6:   Adults learn best in informal environments.
Principle 7:   Use a variety of methods in teaching adults.
Principle 8:   Adults want guidance, not grades. (pp. 31-38)

When planning curriculum for adults, keep these eight principles in mind. They can be used as guidelines to assure that the needs of the learners are being met.

Facilitator's Role

In public school, it is common to associate the word *teacher* or *educator* with the person in charge of delivering the instruction. However, in adult education, that is not the case. Adult educators refer to themselves as *facilitators of learning*. According to Cranton (1992), a facilitator is "a person who makes things easier. A facilitator of learning is a person who makes learning easier" (p. 76). It is like this analogy: a facilitator is like a bridge, connecting the learner to the new knowledge. There are many bridges. Some have few boards, and in some cases, the bridge has to be stronger to support more knowledge. In other cases, the learner will have more boards to contribute to the learning bridge. The facilitator must use whatever materials it takes to create a complete bridge of learning for everyone.

As a facilitator for adult learning, it is imperative to be as prepared to teach as possible. Going into a learning situation unprepared, especially with adult learners, can create frustration for the learner. In turn, the student may not come back to learn. Adults are different from children in this respect; they will run away before they will have a feeling of discomfort.

Knowles (1980) stated that a facilitator must address the following assumptions within the learning environment:

- The adult learning climate
- Self-diagnoses of adult learning needs
- The planning process
- Learning experiences
- Evaluation of learning (pp. 47-49).

Knowles goes on to say that "the single most difference between children and adults as learners is the differences in assumptions we make about our self-concepts, and this is why these assumptions and their technological implications have been dealt with such detail" (p. 49).

It is important to remember that not every situation is suited for the facilitator role. Many times, as a graduate instructor, I have had to put on my classroom management hat and discipline my students. In this case, I revert back to my pedagogical experiences and teacher voice. Also, there are times when the content of the lesson, such as when a student is learning how to operate a piece of equipment, demands *instructor* control. Imagine how a student would look at the facilitator if asked, "How do you think you should operate that machine?" (Cranton, 1992, p. 78). Under such circumstances, this tactic is not ideal. In fact, it is not safe, because the learner will disengage. Therefore, some content is not appropriate for learner choices.

How to Engage the Adult Learner

Learner engagement is equal to learning. Without it, learning can not occur. Unfortunately, engagement is one of the hardest teaching skills to master. What works for one set of learners may not work for another set of learners. It can also be that the learner is engaged with the content, but how the facilitator delivers it is not engaging. Many factors go into engaging the learner. In the following paragraphs, we will address some skills to keep in one's repertoire as a facilitator of adults.

Sequencing Effective Instruction

Before thinking about sequencing instruction, facilitators must go through two of the most critical steps in instructional design: *task analysis* and *procedural analysis*. According to Cranton (1989), task analysis is the "procedure for determining which specific aspects of learning must precede others in order that tery of an objective or goal can take place" (p. 54). Procedural analysis "emphasizes the actual order in which a learner performs a task, opposed to the hierarchy of skills involved" (p. 54).

Morrison, Ross, and Kemp (2004) state that "task analysis solves three instructional design problems:

1. It defines the content required to solve the performance problem or alleviate a performance need. This step is crucial since most designers work with unfamiliar content.
2. Because the process forces the subject matter expert (SME) to work through each individual step, subtle steps are more easily identified.
3. During the process, the designer has the opportunity to view the content from the learner's perspective. Using the perspective, the designer can often gain insight into the appropriate teaching strategies." (p. 78)

For a deeper understanding of the process of task analysis, let's examine what Jonassen, Hannum, and Tessner (1999) say about what designers of instruction are trying to establish when conducting a task analysis:

1. The goals and objectives of learning;
2. The operational components of jobs, skills, learning goals or objectives, that is, to describe what task performers do, how they perform a task or apply a skill, and how they think before, during, and after learning;
3. What knowledge states (declarative, structural, and procedural knowledge) characterize a job or task;
4. Which tasks, skills, or goals should be taught, that is, how to select learning outcomes that are appropriate for instructional development;
5. Which tasks are most important—which have priority for a commitment of training resources;
6. The sequence in which tasks are performed and should be learned and taught;
7. How to select or design instructional activities, strategies, and technique to foster learning;
8. How to select appropriate media and learning environments; and
9. How to construct performance assessments and evaluation. (p. 3)

For further reading on task analysis, I recommend the *Handbook of Task Analysis Procedures* by Jonassen, Hannum, and Tessner (1999).

There are many different procedures of task analysis. The facilitator must determine which ones to utilize by taking into account the purpose, content, learner, and the environment in which the task will be delivered and performed. In the next section, I will go into detail about how a facilitator of adults can select the type of task analysis and conduct the task analysis.

Selecting the Type of Task Analysis

According to Gagné and Briggs (1979), there are three different approaches of task analyses that can be performed on the objectives to be learned: (1) information-processing analysis; (2) task classification; and (3) learning task analysis. When conducting an information-processing analysis approach, the facilitator categorizes the sequence of decisions related to events that will be involved in applying the objective. Simply stated, it describes the steps involved.

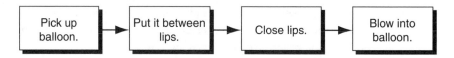

To employ the task classification approach, the facilitator must determine the target objectives, and then the objectives can be classified into: (1) intellectual skills; (2) cognitive strategies; (3) information; (4) attitudes; or (5) motor skills. The authors state that "The purpose of the approach is to determine the conditions for learning." The last approach, learning task analysis, will guide the facilitator in planning the prerequisites involved in learning called "enabling objectives" (p. 100). A facilitator must conduct an extensive amount of investigation prior to the lesson being taught.

Conducting a Task Analysis

The following list, developed by Cranton (1989), is intended to help adult facilitators determine the steps associated with conducting a task analysis:

Step 1:   Select the objective in which you will conduct the analysis.

Step 2:   By examining one objective at a time, determine the information necessary for the learner to have prior to instruction of the objective.

Step 3:   Reflect upon the list made in step 2, and for each item make another list with the answers to the following question: "What does the learner need to know to start this task?"

Step 4:   Repeat, repeat, repeat this process until you feel as though you are comfortable with the level of instruction for the learner. This decision can be very difficult, and many first time facilitators provide too much information. Nevertheless, the more you teach the better you will get.

Step 5:   After completing this task, examine the list you created in steps 3 and 4 and arrange a "tree structure."

Step 6:   Any time you are creating something for the first time, it is advisable to get the opinion of a content specialist in the field in which you are conducing the task analysis. So have the specialist read it over to determine accuracy.

Step 7:   Reflect upon the critique of the content specialist, and employ the task analysis in your instruction with observation and evaluation of the learner. After conducting the task analysis, reflect again and jot down some notes for the next time. (Cranton, 1989, p. 56)

For further reading on the steps involved in task analysis, please refer to Cranton's (1989) book *Planning Instruction for Adult Learners*.

Selecting Instructional Content

Before sequencing is discussed, selecting content is an important area to address. Caffarella (2002) recommends "playing with content, letting the objectives surface" (p. 172). She states that "key topics and points will develop as you glean the content for learning objectives" (p. 172). Different instructors use different techniques for selecting content to be taught. As instructors rethink and reflect on the content, some of it is dropped, and other content is added. Some instructors create concept maps to assist in the process of selecting content. By doing this, they can see the big picture before the material is taught. Other instructors talk through the content using a combination of methods.

Caffarella (2002) states that "instructors should ask themselves three questions when selecting content:

1.   What must the participants know?
2.   What should the participants know?
3.   What could the participants know? (p. 173)

By asking these questions, educators can create content that is appropriate for the learner. She also concludes that educators must keep in mind three common pitfalls: "they create too much material for the time allowed; instructors want to impart more than learners are motivated to absorb; and they discount the context in which the learning is to be applied" (pp. 173-174). According to Knowles (1980), "three major criteria must be met in building an effectively organized group of learning experiences: (1) continuity, (2) integration, and (3) sequence" (p. 235).

Creating Performance Objectives

One other aspect of instruction that must be addressed before entering into the realm of sequencing is the objective of the lesson. The objective of a lesson is a description of what the learner will be able to do at the end of instruction, and it is this objective that the educator will eventually sequence. If the objectives are not determined before instruction starts, the lessons will not flow logically, and the learners will be left without any insight into what they are learning. Example objectives include:

1. The learner will master the terms associated with the Dunn and Dunn learning style instrument.
2. The learner will be able to construct a diagram that organizes the Dunn and Dunn model of learning styles.
3. The learner will be able to apply the Dunn and Dunn model of learning styles in a theoretical classroom setting.
4. The learner will be able to recognize unstated assumptions within the Dunn and Dunn model of learning styles.
5. The learner will be able to design a classroom using the Dunn and Dunn model of learning styles.
6. The learner will be to evaluate the effectiveness of the Dunn and Dunn model of learning styles within one's classroom.

What Is Sequencing Instruction?

So, what is sequencing? Let's examine several leading theorists' definitions of sequencing instruction. Gagné (1973) states that "sequencing of instruction is primarily, and perhaps entirely, a matter of convenient arrangement of a succession of events that must be spread over time, because they are too lengthy to be accomplished" (p. 9). Whereas, the father of adult education, Knowles (1980), states that sequencing instruction is "higher levels of treatment with each successive learning experience" (p. 235). According to Cranton (1989), sequencing instruction is "determining the order with which topics or objectives will be taught" (p. 52). She also goes on to say that one cannot define sequencing without defining *instructional analysis.* She claims that instructional analysis is "the process of determining which learning must precede which other learning" (p. 52) . . . "simply a systematic procedure for sequencing instruction in order to optimize learning" (p. 54). Based on the definitions of the leading theorists, one could assume that sequencing instruction is a convenient arrangement of procedures delivered to the learners. On the contrary, this chapter will show that there is much more to sequencing instruction than what is depicted in these definitions.

According to Brown and Green (2006), sequencing instruction serves one of two purposes: (1) "to isolate a piece of knowledge (a concept or principle) to help students comprehend its unique characteristics or (2) to relate the concept or principle to a larger organized body of knowledge" (p. 161). No matter which purpose is selected, proper sequencing has several advantages:

1. [it] ensures that skills and knowledge are developed in an orderly and progressive manner;
2. [it] prevents unnecessary repetition or duplication, and gaps or omissions in the instruction;
3. [it] provides organization and certainty for your learner (Cantor, 2001, p. 121).

As a facilitator develops an instructional sequence, the objectives are prepared to be presented in a manner that creates effective instruction. This preparation will also provide avenues of facilitator remediation before entering into the classroom, and an educational map that the facilitator can follow in selecting strategies and materials for the learners to be successful.

The issue of sequencing instruction is not often recognized or encountered in the preparation of the facilitator. Most facilitators are worried about the content, rather than in what order it is to be delivered. However, it should be the opposite, because sequencing plays a massive role in curriculum development. In fact, there is a direct relationship between how instruction is sequenced and the success of the learner.

As a learner, you have surely been aware of a situation in which the facilitator was not organized. Think back on how this made you feel as a learner. When information is not organized properly, the learner has a sense of isolation, fear, and abandonment, all of which will scare adult learners out of the learning. Therefore, just the mere thought of how instruction should be sequenced will provide an avenue in which to outline, plan, and prepare lessons. In turn, this will ensure the most effective learning environment for the learners.

If you look up "sequencing instruction" at the library, a host of books will appear that attempt to describe, in one sentence, what sequencing instruction is all about. This chapter delves into sequencing instruction as never before in adult education. In turn, this will enlighten, and, hopefully empower you as an adult facilitator.

Levels of Sequencing Instruction

In any given teaching situation, there are levels of sequencing. Gagné, Wager, Golas, and Keller (2005, p. 176) discuss the following four levels, shown in Figure 5.1.

1. Course sequencing
2. Unit or topic sequencing

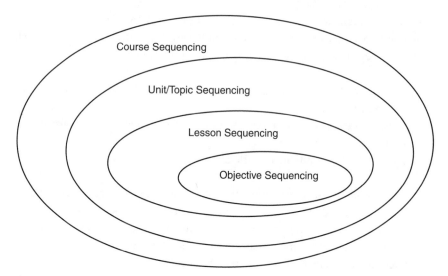

Figure 5.1: The levels of sequencing and how they are interrelated.

3. Lesson sequencing
4. Objective sequencing

  Course sequencing deals with asking yourself, "How am I going to set up the course, and how should the topics be presented for the learner to be most effective?" First, you must be able to address the issue of prior learning. Will the learners have the knowledge they need for the facilitator to perform as a teacher? You would not put a learner in a college algebra class if the student has not had elementary algebra. You would not start to teach a student the parts of speech if the learner did not know how to read. This assessment of prior knowledge is a necessary issue that facilitators need to address when sequencing course content.

  A unit or topic can lend itself to a certain sequence; on the other hand, it may not always be so. Topic sequencing, in my opinion, is very difficult. What sounds plausible to an educator may not be the same for the learners. This is where teaching experience is useful. As the content specialist teaches content over and over again, a natural sequence of the topics will emerge. It also helps to be incredibly reflective. At the end of a topic, make it a point to reflect upon the topic and write down notes answering the following questions about the sequence:

1. What worked?
2. What did not work?
3. What can be changed to make learning more effective?

In answering these questions, you will gain the knowledge needed to assure that the sequence of the topic is accurate and effective. Posner and Rudnitsky (2006) recommend the following seven questions for unit sequencing:

1. In what subject matter areas is unit organization (sequencing) most important? Why?
2. Are there courses of study that will include divergent, practically unrelated units in which organization (sequencing) will serve little or no purpose?
3. What are the criteria for choosing one principle of unit organization (sequencing) over another?
4. Think of one of the best courses you have taken. Do you recall how the units were organized (sequenced)? Did that make a contribution to the quality of that course?
5. Think of one of the poorest course you have taken. Do you recall how the units were organized (sequenced)? Did that affect the quality of the course?
6. What would be the effect if, due to unexpected questions in class, the instructor teaching your course were to teach a unit out of sequence? Would this significantly weaken your course?
7. To what extent should the student be consciously aware of the unit organiza= tion (sequencing)? (p. 143)

These kinds of deep synthesis questions about how the lesson is sequenced will, in turn, create a more effective learning environment.

The next level, lesson sequencing, is very similar to that of topic sequencing. In fact, I would recommend using the same reflective technique, at a deeper level, and at the end of every lesson. The first three questions will remain the same, but you will add the following new questions:

1. What worked?
2. What did not work?
3. What can I change to make learning more effective?
4. What parts of the lesson engaged the learner?
5. What did not engage the learner?
6. If I had taught that lesson in a different sequence, would I have had as many questions from the learners?

The last level of sequencing that Gagné et al. (2005) elaborate on is the lesson objective sequence. In some respects, this level is the most crucial and the most effective—if sequenced properly. The sequencing of objectives might be more effective if the facilitator asks, "What might the learner need to know to learn this objective?" Then, the facilitator perceives it being taught. "How can I build on what the students already know? How can I get the learners to use past experiences to enhance the objective?"

Role of the Students in Selecting and Sequencing Instruction

According to Cranton (2003), most teachers oppose involving students in the decision-making process for content choices, let alone the sequence. She states that teachers argue that the learner is not the content specialist, facilitators are. Therefore, to allow them the opportunity to be involved in the curriculum decision-making process would, in turn, lessen the quality of instruction (p. 41). However, according to Knowles (1990), adults are self-directed, and nevertheless "a mechanism must be provided for involving all the parties concerned in the educational enterprise in its planning" (p. 125). Kidd (1959) also emphasizes this by saying "the adult learner, far more than the child, may expect to take a much more active part in the consideration and selection of what he is to" learn (p. 273). He also states "when the facilitator and learner are making such curricular choices, that it is essential to include application of such knowledge (p. 273). Knowing this, it is imperative to involve the learners on some level of planning. From experience, I have discovered that by asking the learner to be a part of the process, the learner then has ownership in the learning experience. Consequently, the quality of learning increases.

Methods for Sequencing Instruction: Theorists and Theories

Prerequisite/Hierarchical Method (Gagné)

Gagné's prerequisite/hierarchical method can not be discussed without first presenting information about his *condition of learning theory*. This theory describes a prerequisite/hierarchical set of cognitive processes that are taking place in relation to nine instructional events. The nine cognitive processes are:

1. Gain attention of the learner to focus upon the task at hand.
2. Inform the learners of the objective to communicate the task at hand and what the learning outcomes are.
3. Stimulate recall of prior learning, to stimulate prior knowledge and experiences.
4. Present the stimulus material to provide the learner with a resource for the objective.
5. Provide a learning guidance to connect what they know to what is being learned.
6. Elicit performance to stimulate actual internal integrating.

7. Provide feedback to confirm what has actually been learned.
8. Assess performance to confirm the learners' perspective of the objective is accurate.
9. Enhance retention and transfer to enhance the learners' ability to recall or apply the newly gained knowledge. (Gagné, Wager, Golas, & Keller, 2005)

For Gagné, these nine conditions of learning provide a foundation for sequencing instruction (Gagne, 1950; Gagné, 1973; Gagné, 1974; Gagné, 1985; Gagné et al., 2005; Knox, 1977). Gagné is one of the leading theorists in sequencing instruction through prerequisite relations. Gagné's *prerequisite/hierarchical sequence* states "A prerequisite is a simpler intellectual skill, but such a characterization does not adequately identify it because one could name a number of intellectual skills that are simpler than the lesson objective described" (Gagné et al., 2005 p.183). This skill is related to supporting the learners' prior learning by starting with simpler component skills (Gagné, 1974). For example, in some areas, it is required that the learner know the meaning of certain words to understand the concepts to be learned. If the meanings of the prerequisite words are not acquired before learning, then the learning of the new concepts will not take place.

Sequencing Schemes (Posner and Strike)

Posner and Strike (1976) present five categories for sequencing instruction in their model called *categorization scheme for sequencing instruction*. They conclude that sequencing is not as simple as most individuals think. However, they suggest that before the facilitator begins teaching, two questions should be asked: "How should content be sequenced?" and "In what ways can content be sequenced?" (p. 665). To adult facilitators, these are two very important questions, and should be addressed prior to developing instruction for adults.

The framework for Posner and Strike's categorization scheme is summarized in the following principles:

1. What are the empirically verifiable relationships between the phenomena in the world about which the pupil is to learn, and in what ways can the content be sequenced so that the organization is consistent with the way the world is?
2. What are the conceptual properties of the knowledge that the pupil is to learn, and in what ways can content be sequenced so that it is logically consistent in organization to the organization of the concepts?
3. How do propositions and concepts come about, and in what ways can content be sequenced so that it is consistent with this process of inquiry?
4. How does the pupil learn, and in what ways can the content be sequenced so that it is consistent with the learning process?

5. How will the pupil utilize the content after learning it, and in what ways can the content be sequenced so that it is consistent with the utilization process? (p. 667)

Using these questions, Posner and Strike (1976) were led to develop five categories for sequencing instruction: (1) world-related sequencing; (2) concept-related sequencing; (3) inquiry-related sequencing; (4) learning-related sequencing; and (5) utilization-related sequencing.

World-Related Sequencing

"World-Related Sequences are those sequences in which there is consistency among the ordering of content, on the one hand, and the relationships between phenomena as they exist or occur in the world on the other hand. The content structure reflects empirical relationships among events, people, and things" (Finch & Crunkilton, 1989, p. 672). For example, the content of time is arranged chronologically from the earliest to the latest occurrence. According to Finch and Crunkilton (1989), world-related sequencing is most related to the natural structure of content. The subsets within world-related sequencing are space, time, and physical attributes (Hlebowitsh, 2005).

Imagine creating a lesson for an adult facilitator on designing a classroom for learning. Does the furniture in the room come first? Does the location of the whiteboard come next? What about the location of the facilitator's desk? How about the types of desks and chairs that are needed for the learner to be successful? Should the types of lighting that are effective for learners take precedence? Is the greatest concern how the learner views the classroom? According to Morrison, Ross, and Kemp (2004), "Content that represents objects, people, and events is presented in a sequence that is consistent with the real world" (p. 139). Organization designed from the point in which you come in the classroom door and walk around would be considered *spatial organization*. Organization that starts with the physical aspects of the classroom such as lighting, chairs, desks and whiteboards is *physical phenomena*. Sequencing that begins with the historical aspect of classrooms, starting with the one-room classroom and moving toward the history of an adult-learner classroom, is grouping by *temporal* or *chronological sequence*.

Concept-Related Sequencing

Concept-related sequences reflect the organization of how concepts are or can be connected to each other—in other words—"a sequence in which a concept is structured in a manner consistent with the way the concepts themselves related to one another" (Posner & Strike, 1976, p. 673). For example, it is logical to understand that one concept comes before another, such as World War I came before World War II, or beginning addition comes before multiplication. The four schemes for sequencing conceptual content are class relations, propositional relations, sophistication, and logical prerequisite.

Within *class relations*, it is appropriate to group events that are similar. The second concept-related theme is *propositional relations*. Within this framework, information is sequenced with examples first; then comes the proposition. The third concept-related sequence is *sophistication*. Within this theme, the simple proceeds to complex; concrete to abstract. The last method is *logical prerequisite*. Within this scheme of teaching, the logical prerequisite concept would be taught first, and then content builds up to the main concept.

Inquiry-Related Sequencing

Briggs describes inquiry-related or guided discovery sequencing as "providing a sequence of questions designed to stimulate thinking about problems by the learner" (Briggs, 1977, p. 189). The subsets within inquiry-related sequencing are logic, or inquiry, and the empirics of inquiry. Within the inquiry-related sequence, content is sequenced in a way which gives the student more control of the learning situation. Content is provided through questions, and discussion is guided by the facilitator. Depending on the comfort level of the facilitator, the amount of information provided to the learner can vary. Some facilitators might only provide the objective of the lesson; others will guide the learner with prerequisite information. This category of sequencing is less rigid, and many times does not have a sequence to follow.

Learning-Related Sequencing

Learning-related sequencing "draws primarily on knowledge about the psychology of learning as a basis for curriculum" (Posner & Strike, 1976, p. 677), and is based on the needs of the learner. In adult education, it makes sense for the needs of the learner's sequencing to be addressed prior to the content's sequencing. An example of this is recognizing when the learning of one skill outweighs the learning of another. Basic skills should be taught first, and then the application of that skill can be taught. The subsets within learning-related sequencing are empirical prerequisite, familiarity, difficulty, development, interest, and internalization (Morrison, Ross, & Kemp, 2004).

Imagine applying this concept of development to a course for English language learners (ELL). The educator might want to start by breaking the reading process up into teaching phonemic awareness, then decoding words, then reading in English. However, students may lose interest in the subject by starting this way. According to the learning-related sequence, the facilitator may want to empower the students by addressing the learners' needs. By asking the learner to be involved in the learning process, the sequence of instruction would vary based upon each learner. Adult learners bring varying experiences to the learning situation, and these experiences should be taken into account.

Utilization-Related Sequencing

Utilization-related sequencing is "organizing content around personal and social needs of the learner" (Posner & Strike, 1976, p. 680). Utilization-related sequencing is used primarily in training programs where adults must learn procedures or processes to complete their jobs. It is imperative to make sure the order of sequencing correlates with the actual job sequence, or is in the order that tasks are performed. Utilization-related sequence is a relative and important aspect of adult education. Many adults are facing retraining due to the introduction of technology into their jobs. Facilitators must be aware of the aspects of the new tasks before training starts. The subsets within utilization-related sequencing are procedure (steps in a process) and anticipated (frequency of phenomena's occurrence) (Posner & Strike, 1976, pp. 680-681).

Posner and Strike (1976) developed this categorization scheme to provide facilitators with the tools to facilitate instruction. Use of this model allows facilitators to choose a sequence that is most appropriate for the situation, which, in turn, can lead to more flexibility. These five schemes for sequencing instruction are useful for facilitators in curriculum development. However, within this model, basic need factors are emphasized, such as how location of the school, climate, and teachers' interests all affect the sequencing of instruction. The actual decision of how instruction is sequenced must take into account the nature of the learner and the content to be delivered.

Elaboration Theory (Reigeluth)

Reigeluth developed an instructional design method called the elaboration theory in the 1980s, which focused on organizing and sequencing instruction exclusively at the macro level; "organizing the instruction on a single idea" (Reigeluth, 1983, p. 19). Like Gagné, Reigeluth's elaboration theory's key idea is to present information from simple to complex. However, his theory goes one step further. He states that information should be presented to learners in increasing order of complexity, which he calls *elaborative sequence*. This elaborative sequence has two distinctive components: (1) most general ideas epitomize rather than summarize the content and (2) there are three different sequences surrounding one subject matter (concept, procedure, and principle).

The first component, which is how most general ideas epitomize rather than summarize the content, states that epitomizing differs from summarizing in two ways: "(1) presenting a very small number of ideas that are to be taught in the course; and (2) presenting them at a concrete, meaningful, application level" (Reigeluth, 1983, p. 343). In contrast, summarizing is presenting a large scale of information, more at the memorization level. For example, if one is teaching a course on learning styles, the summary of learning styles would go into the most important principles of learning styles, whereas the epitome would be to teach one or two fundamental aspects of how people learn differently.

In regard to the second component, the three content orientations (concept, procedure, and theoretical), the elaboration theory considers that the idea of sequencing instruction from simple to complex must differ based on the type of content involved, and the relation of the content to the goals of the instruction. So the facilitator must ask, if *concepts* are important, then select the most important concept, and create lessons that sequence from the most fundamental idea to the most complex idea. If the *procedure* concepts are the most important, then sequence instruction based on the simplest task, and gradually add procedural knowledge until you reach the higher level. If *theoretical* content is most important, then facilitators need to identify all the necessary theoretical principles that need to be learned and sequence content based upon the priority of each principle. In some respects, the elaboration model does have a fourth sequence based upon Gagné's prerequisite sequences, but it is called "learning prerequisite" by Reigeluth. This sequence is based upon a learning structure, or learning hierarchy. According to Reigeluth (1983), a learning hierarchy consists of a "structure that shows what facts or ideas must be learned before a given idea can be learned" (p. 357). So if *prerequisite* content is most important, then the facilitator must identify the prerequisite knowledge necessary for the learner to be successful later on in the lesson, and sequence that at the beginning of the lesson to assure that the learner does not go forth without that knowledge base.

The elaboration model has seven themes that are immersed throughout the model:

1. Motivate.
2. Present an analogy.
3. Organize content ideas.
4. Support content ideas.
5. Summarize.
6. Synthesize.
7. Create cognitive-strategy activators.

These seven themes allow Reigeluth to talk about a general model of instruction. In general, the epitome will start with a motivational strategy to pull the learner into the lesson; then present an analogy to further draw the learner in; then organize the content ideas from simple to complex to ease the learning process for the learner; then support the content ideas with examples or principles that are related to the learner; then summarize and synthesize the information to pull the knowledge back into perspective for the learner; and finally create cognitive-strategy activators as additional motivators for the learner.

According to Reigeluth (1983), the elaboration model "helps to ensure that the learner is always aware of the context and importance of the different ideas that are being taught" (p. 341). On some levels, it allows the learners to have control over their learning process by allowing the learners to learn at the appropriate level of complexity. The elaboration model especially prevents the learners from struggling through learning processes that are too complex for them.

Acknowledging these models is important, because if content is not sequenced, it appears that the educator is disorganized and disconnected from the proper way instruction should be delivered to make learning meaningful.

How Should Instruction Be Sequenced?

What is the goal of instruction? The goal is to transfer information from the facilitator to the learner. Subsequently, how is information ordered in a meaningful manner that the learner will absorb, retain, and apply it? In most circumstances, there are numerous ways to accomplish this. Recall the purpose of sequencing instruction, which is: (1) "to isolate a piece of knowledge (a concept or principle) to help students comprehend its unique characteristics or (2) to relate the concept or principle to a larger organized body of knowledge" (Brown & Green, 2006, p. 161). Cantor (2001) states that to accurately sequence instruction, "two questions must be answered:

1. In what order will the objectives be taught and learned?
2. How will the learning content for each objective be arranged?" (p. 122).

He states that if a facilitator tries to answer these questions, it must first be determined how instructional objectives will be taught. These are all issues that must be addressed. In the following pages, based on what the theorists say about how instruction should be sequenced, this skill can be mastered.

Content-Specific Sequencing

Facilitators might find that the curriculum lends itself to a certain sequence. However, it is not always clear how to sequence content. The intent in sequencing content is to provide students with quality instruction without jeopardizing the students' abilities to master the curriculum. The following approaches have been selected based upon the appropriateness for adult learners; many are appropriate for public schools as well. In the following section, six types of content sequencing will be discussed:

1. Inductive sequencing: General to specific; simple to complex
2. Deductive sequencing: Whole to part
3. Chronological sequencing
4. Logical sequencing
5. Interest related sequencing
6. Spiral sequencing

Inductive Sequencing

In inductive sequencing, content is sequenced from known to unknown; easy to difficult; concrete to abstract; general to specific; and simple to complex. Content is arranged from the simplest form to more complex ideas. Traditionally, facilitators are more familiar with (and use) this type of sequencing. Significantly, this is probably how most content was delivered to facilitators as learners. It makes sense for educators to deliver content in this way to students because, theoretically, it makes learning easier. Using Bloom's taxonomy is an example of inductive sequencing.

To apply inductive sequencing to teaching a lesson on learning theories, a facilitator should start by defining learning, then discuss theories of learning, and finally, ask the learners to apply the theories of learning in the classroom. In teaching an adult learner to prepare for the mathematics section on the General Educational Development (GED), this type of sequencing would be appropriate, because mathematics naturally lends itself to be taught from general to specific by building on concepts already taught (Cantor, 2001).

Bloom's Taxonomy of Educational Objectives

Bloom's taxonomy was developed in 1956 by Benjamin Bloom and his colleagues and cited in the book *Taxonomy of Educational Objectives*. Within this theory, Bloom categorized the development of intelligence into the following three categories: (1) the cognitive domain, (2) the affective domain, and (3) psychomotor domain. The most well-known category, the cognitive domain, contains six levels arranged from the lowest cognitive knowledge, of recalling facts, to the highest, where knowledge is evaluated (see Table 5.1). The general purpose of his theory is to provide a framework for educators to develop educational objectives.

Kibler, Cegala, Miles, and Barker (1981) have proposed sequencing instruction based upon Bloom's taxonomic classifications using the task analysis approach. Cranton (1989) states that task analysis is the "procedure for determining

Table 5.1

Bloom's (1956) Taxonomy (Cognitive Domain)

Level	Description.	Example Objective
Knowledge This lowest level is the simplest form of learning.	Knowledge that emphasizes remembering by recalling facts and ideas.	The learner will master the terms associated with the Dunn and Dunn learning style instrument.
Comprehension	At this level, learners are able to comprehend certain aspects of content.	The learner will be able to construct a diagram that organizes the Dunn and Dunn theory of learning styles.
Application	At this level, learners are able to apply knowledge learned in solving problems.	The learner will be able to apply the Dunn and Dunn theory of learning styles in a theoretical classroom setting.
Analysis	At this level, learners are able to understand relationships among concepts.	The learner will be able to recognize unstated assumptions within the Dunn and Dunn theory of learning styles.
Synthesis	Just as the word implies, learners are able to synthesis information to create one idea out of many concepts.	The learner will be able to design a classroom using the Dunn and Dunn theory of learning styles.
Evaluation This is the highest level.	At this level, learners are able to make an evaluation based upon facts.	The learner will be to evaluate the effectiveness of the Dunn and Dunn theory of learning styles within the real classroom.

which specific aspects of learning must precede others in order that mastery of an objective or goal can take place" (p. 54). However, in 1974, Gagné was the first to introduce task analysis in his book, *Essentials of Learning for Instruction*. The steps involved in completing a task analysis will be discussed later in this chapter. Based upon Kibler et al.'s (1981) theory of sequencing instruction, the facilitator starts at the lowest level of Bloom's taxonomy, provides facts of basic knowledge, and sequences the instruction to the highest level, encouraging critical thought and synthesis.

Marzano's New Taxonomy of Educational Objectives

Marzano (2001), the author of *Classroom Instruction that Works,* has developed a new *taxonomy of educational objectives.* Marzano has theoretically improved upon Bloom's taxonomy in two distinct ways: first, "it presents a model or a theory of human thought as apposed to a framework," and second, "it allows for the design of a hierarchical system of human thought from the perspective of two criteria: (1) flow of information and (2) level of consciousness" (pp. 12-13).

Within his taxonomy, he discusses three systems of thinking that are at the heart of his theory: (a) the self system; (b) the metacognitive system; and (c) the cognitive system. Contained within the cognitive system are four ordered hierarchy elements: (1) retrieval; (2) comprehension; (3) analysis; and (4) knowledge utilization (p. 30) .

Just as Bloom's taxonomy was developed to create educational objectives, it is also the intent of Marzano's (2001) new taxonomy. However, the objectives within his taxonomy are not intended "to prescribe the objectives that a school or district should adopt, only to articulate the range of possible objectives that a classroom teacher or entire school or district might focus on, given the understanding of how the human mind operates" (pp. 106-107). It is intended to involve the learner in the mixed processes of learning using the three systems of thinking.

Traditionally, Bloom's taxonomy has focused on knowledge that the learner is supposed to retain and process. Therefore, the learner must acquire an exorbitant amount of knowledge to be successful. Regrettably, classrooms in today's society do not move beyond the acquisition of knowledge. Inherently, this leaves the learner with an abundant knowledge base of memorized facts that are easily lost, or occasionally filled within the brain for later recall. Within Marzano's domain of knowledge, the acquisition of knowledge is accounted for through information, mental procedures (how-to), and psychomotor procedures (if, then). It is these categories that propel Marzano's taxonomy beyond that of Bloom's (Marzano, 2001, pp. 16-17).

To contrast these two models, take the sample objective of a lesson's instruction; that "The learner will master the terms associated with the Dunn and Dunn learning style instrument." Within Bloom's, this objective is at the lowest level of the cognitive domain; therefore, the learner has only to memorize the terms to be successful. Within Marzano's, the objective would exceed memorization and encompass the following:

- Vocabulary (information): There are 21 elements in the learning styles instrument.
- Generalization (information): All learning styles instruments have these elements.

- Mental Procedures (how-to): Learn to interpret the learning styles instrument.
- Psychomotor Procedures (if, then): Interpret a learning styles instrument.

Allowing learners to engage more extensively in the manipulation of knowledge creates a better understanding of the information, as well as the ability to retain it and eventually apply it (Marzano, 2001).

Deductive Sequencing

Deductive sequencing is reversed from that of inductive sequencing. Content is sequenced from the whole to part; the big picture to the specific; or the content begins with an overview and then narrows. Some content lends itself naturally to deductive sequencing. Politics is one such topic; it is easier for the learner to understand the global aspects of politics, and then go into the specifics of parties and how they work.

To apply deductive sequencing to teaching a lesson on learning styles, the main concept that everyone learns differently is introduced. This branches off into specific learning style philosophies, and finally, different types of learning styles are discussed in detail.

Chronological Sequencing

In chronological sequencing, content is "sequenced from the earliest event to the most recent event", thus, this type of sequencing is usually seen in historical content (Posner & Strike, 1976, p. 673). When historical content is sequenced, it is best for the facilitator to focus on the earliest time periods and move forward in time. This type of sequencing does not mandate content be sequenced in this matter, but it most commonly seen this way (Armstrong, 2003).

Posner and Strike (1976) depict chronological sequencing under the category of world-related sequencing (which was discussed earlier in this chapter). "World-related sequences are those sequences in which there is consistency among the ordering of content, on the one hand, and the relationships between phenomena as they exist or occur in the world on the other hand. The content structure reflects empirical relationships among events, people, and things" (p. 672).

Logical Sequencing

In logical sequencing, content is logically arranged "to understand the first concept or proposition in order to understand the second" (Posner & Strike, 1976). Posner and Strike illustrate sequencing under the category of concept-related sequencing (which was discussed earlier in this chapter). Concept-related sequences are those sequences in which "a concept is structured in a manner consistent with the way the concepts themselves related to one another" (p. 673). The authors state that it would be logical to teach what velocity means first, and then teach what acceleration means. Some content lends itself to logical sequencing, especially within the elements of job performance. For example, in on-the-job training, the learner first needs to understand how certain machinery operates before attempting to fix it. This is what is referred to as logical sequencing (Cantor, 2001).

Ausubel's Advance Organizers

Ausubel's (1968) idea of advance organizers can be defined as "appropriately relevant and inclusive introductory material . . . introduced in advance of learning . . . and presented at a higher level of abstraction, generality, and inclusiveness" than the learning material itself (Ausubel, 1968, p. 148). The idea of advance organizers can be viewed as a form of logical sequencing. He states that facilitators who are experts in the field being taught should be able to sequence knowledge in such a way that new ideas are integrated into existing content in the most logical format possible (Ausubel, 1963).

Face Validity

No matter how logical it seems that content should be sequenced, curriculum developers must take into account that facilitators play an important role in how successful the content is delivered. Therefore how comfortable facilitators are with the sequencing of the content must be addressed. Face validity sequencing addresses this very topic. According to Finch and Crunkilton (1989), face validity sequencing "encompasses the extent to which teachers accept sequencing as being logical and meaningful" (p. 192).

Thematic Sequencing

Thematic sequencing is when content is sequenced based upon themes or units. This type of sequencing is commonly seen in public schools. However, thematic sequencing can be very pertinent to adult education. In the instance that an adult comes back to school to pass the GED, the curriculum may be sequenced based upon the sections of the GED exam. Posner and Strike (1976) call thematic sequencing as *class relations*, "a concept that selects or groups a set of things or events as instances of the same kind of thing because they share common properties" (p. 674). Therefore, the sequence of content is based upon the most logical theme for student learning. Other content areas that are relevant for thematic sequencing are art, creative writing, plays, and poetry (Armstrong, 2003).

Interest Related Sequencing

Sequencing content in relation to interest means to start with the content that most interests the learners. This type of sequencing will maintain student engagement (Mager & Beach, 1967). As it can be deduced from earlier in this chapter, adults must be interested in the content and be able to apply it to real life. If the instructor first obtains student attention by selecting content that will be of interest to the learner, and moves into the content that is not so inherently interesting, then more learners will be engaged by that time. For example, most learners are not interested in the history of learning styles, but if the facilitator makes it personal and starts the content discussions with questions like, "How do you think you learn?" this gets the learner engaged. Then, it is easier to move forward to types of learning styles, and on to the history of learning styles. In relation to this approach, learners are ultimately more successful. Interest related sequencing is not widely used or known in curriculum development. However, if curriculum were delivered in such a manner, more adult students might be more successful in educational endeavors.

Spiral Sequencing

According to Bruner (1960), spiral sequencing reintroduces the content at periodic intervals throughout the lesson. His intention is to remediate and review content that has already been taught, while simultaneously elaborating on the content. This, in turn, improves retention and broadens understanding of the content (Gagné & Briggs, 1979). If this type of concept sequencing were used not only in one lesson, but throughout a learners' entire educational career, then previous knowledge would be continually reinforced. Therefore, learners would have a better understanding and retention of the concepts learned. This would also reduce the amount of memorizing, and enhance the learners' ability to apply new concepts. Important concepts would be introduced, and then while the content continued to develop and grow, previous ideas would be continually reintroduced for the learner to process and absorb. However, Bruner was unclear as to how to implement spiral sequencing, or how and when to reintroduce the concepts in the spiraling cycle; hence, this type of sequencing is difficult to utilize.

Spiral sequencing could be implemented when teaching an adult learner how to speak and write English. The spiraling effect would enhance the learners' ability to grasp the foreign language and take it to a deeper understanding. This type of sequencing content would be the similar to being immersed in the new language.

Career Sequencing

When instruction is arranged in the exact order that a learner will perform an on- the-job task, it is called career sequencing. In adult education, this type of sequencing is encountered a great deal. If the instruction is based upon how the job will be performed, the learner is more likely to repeat the sequence at work, and therefore, become more successful. An example of this would be teaching someone how to operate some kind of machinery. The facilitator would not only want to make sure to sequence the instruction in the order of operating the machine, from turning it on to turning it off, but would also be very detailed and specific and not leave out any steps. If steps were left out, the learner would not be able to perform the task, and this could lead to job termination. In most cases, it would benefit the learner to be able to practice and apply the sequence, while learning, before the end of the instruction. According to Mager and Beach (1967), "at least 5% of course time should be devoted to such practice" (p. 61) for the learner to retain the skill (Cantor, 2001; Finch & Crunkilton, 1989; Mager & Beach, 1967; Posner & Strike, 1976).

The following approaches have been selected based upon the appropriateness to adult learning; many types of occupational sequencing are also appropriate for public school. In the following section, two types of career sequencing will be discussed:

1. Frequency sequencing
2. Application-based sequencing

Frequency Sequencing

Frequency sequencing is obtained by prioritizing the skills needed most, and then sequencing the rest of the instruction. Sometimes, it is better to sequence instruction with the most pertinent task first, and then to progress toward the rest of the tasks. Unfortunately, time is a factor in adult education. Being adults, such learners have a tendency to attend until it is felt that needs have been accomplished. Or, similarly, because of money constraints, students may only be able to attend classes for a limited amount of time. Therefore, if the most crucial task is first and there are some dropouts, at least the learner will have some skills to be successful (Mager & Beach, 1967).

Application-based Sequencing

Application-based sequencing is most beneficial when application of skills and practicing such skills are crucial to the learners' success rate. For example, no one wants to be the patient of a surgeon who has not actually applied the skill before. The same is true for employers who depend on workers to be able to apply the skills learned at the training session. Time lost is a loss of money, in the employers' eyes.

Technology-based Sequencing

The following approaches have been selected based upon the appropriateness to adult learners: online-based sequencing and knowledge-based sequencing.

Online-based Sequencing

Within an online environment, it is imperative to sequence instruction to make it meaningful for adult learning. Since the facilitator is online, the instructor must convey the information through the computer instead of face to face. Gagné, Wager, Golas, and Keller (2005) address online-based sequencing by stating "the goal of curriculum sequencing is to provide the student with the most suitable individually planned sequence of knowledge units to learn, as well as a sequence of learning tasks to work with" . . . "in other words helping the students find the optimal path" (p. 186). This can be difficult, because written words are not always interpreted the same way as when spoken. It is imperative for educators to provide the information through pictures, diagrams, and online discussion boards as well as text.

Knowledge-Based Sequencing

Gagné et al. (2005) state that knowledge-based sequencing "is based upon the notion that certain patterns can be used to guide the design of instructional hypermedia" (p. 185). Within this frame, sequencing is developed by someone other than the facilitator. This can be hazardous to online learning. As the old saying goes, "If one wants to know content, one should teach it." However, if the curriculum has not been developed or sequenced in the manner that the facilitator is most comfortable with, then it will be very difficult to teach it, especially online. As can be expected, when an educator develops the curriculum, it is known thoroughly. If someone else develops it, and the educator is not familiar with the sequencing style, adult students will notice, and this can lead to the facilitator's loss of credibility.

Sequencing Rules

In general, sequencing should depend on the content of the material being sequenced. However, Cantor (2001) provides a universal outline:

1. Whenever possible, place easily learned objectives early in the sequence.
2. Introduce concepts at the first point where the understanding of the concepts is necessary for performance. For example, component operation may be taught just before inspection procedures.
3. Introduce a concept or skill into the course where it is to be used.
4. Introduce instruction on prerequisite skills prior to the time where they must be combined with other skills or where they are to be applied.
5. Teach procedural skills and knowledge in the same sequence as required in the work environment and facilities.
6. Place complex skills late in the sequence (p. 124).

Factors that Impact Sequencing Instruction

There are several factors that can impact sequencing instruction that are outside of the facilitators' control:

1. Textbook companies
2. Curriculum alignment
3. Learner background
4. Availability of resources
5. Time

Cranton (1992) elaborates on this idea in her book *Working with Adult Learners*, by stating several factors that can impact not only sequencing, but instruction: (1) too much material, too little time; (2) lack of learner experience; (3) impossible learner goals; (4) unknown learners; (5) resistant learners; (6) mandatory attendance; (7) minimum effort; (8) physical constraints; and (9) financial constraints. It is imperative for adult educators to not be impaired by these constraints, but to see them as challenges that can help facilitate the development and organization of appropriate curriculum for adult learners. The educator's commitment to maintaining flexibility in such respects during the learning process will create a safe climate that is conducive to the adult learner.

Sequencing in Relation to Mastery Learning

It is not possible to write a chapter about sequencing instruction without touching on the topic of mastery learning. No matter how educators sequence instruction, the goal is for students to retain as much information as possible and apply what is learned when it is appropriate. This is why it is imperative to discuss issues of mastery.

According to Bloom (1976), the "key to the success of mastery learning strategies largely lies in the extent to which students can be motivated and helped to correct their learning difficulties at the appropriate points in the learning process" (p. 5). His theory of mastery learning has three interdependent variables:

1. The extent to which the student has already learned the basic prerequisites to the learning to be accomplished.
2. The extent to which the student is (or can be) motivated to engage in the learning process.
3. The extent to which the instruction to be given is appropriate to the learner. (pp. 10-11)

If one remembers, these three issues are also mentioned within the theories of sequencing instruction earlier in this chapter. Thus, there is a direct relationship between sequencing instruction and mastery learning.

Bloom (1976) states that within the theory of master learning, learning tasks are grouped by "preferred or convenient order as viewed by the curriculum makers, the textbook writer, or the teacher" (p. 34). However, in true mastery sequencing, tasks are sequenced based upon the first task being mastered, then moving on to the next sequential task, and when it is mastered moving on the next sequential task, and so on. Thus, students have a strong understanding of the first task before moving to the next, which in turn nurtures a learner who has ownership in learning process. This fosters engagement, and internal motivation. Since these characteristics are important to the adult learner, mastery is key to the instructional process.

Gagné (1997) supports Bloom's idea of mastery and instructional design by concluding that "two sources are both involved in the formulation of the events of instruction. These events are as follows:

1. Gaining attention
2. Informing the learner of the objective
3. Stimulating recall of prior learning
4. Presenting the stimulus
5. Providing learning guidance
6. Eliciting the performance
7. Giving informative feedback
8. Assessing performance
9. Enhancing retention and transfer" (p. 13).

These nine events of instruction are "capable of supporting internal processes of learning" (Gagné, 1997, p. 13), with the exception of learners who are intrinsically able to do so. Therefore, if these events of instruction are used appropriately, educators will be able to "(a) enhance prerequisites, (b) provide content organization, (c) assure student participation and (d) use informative and corrective feedback" (p. 14). Incorporating these events into instruction helps to enhance the learning environment.

Summary

Finch and Crunkilton (1989) point out that the effectiveness of theories of sequencing instruction are still in question and needs to be researched further. They state the following conclusions:

1. ***Sequencing effects are long range.*** The advantages or disadvantages of using any particular sequencing scheme are not likely to appear immediately. Therefore, end-of-course evaluative measures should be used for evaluating the effectiveness of sequencing techniques. Within-course evaluative measures of small portions of the material are not likely to reveal the true effects of sequencing.

2. ***Sequence is important to low aptitude students.*** Students who have a high aptitude for the subject matter will learn the material in spite of sequencing. The lower the aptitude of the learner for the content, the more important it becomes that some type of sequence and structure be provided.

3. ***Sequence is important when students are given unfamiliar materials.*** Students who are familiar with the materials will learn, regardless of the order of presentation. But as material becomes increasingly unfamiliar to the student, the important of the sequence increases.

4. ***Sequence is important when used to help teach non-redundant materials.*** Some curricular materials are especially redundant, stating important points over and over again. Sequencing is not especially important with these materials, because the student can attain things the second time they are addressed. But if the materials are non-redundant (state their points only once), it is important that they be sequenced according to some rationale. (pp. 196-197)

This chapter explored the different theories and types of sequencing instruction, as well as the implications concerned with sequencing instruction for adult learners. The age and experience of the adult learner will be complementary to the learning process if the contents of classes are sequenced correctly for instruction and learning. However, all of these aforementioned elements are appropriate, especially to the adult learner. Educators should not forget the delicate dance between experience and inexperience that the adult learner does in adult education. Facilitators should use the means of sequencing that works in the context of the individual classroom, and should always be open to new ideas for sequencing material.

References

Armstrong, D. G. (2003). *Curriculum today*. Upper Saddle River, NJ: Merrill/Prentice Hall.

Ausubel, D. P. (1963). *The psychology of meaningful verbal learning: An Introduc_ tion to school learning*. New York: Grune & Stratton.

Ausubel, D. P. (1968). *Educational psychology: A cognitive view*. New York: Holt, Rinehart, & Winston.

Birkenholz, R. J. (1999). *Effective adult learning*. Daneville, IL: Interstate Publishers, Inc.

Bloom, B. (1956). *Taxonomy of educational objective: Cognitive and affective domains*. New York: David KcKay Company, Inc.

Bloom, B. (1976). *Human characteristics and school learning*. New York: McGraw Hill.

Brown, A. B., & Green, T. D. (2006). *The essentials of instructional design: Connecting principles and practice*. Upper Saddle River, NJ: Merrill/Prentice Hall.

Briggs, L. (1977). *Instructional design*. Englewood Cliffs, NJ: Educational Technology Publishers.

Bruner, J. S. (1960). *The process of education*. Cambridge, MA; Harvard University.

Caffarella, R. (2002). *Planning programs for adult learners*. San Francisco: Jossey-Bass.

Cantor, J. A. (2001). *Delivering instruction to adult learners* (2nd ed.). Toronto, Canada: Wall & Emerson, Inc.

Cranton, P. (1989). *Planning instruction for adult learners*. Toronto, Canada: Wall & Thompson

Cranton, P. (1992). *Working with adult learners*. Toronto, Canada: Wall & Thompson

Cranton, P. (2003). *Finding our way*. Toronto, Canada: Wall & Thompson

Finch, C. R., & Crunkilton, J. R. (1989). *Curriculum development in vocational and technical education: Planning, content, and implementation*. Needham Heights, MA: Allyn and Bacon.

Gagné, R. M. (1950). The effect of sequence of presentation of similar items on the learning of paired-associates. *Journal of Experimental Psychology, 40*, 61-73.

Gagné, R. M. (1973). Learning and instructional sequence. *Review of Research in Education, 1*, 3-33.

Gagné, R. M. (1974). *Essentials of learning for instruction*. Illinois: Dryden Press.

Gagné, R. M. (1985). *Conditions of learning and theory of instruction* (4th ed.). New York: Holt, Rinehart, & Winston.

Gagné, R. M. (1997). Mastery learning and instructional design. *Performance Improvement Quarterly, 10*(1), 8-19.

Gagné, R. M., & Briggs, L. J. (1979). *Principles of instructional design*. New York: Holt, Rinehart, & Winston.

Gagné, R. M., Wager, W. W., Golas, K. C., & Keller, J. M. (2005). *Principles of instructional design*. Canada: Thompson Wadsworth.

Hlebowitsh, P. (2005). *Designing the school curriculum*. Boston: Allyn and Bacon.

Jonassen, D. H., Hannum, W. H., & Tessner, M. (1999). *Handbook of task analysis procedures*. New York: Praeger.

Kibler, R., Cegala, D., Miles, D., & Barker, L. (1981). *Objectives for instruction and evaluation* (2nd ed.). Boston: Allyn and Bacon.

Kidd, J. R. (1959). *How adults learn*. New York: Association Press.

Knowles, M. (1980). *The modern practice of adult education: From pedagogy to andragogy revised and updated*. Chicago: Association Press.

Knowles, M. (1990). *The adult learner: A neglected species*. Houston, TX: Gulf Publishing Company.

Knox, A. B. (1977). *Adult development and learning*. San Francisco: Jossey Bass.

Mager, R. F., & Beach, K. M. (1967). *Developing vocational instruction*. Belmont, CA: Lear Siegler, Inc./ Fearson Publishers.

Marzano, R. J. (2001). *Designing a new taxonomy of educational objectives*. Thousand Oaks, CA: Corwin Press.

Morrison, G. R., Ross, S. M., & Kemp, J. E. (2004). *Designing effective instruction*. Hoboken, NJ: John Wiley & Sons, Inc.

Posner, G. J., & Rudnitsky, A. N. (2006). *Course design: A guide to curriculum development for teachers*. New York: Allyn and Bacon.

Posner, G. J., & Strike, K. A. (1976). A categorization scheme for principles of sequencing content. *Review of Educational Research, 46*(4), 665-690.

Reigeluth, C. M. (1983). *Instructional design theories and models: An overview of their current status*. Hillsdale, NJ: Lawrence Erlbaum Associates, Publishers.

Sork, T. J., & Caffarella, R. S. (1989). Planning programs for adults. In A. L. Wilson, & E. R. Hayes (Eds.), *Handbook of adult and continuing education* (pp. 233-245). San Francisco: Jossey-Bass.

Van Patten, J., Chao, C., & Reigeluth, C. M. (1986). A review of strategies for sequencing and synthesizing instruction. *Review of Educational Research, 56*(4), 437-471.

Chapter 6
Expanding Curriculum Development Models
Mary Ziegler

Introduction

Educational programs are the heart of adult education and the process of planning them is foundational to the practice of adult education. With rapid technological growth, increased mobility, and almost instant global electronic communication, the world at the beginning of the 21st century offers additional challenge and opportunity to those who plan educational programs. Numerous authors suggest that adult education is uniquely poised to address not only the educational interests of adults but also to consider how global changes affect people's lives (King & Wang, 2007; Merriam, Courtney, & Cervero, 2006). However, "given the injustice, inequality, and environmental degradation that exist in the late twentieth century, we have a lot of learning to do in a short time" (Sork, 2000, p. 187). Although the planning and implementation of curriculum have a long history of scholarship and practice, the models for adults not only differ but also are contested, particularly since not all curriculum for adults embraces the learner-centered values of adult education (Wang, 2007).

This chapter describes curriculum development and program planning, and the usefulness of models. For the purposes of comparison, the models are placed on a continuum from functionalist to empowerment, two distinctions derived from practice. The functionalist approach, sometimes called the technical or the technical/rational approach, grows out of the objectivist paradigm that assumes knowledge is objective and lies outside the learner. In this approach, the curriculum begins with identifying the gap in the learners' knowledge in relationship to a norm set by an expert. The role of the adult educator is to help learners access that knowledge and fill the gap in their learning (Lave & Wenger, 1991). On the other hand, the empowerment approach grows out of a subjectivist paradigm that has an assumption that knowledge is subjective and socially constructed (Gergen, 1992). From this perspective, the curriculum is the learners' lived experience. The curriculum begins with the assumption that the learners have expertise. The role of the educator is to help learners become critically aware of their experience in a way that leads to action. The chapter concludes with a look at emerging models, implications for practice, and possible directions for the future of curriculum planning in a global environment. Reviewing planning models provides an opportunity for experienced planners to reflect on the connection between these theories and their practice. Novice planners can see the variety of ways that curriculum planning can be conceived. A hint of some of the complexities of the task of situating adult education within a global environment can be seen in the use cf the terms *curriculum development* and *program planning*.

Curriculum Development or Program Planning

Use of the term *curriculum* is uncommon in adult education in the United States. "Curriculum" often refers to formal schooling while "program" refers to the broad range of education for adults. Apps (1979) suggested that a program may contain a curriculum but a curriculum is not necessarily a program. In contrast, Jarvis (2004) suggests that "programme" may be more commonly used in the United States because of the traditionally nonformal nature of adult education; however, "curriculum" has been more popular in Britain until recently. In many cases, the terms *curriculum* and *program* are used interchangeably. For example, in the index of the *Handbook of Adult Education* (Wilson & Hayes, 2000) the entry for "curriculum development" says "see program planning" (p. 726). Most dictionaries define curriculum as a course of study whereas a program is a plan or schedule of activities or procedures to be followed. Curriculum or program models in adult education have undergone comparatively little change in decades (Sork, 2000). Practitioners use the terms *curriculum* and *program* broadly to describe the course of study for an entire school or narrowly to describe the course of study for a particular event such as a seminar or workshop. Since this chapter focuses on the process of developing teaching/learning activities for adults rather than the content of those activities, the terms *program* and *curriculum* will relate to the particular model being described. Next is a clarification of the term *model* and its use in planning.

Use of Models

A model is often used in order to better visualize something that cannot be directly observed. Models provide a vantage point from which to ask questions, to interpret practice, or to test hunches or hypotheses. A conceptual model is foundational in any theory development. According to Sztomka (1979), a conceptual model is " . . . a general, comprehensive image of the subject matter . . . embracing the main principle of its constitution, operation and transformation" (p. 87). More than anything, models reflect the values of the model builder and describe what

the model builder considers important. Thus, "a model is always an approxima-
tion, usually a simplification, and hopefully an aid to insight" (Borko, 1967). The
purpose of a model is not to represent the phenomena exhaustively or in its en-
tirety but rather to make parts of the phenomena more visible and accessible
(Sztomka, 1979). In adult education, Boone (1992) refers to a model as a graphic
structure that is useful for guiding the thoughts and actions of the adult educator.
The curriculum and program planning models that have evolved in adult education illuminate aspects of practice and how these differ. Although adult education
program planning models differ in many ways, many seem to share functionalist
assumptions such as measurable objectives that directly relate to what an adult
learns.

Functionalist and Expanded Functionalist Models

Most adult education curriculum and program planning is consistent with a
functionalist approach, which is based on the assumption that knowledge is stable,
objective, and lies outside the leaner. The curriculum, standardized for efficiency,
guides the teacher and the learner through knowledge that has been predetermined. Most prevalent in the United States, the functionalist approach has been
labeled rational, technical, or positivist and undergirds most curriculum and program planning models (Boone, Safrit, & Jones, 2002; Cervero & Wilson, 1994;
Pinar, Reynolds, Slattery, & Taubman, 1996; Sork, 2000). An assumption of this
approach is that what is to be known can be structured and sequenced in such a
way that it is standardized for all learners and will lead to all learners having the
same knowledge (Doll, 1993). Books that promote procedures for instrumental
and technical problem solving are the most popular books in adult education
(Wilson & Hayes, 2000). How did this approach become so prevalent? The functionalist approach is pragmatic. Often focused on specific identified problems in
ways that can be described, measured, and evaluated, the functionalist approach
has proven its value in helping adults learn in a host of different venues. First
identified by Ralph Tyler, the key elements of this approach are captured as a part
of what has been termed the Tylerian rationale long used because of its effectiveness and apparent simplicity.

Tylerian Rationale
The Tylerian rationale, the foundation of the functionalist approach to curriculum development, is based on the book by Ralph Tyler (1949) that has dominated curriculum since its publication (Slattery, 1995). "Most current theoretical
formulations of program planning in continuing education are borrowed from
Tyler's seminal work in curriculum development" (Pennington & Green, 1976, p.

14). Although the Tylerian rationale has been criticized for its lack of attention to context, its neutrality with regard to social stratification, its lack of specificity, and its technical-rational emphasis (Jarvis, 2004; Slattery, 1995; Sork, 2000), this approach forms the foundation of most of the program planning models commonly used in adult education. Reviewing the Tylerian rationale shows how these ideas have influenced adult educators, primarily because of their practicality and the seeming focus on learners' needs. The rationale consists of four questions to answer when developing a curriculum.

What educational purposes should the school seek to attain? At the heart of the purpose are learning objectives. In fact, Tyler considered objectives so important that he dedicates almost half of his book to explaining this step. The sources of objectives are subject matter experts, the needs of learners, and the needs of society. Ultimately though, objectives must be stated in relationship to a norm or standard. Thus, objectives could be stated in quantifiable, behavioral terms. These in turn provide a guide for instructors as they select teaching methods.

What educational experiences can be provided that are likely to attain these purposes? Tyler's second question involves deciding what kinds of experiences will lead to achievement of the learning objectives. Criteria for the selection of learning experiences include those that provide opportunities to practice the behavior implied by the learning objective. Objectives can be met by a wide range of methods.

How can these educational experiences be effectively organized? The third question addresses the criteria for organizing learning experiences including continuity, sequence, and organization. Sequencing means building a unified picture from specific parts.

How can we determine whether these purposes are being attained? Answering the final question is evaluation. "The process of evaluation is essentially the process of determining to what extent the educational objectives are actually being realized by the program of curriculum and instruction" (Tyler, 1949, p. 106). Evaluation consists of appraising student behaviors on more than one occasion to see if change has taken place as the result of instruction. Over the years, Tyler's four questions have been distilled to four components: purpose, objectives, method, and evaluation. Although these components form the foundation for curriculum and program planning, adult educators have added elements to Tyler's rationale in an effort to make it more suitable for adult learners and more comprehensive in its application.

Some would argue that the predominance of Tyler's model has shifted adult education's focus from developing a more just and equitable society to a more individual, instrumental focus (Faillos, 2006). The different models of program or curriculum planning support this perspective. Where adult education departs from the Tylerian rationale is in seeing the role of education in actualizing of human potential. Beginning with Houle (1972), adults as a unique group of learners became a part of adult education planning models. Unlike children, adults were thought to participate in educational activities for many different reasons in a myriad of contexts. Often, they were volunteers, meaning they had a choice in whether or not they would participate. This element of choice and the experience an adult brought to the educational activity were two aspects that made adult education unique. Following are examples of the functionalist approach to adult education and models from Houle (Houle, 1972, 1996), Sork (Sork, 1997, 1998, 2000), and Caffarella (Caffarella, 2002). After a description of the components of each model is an application of the model in practice that concludes with a summary of the model's key points with regard to the role of the educator and adult learner, context, content, key strategies, and focus. Houle (1972) was one of the first to build on the Tylerian rationale and devise a systematic approach to adult education curriculum development.

The Fundamental System

Houle (1972, 1996) claimed that although Tyler's rationale has undergone amplification and been subject to disagreement over the years about how to define each of the components, "the fundamental way of thought that Tyler suggested still remains intact, underlying the discussion and practice of most education today" (Houle, 1996, p. 15). Building on the Tyler rationale, Houle expanded these ideas for relevance in adult education. His model identifies assumptions about adult education, categories of educational situations, and a framework that underlies these situations. Among the assumptions he makes about curriculum, two are noteworthy. First is the profound influence of context on the teaching/ learning process and the understanding that no curriculum exists in a vacuum. Even a standardized curriculum may be different depending on the context in which it is delivered (Cookson, 1998). Second is the assumption that learners may initiate a learning activity and it is up to the educators to provide support and resources. In addition to assumptions about adult education, Houle (1996) classified education activities into a framework with 11 different educational situations designed either by an individual, group, or institution. This framework spans self-directed learning on one hand to television programs for a mass audience on the other (Jarvis, 2004).

What makes Houle's model a fundamental system is that regardless of the context, planner, or audience, all educational activities follow the same type of design system. In other words, his model is generic to educational activities designed for adults in all types of contexts depicting what occurs naturally in the planning process. Houle proposed the model "in a spirit of pragmatic utilitarianism" (1996, p. 70). Although he says that his model is not linear, in practice, the steps do seem to occur in a linear manner (Sork, 2000). Following are the key components of the model.

A possible educational activity is identified. An individual, group, institution, or community can initiate an educational activity that may be the result of a need or an opportunity.

A decision is made to proceed. If the decision is negative, the planning activity ends; if it is positive, then planning activities continue.

Objectives are identified and refined. This step consists of identifying what the program will achieve. Generally, a hierarchy of objectives emerges.

A suitable format is designed. This step includes the selection of learning resources, leader(s), and methods; and creation of a time schedule and sequence of events. Other aspects of format include providing for social reinforcement of the learning; consideration of the nature of each individual learner; clarification of roles and relationships; and design of the educational activity.

The format is fitted into the larger patterns of life. This component is a unique aspect of Houle's model as he suggests that the adult's life roles (work, home, civic, and other responsibilities) must be taken into consideration when planning an educational activity for adults (Boone et al., 2002). Considerations in this step include guiding learners into and out of the activity; making lifestyle modifications so that learners can accommodate the activity into their schedules; financing; and interpreting the program to the public.

The plan is put into effect. As the plan is implemented, adaptation will be necessary because a plan is abstract and the concrete situation will likely have differences from what was intended. Changing situations may require a change in format.

The results are measured and appraised. Measurement is based on quantitative data and appraisal is based on the subjective judgment of the planner that goes beyond the data; these two activities make up evaluation.

The situation is again examined in terms of a new possible educational activity. The critical examination of the program either ends the program or begins the planning cycle anew.

Applying the Fundamental System

Houle (1996) provides interesting examples of how the "fundamental system" can be applied in both formal and nonformal contexts. For example, he describes "A Hobo School" (Ely, 1936) that took place after World War I where one man, a self-described hobo who was able to read, realized that another man in a similar situation wanted to read so he could understand the comic pages of the newspaper. After devising a way to teach reading, others described as vagrants by the story's author, wanted to participate, each for a different reason. The hobo taught men to read by focusing on their interests, whether it was to read the comics, or understand a work manual, or improve vocabulary. Regardless of the interests of the individual, the "teacher" followed the steps in the *fundamental system*. Other activities that apply the model occur in a rural community, the army, a club, and a hospital. What is noteworthy about each of these distinct cases at the individual, group, and institutional level is that each incorporates components of the *fundamental system* of program design. However, incorporating these components occurred pragmatically and was driven by the experience of the decision-makers. In this sense, Houle built his model from experiences in practice rather than fitting practice to a theoretical model. The pragmatic, utilitarian purpose of this model places it in the functionalist approach.

Key Points

The role of the educator is to be a leader who provides "focus, direction, and content" (Houle, 1996, p. 48) and generally possesses knowledge or experience that the learner must master. The learner is an adult "whose learning is shaped and led" (p. 48) through key strategies such as measurable objectives and evaluation. The context is any situation where adults engage in systematic learning and the context will shape the fundamental system. The focus of the learning is the individual, although the need for a program can be initiated by individuals, groups, institutions, or communities.

Houle made important contributions to adult education and his thinking contributed to the models that were developed after his. Other theorists included the importance of the learner's needs and the context. As models were critiqued, they evolved to include both the functionalist aspects of a curriculum suggested by Tyler (i.e., needs, objectives, methods, and evaluation) but they expanded on other aspects of planning to move beyond the purely instrumental approach. The evolution of Sork's (2000) question-based model is an example.

Question-based Framework of Program Planning

Sork's (1998) question-based model of program planning began as a functionalist model that incorporated the components of the Tylerian rationale. Similar to Houle (1996), he sought a generic process that would apply to different types of adult education activities but wanted simultaneously a generative process that would lead to innovation. Several aspects of the model make it distinctive. Rather than following a list of tasks, Sork (1997) proposes that planners ask questions, which he suggests will lead to more effective practice. For example, when considering who should be represented on a planning group, a planner might ask, "Who is not here who should be here?"

Although incorporating the four curriculum components in the Tylerian ratio-nale, the question-based approach indicates that the answers are not necessarily predictable. The approach is useful for guiding or analyzing planning (Sork, 2000). To *guide planning*, planners can pose questions that enable them to elicit the information they need and consider which techniques from among the vast num-ber available might help answer each question. "When used to *analyze planning*, the framework can serve to organize questions that are posed explicitly or sug-gested implicitly by the decisions or actions of the planners" (p. 180).

The question-based framework consists of six descriptive categories, each representing "a cluster of possible questions, decisions, and actions" related to an element of the planning process. Similar to Houle, Sork suggests that the frame-work is nonlinear in nature. In a graphic representation of the model, Sork arranges elements of the framework in an oval that contains each element of the model. On the outside of the oval is a path indicating that the planner can move from element to element in any order. Formative evaluation sits at the center of the oval indicat-ing that it influences each element of the planning process. The model has six steps that are proposed as clusters of questions rather than steps in a process as described below.

Analyze context and learner community. The context is dynamic rather than static and understanding it is a precursor to acting upon it. The learner community consists of the adults who might participate in the program and their characteris-tics relevant for planning.

Justify and focus planning. Needs assessments are only one way of determin-ing why it is valuable to devote resources to a particular program and what the characteristics of the program will be. Other approaches to justify and focus plan-ning are interest inventories, problem analyses, trend analyses, and market testing (Sork, 1987).

Clarify intentions. Clarifying intentions addresses what the planners intend for the program. Although planners can take different approaches to clarifying their intentions about a program, defining objectives are still the most prevalent. Sork (1998) does say that objectives are useful for clarifying intentions and that they are not necessarily behaviorist.

Prepare instructional plan. The instructional plan is the heart of the program where method and content merge with how the planner visualizes adult learning. Technology use often influences instruction.

Prepare administrative plan. Every instructional decision has administra-tive implications. Programs fail not only because of poor instruction but also because of poor administration.

Develop summative evaluation plan. The evaluation determines the worth or value of an educational program and whether the program fulfilled its intent.

Evaluation also depends on the information that the stakeholders want and the resources available for conducting an evaluation.

Each of these elements include Tyler's rationale, but Sork (2000) attempts to extend it by using more expansive language than Tyler, for example, rather than defining objectives, he suggests that the planner clarify intentions, which allows for a wider variety of learning experiences. Sork describes these elements of the model as technical because they emphasize the craft of planning. Recently, he added two additional dimensions that move beyond the technical and attend to the artistry of planning: the sociopolitical dimension and the ethical dimension.

The sociopolitical dimension includes power and interests of the various stakeholder groups (Cervero & Wilson, 1994). The focus is on how people engage with one another. "Working effectively in the sociopolitical domain of planning involves becoming aware of the role of power, ideology, and interests and how these interact when people work collectively to make decisions about intentions and actions" (Sork, 2000, p. 177). In the ethical domain, questions that concern values are more challenging. An ethically responsible planner will "recognize the moral commitments they are making as they develop programs" (p. 178). Practitioners interpret this model in different ways; however, the example that follows shows a functionalist application suggesting that the "artistic" layers of the model are not yet fully articulated.

Application of the Question-based Model of Program Planning

Mansfield (1999) used the question-based model to develop a training program intended to teach members of the Insurance Brokers Association of British Columbia (IBABC) how to use the Internet safely. An analysis of the context and learner community revealed that a short-term program held in computer labs in major cities throughout British Columbia would best meet the needs of the learners. Justification for the program was derived from answers to a survey indicating that only 32.5% of the brokers used the Internet for business purposes and they rated their skills in using email or searching the Internet as poor to fair. Therefore, the planners determined that the program would focus on e-mail and Internet usage skills at both the basic and intermediate levels that were relevant to the effective communications, research, and marketing opportunities that the Internet offers. These intentions were subsequently clarified by the development of measurable objectives for each topic. Instructional plans included lecture, group discussion, demonstration, and time for learners to practice their new skills. Administrative planning and course instructors were provided by the IBABC's Education Department. Summative evaluation consisted of assessments of "changes in learner knowledge, skills and attitudes; the design and implementation of the course; the level of learner satisfaction; and the level of learner participation" (p. 5).

Key Points

The technical, sociopolitical, and ethical domains of the question-based model build on Tyler's framework but begin to expand these concepts beyond the purely technical/rational. The role of the educator is to engage learners in learning tasks, promote inclusiveness and accessibility, and assure a smooth flow of the learning process (Sork, 1997). The learner is part of a community that has some type of common demographic, geographic, or social characteristic. When planning a program "their biography, their life circumstances, their ideological commitments, their aspirations" (Sork, 2000, p. 182) should be taken into account. Context determines what is possible when developing a program including not only the environment in which the program is conducted by also factors that limit or constrain the program. Content is part of the instructional plan that incorporates learners' characteristics such as gender, cultural background, education, facility with language, abilities, or disabilities. The key strategy is asking questions. The focus of this model is on changing the individual—physically, socially, intellectually, and/or emotionally.

Other planners have developed models that add to the fundamental system and the question-based models. For example, Caffarella (2002) builds on the instrumental aspects of planning, including the context and ethical dimensions emphasized by others, but adds the role of the planner and transfer of learning. Her *interactive model of program planning* attempts to go beyond the foundational models because "by design, it is interactive and comprehensive; people and place are acknowledged as important in the planning process; differences among cultures are taken into account in the planning process; and practitioners find the model useful and therefore a practical tool" (p. 20). The model takes into account the technical tasks that program planners undertake and these are included in a checklist (p. 23). What makes her model distinctive is that not all planners will use all steps of the model because of the contexts in which they work. For example, a program that recurs yearly may not have to build a base of support each year. Like Sork (2000), Caffarella (2002) acknowledges that adult education has a global nature, particularly that programs must meet the demands of diverse constituencies. She claims that educators who are in countries that have a teacher-directed curriculum can use the model effectively; however, she advocates a "macro" perspective in planning as programs increasingly cross cultural boundaries.

Although rooted in the functionalist tradition, the models described so far have a humanistic component that addresses the needs and interests of the learner, the differences among learners, and the impact of context on the educational process. Unlike Tyler (1949), these models have added such aspects as context, the role of the educator, a focus on the learners' needs and interests, and the political and ethical dimensions of planning. In this sense, they go beyond the functionalist approach. Yet, the additions to the models surround a very structured process. In general, they do not focus on who decides what will be included in a particular curriculum or program, who benefits from the curriculum, whether expert or practical knowledge is privileged, or who controls how the resources for education will be used. Planning is done before the program begins and is separated from the implementation. These are critical aspects of curriculum planning (Doll, 1993; Jarvis, 2004) that are more central in the empowerment models of curriculum or program development.

The Empowerment Models

The empowerment perspective has the goal of empowering individuals, groups, communities, and societies. "It suggests the purpose of any educational undertaking is to reduce the power and influence that various systems have on our lives – the ultimate goal is to change the system itself and the oppressive conditions it creates for people who are a part of it" (Pearce, 1998). As mentioned earlier, the empowerment perspective grows out of the subjectivist paradigm, which suggests that reality is socially constructed. In these models, the curriculum begins and ends with the learners' experience; the learner's knowledge is privileged over expert's knowledge. Through learning, adults empower themselves to understand their reality in new or expanded ways and this new understanding or transformation leads to emancipation and social action. The empowerment perspective as Pearce describes it is similar to what Cervero and Wilson (1994) call the critical perspective. While the functionalist and empowerment perspectives appear dichotomous, this distinction is more one of convenience, since in practice models may tend more toward a functionalist or empowerment approach, but also embody elements of each. Empowerment models draw on the understanding that curriculum begins and ends with the learners' experience. The Brazilian educator Paulo Freire is an example of the empowerment perspective along with other grass-roots activists.

Freire (1990) developed a model that, for the purposes of this chapter, is referred to as the *emancipatory model*. The most enduring aspect of Freire's work is his emphasis on the political nature of all educational activity (Mayo, 1997). From his perspective, education cannot be neutral. He worked primarily in the area of literacy among the poor in Brazil. In contrast to the Tylerian rationale, Freire (1970) was not advocating objectives or even "clarifying intentions" as Sork (2000) suggests. Freire believed that what was to be learned could not be established before the learning began because the learners themselves needed to be full participants in determining the "content" of their learning. In Freire's approach, the "banking" concept of education, where the teacher talks and the students passively receive more objective information, is replaced by the "culture circle" where teachers and students face one another and discuss issues of concern in their own lives (Freire, 1973). Freire used a limited but powerful repertoire of learning experiences consisting of problem-posing and dialogue. Problem-posing is aimed at raising the awareness of learners so they can describe the problems in their lives and communities. The teacher and the learner are peers, even to the extent that the roles shift back and forth because the learners have the expertise on their lives and experience and therefore become teachers and those who are designated teachers become learners.

As a dialogical approach to a literacy curriculum, Freire's (1990) method consisted of four phases. In the first phase, members of a literacy team spend time in communities where a literacy program is to be implemented, talking with the residents, and listening for recurring words and themes that are relevant to the people and documenting them. In the second phase, the literacy team chooses "generative words" from their vocabulary and thematic lists that they would later use to help learners develop elementary skills in decoding and encoding print. It was Freire's (1973) belief that the generative words should have special affective importance to learners and should evoke the social, cultural, and political contexts in which learners used the words. In the third phase, the generative words and themes are embedded in a symbolic, codified way as a part of drawings of familiar scenes in the life of the community. Each scene depicts conflicts found within the community. The task for the adult participants is to recognize, analyze, and attempt to resolve these as a group. In the course of this problem-posing, learners "name" the embedded generative words and themes, thereby creating their own "texts" for reading and writing. Through dialogue, teacher and learners co-investigate the texts from a critical perspective. Solutions that evolve from the interaction often include actions that require reading and writing skills. By working on aspects of their own lives, learners experience a concrete purpose and application for the literacy skills they are developing (Freire, 1973). Though it shares common elements, Freire's style of practice cannot be reduced to a technique; rather it is a way of being in the world (Mayo, 1997).

While Freire has become an icon of social change through education, his method of program or curriculum development has been criticized from a more functionalist perspective because of its lack of objective evaluation criteria. Outcomes of problem-posing and dialogue cannot be predicted and are therefore difficult to quantify. Freire's (1970) emancipatory model may have more aspects of banking education within it than might appear on the surface because the topics used in problem posing can lead to indoctrination. Another criticism shared by others in popular education is that the educator is often not a part of the community and comes from the "outside" (Egan, 2005). Despite these criticisms,

Freire is one of the educators most cited in Latin America, Africa, and Asia (Smith, 1997).

Application of the Emancipatory Model

Freire's model was used to develop an educational program at a homeless shelter, which focused on generative themes related to motherhood, parenting, and social inequality. Rivera (2000) observed over 1,500 hours of adult literacy classes at the shelter during her three-year study. In keeping with Freire's model, newspaper articles, editorial cartoons, music, pictures, videos, and short skits were used to raise generative themes. As Rivera (2000) noted, "The generative themes were also linked to subject matter that developed and strengthened reading and numeracy skills" (p. 32). Dialogue and writing facilitated critical reflection on the generative themes. "Through a process of collective sharing and reflection, the women in this study began to 'act upon the world,' challenging their internalized oppressions, understanding how structural forces shaped and constrained their lives" (p. 47). They learned what they could do on both personal and collective levels to address these problems. The program inspired the women to help other women, encouraged them to become effective advocates for their legal and personal rights, and helped them become more involved in their children's education. This application suggests that Freire's model is in use in contexts different from those in Brazil, and while the goal may on occasion depart from his original intention to promote radical social change, examples like this affirm Freire's central assertion that curriculum begin with learners' experiences that lead to change individually and socially.

Folk schools, like the Highlander Research and Education Center in New Market, Tennessee, also advocate for an empowerment approach to education in ways similar to that espoused by Freire. The Highlander approach, envisioned by Myles Horton (1990), anchored curriculum in the daily lives, interests, and self-identified needs of adults who faced situations of oppression. Those who were teaching did not advocate answers but facilitated a problem-posing, dialogic process where meaning was collectively constructed (Parker & Parker, 1991). In this model, the teacher is a facilitator who helps to clarify participants' questions, encourages conversation, and assists in the collective discovery of relevant answers. Educational activities focus primarily on group rather than individual learning and development. For this reason, Horton chose to work with leaders of "any kind of cohesive group that had a particular aim compatible with the philosophy of creating some form of democratic society" (Horton, 1990, p. 57). Horton moved away from a view of democracy that focused on individual freedom and autonomy toward a more relational view of democracy that views individuals within larger social contexts (Thayer-Bacon, 2004).

Key Points

In summary, in the emancipatory model, the educator is a peer with the learner and switches roles as necessary. Freire (1970) and Horton (1990) rejected the traditional role of the teacher as a subject-matter expert who imparts knowledge to the learners in favor of the role of educator as facilitator of inquiry and dialogue. Learners' experience is the heart of the learning process. The context for learning is the world of the learners; the content is the set of issues from their lives that concern them. The focus is on changing individuals so that they may bring about radical changes in the society in which they live. Key strategies include problem-posing and dialogue aimed at raising the critical consciousness of learners so they can act on the world with their new knowledge. Educational activities focus primarily on the group rather than individual learning and development.

Highlander's curriculum had significant influence on social changes including the labor movement and the civil rights movement; both Martin Luther King and Rosa Parks attended workshops at Highlander. During a radio interview many years later when Parks was asked what role Highlander had played in her decision not to move to the back of the bus, she answered, "Everything" (Hurst, 2002, p. 9). The empowerment approach underscores the importance of political and social dimensions of program planning and stresses the role of learners' knowledge and experience in shaping the curriculum. Although the empowerment model is considered a "radical" approach, it is highly regarded by many adult educators who have incorporated elements of the model (Rivera, 2000). The legacy of the empowerment model is the continuing importance of the social justice aim of adult education that underscores the role of power and interests in planning. A new generation of planning approaches includes these dimensions.

The Next Generation of Planning Models

The next generation of planning models for curriculum development builds on the functionalist and the empowerment perspectives yet depart from both in new ways. Two examples of the next generation of planning modes include Cervero and Wilson (2006) who focus on the central role of power and interests in program planning and Billet (2001) who situates learning in a workplace community of practice.

The Negotiation Model of Program Planning

Cervero and Wilson (2006) suggest that most curriculum models have focused on educational outcomes and excluded political and social outcomes that either reproduce or challenge existing social and political relationships. The *negotiation model of program planning* (Cervero & Wilson, 1994a) presumes that "planning is essentially a social activity in which educators negotiate with others in answering questions about a program's form, including its purposes, content, audience, and format" (p. 28). While their model is not intended to serve as a prescriptive, systematic guide to curriculum development, it does reveal the complexity of social, political, and ethical dimensions associated with planning education for adults. They propose that adult educators should be committed to a democratic planning process in which all people who are affected by a program should be involved in the determination of what is important for learning. They also argue that program planners must address the questions of *who benefits* and *who should benefit* from adult education programs (Wilson & Cervero, 2001). Cervero and Wilson (1994b) maintain that power relationships and legitimate interests define the context in which planners act and are at the heart of the planning process. Legitimate interests are motivations that drive people, including the program planner, to act in certain ways and can be viewed along a continuum ranging from either congruent to conflicting. "So determining whose interests get to the planning table to produce the program is the fundamental ethical question that every planner has to negotiate" (Wilson & Cervero, 1996, p. 20). They describe two dimensions of power as social (including race, class, gender, and sexual orientation) and organizational (including hierarchical positions) and the need for "substantively democratic planning" (Cervero & Wilson, 2006, p. 3). To show how negotiating power and interests would look in the planning process, Cervero and Wilson (2006) outline four major areas for consideration.

Negotiating the program's needs assessments. Planners must identify stakeholders who will affect or be affected by the program, determine whose interests matter, anticipate how power relations frame a needs assessment, and bring as many different stakeholders as possible to the planning table. Needs connect to historical and social context.

Negotiating the program's educational, management, and political objectives. Stakeholders have educational, management, and political objectives that they hope to achieve in the planning process. Negotiating objectives democratically occurs before and during the program. Conflicting needs complicate this process so it is necessary to anticipate how power relations frame the negotiation of objectives.

Negotiating the program's instructional design and implementation. Planners manage the politics of selecting and organizing instructional leaders, techniques, and content. Democratically negotiating instruction provides learners the opportunity to substantively impact the instructional design.

Negotiating the program's administrative organization and operation. Planners evaluate programs democratically based on three types of objectives: educational, management, and political. Power relations frame formal and informal program evaluations and the planner anticipates these.

Depending on the politics of the context and the inclinations of the planner, there are eight strategies that a planner can utilize in these negotiations: reasoning, consulting, appealing, networking, exchanging, bargaining, pressuring, and counteracting (Yang, Cervero, Valentine, & Benson, 1998). Every aspect of this model addresses the questions about who benefits and who determines the outcomes. Unlike other models (Caffarella, 2002; Sork, 2000), the negotiation model illustrates how context and program are inextricably entwined.

Application of Negotiation Model of Program Planning

Umble, Cervero, and Langone (2001) utilized a case study approach toward a continuing education course for public health professionals. "The course was a product of historical processes and organizational relationships that created a strong conceptual frame into which the course had to fit: policy implementation. That frame strongly shaped the course content and audience" (p. 142). Various stakeholders whose interests were not being met, including a course instructor, an epidemiologist, and a nurse, used negotiation to change the power relationships and substantive negotiation to alter the course content and audience. "The course emerged, then, from a social process of negotiation of personal, organizational, and societal interests within relations of power and from negotiations about those relations of power" (p. 142).

Key Points

The focus of the *negotiation model* is on the influence, tactics, and power of adult educators in program planning. The role of the educator is to negotiate the form of the program with stakeholders. The learners have legitimate interests in the program and the right to make a substantive contribution to its plan. The context of this model revolves around socially constructed power relationships in which race, class, gender, and other aspects of diversity are taken into consideration. Curriculum content encompasses multiple objectives and includes needs that are both ascribed to and consequential for those involved. The key strategy is negotiation to satisfy and balance the sometimes competing needs of stakeholders.

The *negotiation model* (Cervero & Wilson, 1994a, 2006) focuses on relationships in a particular context that embody differences in power and interests. From a different perspective, the *guided learning model* (Billett, 2001) presents a curriculum for the workplace that extends the focus on relationships to include the way meaning-making occurs in the context of a community of practice. Both models stress the importance of democratic planning. Most curriculum models for workplace learning follow the tenets of the scientific management movement (Taylor, 1911) that adopted the language of technical rationality. In many ways, these models followed the functionalist tradition that supported education as contributing to economic capital (Tyler, 1949). In the workplace, workers had little voice regarding what or how they would learn because learning/training was controlled by experts for the purposes of increasing efficiency. In contrast to this view of worker as object and learning as production, Welton (1991) advocates a worker-centered perspective in workplace education. An emerging model of workplace learning views work as developmental, participatory, and self-authorizing if not democratic (Dirkx, 1996).

Guided Learning at Work

Billett's (2001) *workplace curriculum model* supports the perspective that learning in the workplace can follow the principles of adult education and aim for what Welton (1991) calls "opportunities that develop worker wellbeing" (p. 32). Billet's evidence-based curriculum model emphasizes the learning that occurs through everyday participation in work activities guided by expert coworkers, peers, and the environment itself. The goal of the curriculum is to provide a framework for developing the knowledge required for expert performance. This type of knowledge goes beyond technical skills and includes the capacity to resolve non-routine problems and become a full participant in the work; in this way, workers can shape the work.

Drawing on the work of Lave and Wenger (1991), Billet describes his model of workplace learning as situated in a particular work context and views work as participation. As a novice, a worker has only peripheral participation in the workplace "community of practice" because of limited knowledge. Through guided learning at work, an individual moves along a pathway to full participation in the workplace. Full participation includes being able to influence the workplace processes and procedures. Although the context shapes what and how learning occurs, Billet claims, "individuals in the workplace still determine what and how they will learn" (p. 37). The workplace will always be contested ground because of competing interests. Regardless, work is a major aspect of many people's lives around the globe and cannot be ignored as a major context of learning.

A curriculum that focuses on the process of learning as it occurs naturally in the workplace can help workers develop or improve their vocational knowledge. Billett's (2001) model consists of four components: movement from peripheral to full participation; access to goals for performance; direct guidance of experts and others; and indirect guidance provided by the physical and social environment of the workplace. Through a series of activities, workers can gain access to complex, nonroutine knowledge that is difficult to learn. Direct guidance of experts and others "is most salient when it makes knowledge accessible to learners that would otherwise remain inaccessible. Learning this knowledge alone may be too difficult (e.g., the knowledge is hidden) or inappropriate (e.g., imprudent shortcuts might be learned)" (Billett, 2002, p. 32).

Application of the Workplace Curriculum Model

Billett (2004) describes how the model was applied in vocational training for hairdressers. Initially, students participated in activities of low complexity such as cleaning the salon workstations. Their movement to full participation in their chosen occupation came about as they received direct guidance on tasks and performance goals related to proficiency in duties such as cutting or coloring hair. "This development includes the learning of heuristics (e.g., tricks of the trade) that assist with easy performance with workplace tasks" (Billett, 2002, p. 33). Indirect guidance provided a means for learners to become acquainted with the nontechnical aspects of practice in their vocation. "For instance, in one hairdressing salon to be an expert hairdresser required knowing the names of relatives and their relationships to the elderly clientele who came to the salon, as much for social contact as to have their hair dressed" (Billett, 2004, p. 27). Billet argues that understanding and shaping the discourse are more important than technical knowledge. In this model, the curriculum emerges from the demands of work, rather than being driven by predetermined content. This is different from practice-based education where curriculum focuses on problems taken from practice but is under the control of training or education providers (Garrick, 2000). Billet (2004) criticizes his own model saying that it will be difficult to identify the pathways of learning and the workers who have the capacity to be guides. Regardless of the criticism, the model makes a contribution to curriculum development in the workplace.

Key Points

In the *guided learning model*, the role of the educator is filled by an experienced worker who provides guidance to less experienced workers so they can become full participants in the community of practice. The learner moves from peripheral participation to full participation and can thus influence the work itself. The context is situated in a particular workplace made up of a community of practice that is dynamic and changing. The content is everyday work activity and gaps in learners' knowledge that prevent their full participation. The key strategy is being guided in learning rather than being taught. The focus is on changing the individual learner who in turn changes the workplace. What makes Billet's (2004) model unique is the use of work practice as curriculum content. Billet acknowledges that his model might be seen to be too much in the technical/rational

tradition that focuses on routine or instrumental learning. He reminds practitioners that even instrumental learning can be emancipatory because it provides a
bridge for a new way of being in the world. The model is socially critical, he
claims, because employees do not passively receive learning, nor do they passively comply with workplace values that contradict their own values.

In addition to the functionalist and empowerment models, these two models
provide practitioners with a new direction for curriculum development that builds
on models that have gone before. As adult educators continue to take a more
global view, new perspectives on how to develop curriculum in different cultural
contexts will emerge. For example, Jarvis (2004) focuses on learner-centered curriculum but places it in a global market context that shows how external forces
shape planning. Long an advocate of the importance of social context in the
learning process, Jarvis laments that the market has a more central focus in determining program or curriculum. He describes market influence broadly to include
not only corporate interests, but also those of government exerted through policy
changes, and the public through choice to enroll and pay for educational programs. Because public funding for adult education programs is decreasing, the
private economic market is increasingly driving adult education curriculum. In a
world where resources for adult education are limited, corporate interests are
transnational, and participants can enroll online for courses across the globe, the
market influence on adult education curriculum cannot be overemphasized. In the
changing global environment both the functionalist assumptions and the empowerment assumptions of program planning take on new and different roles, necessi-
tating new approaches to program planning.

A Planning Approach that Foregrounds Learning

Whatever planning perspective one might advocate today, the rapidly changing world of the early 21st century suggests that it will need to be adapted to be
effective. This need for effective planning in a rapidly changing environment
suggests the importance of learning as a fundamental part of planning. Lave and
Wenger (1991) identify learning as an underappreciated element in curriculum.
Learning is pivotal in times of rapid and continuous change or when the knowledge that is needed does not exist yet. Davis and Ziegler (2005) note that adult
education programs have long focused on learning, but that in most cases learning
is primarily associated with program participants, or focused on a specific part of
the planning process such as evaluation. Only rarely is learning extended to the
planning process itself or the planner seen as a learner. Learning viewed from
functional, empowerment, and strategic levels has become increasingly important
in leadership studies (Heifetz, 1994), organizational change (Bergquist, 1993),
educational reform (Fullan, 2001), organizational learning (Easterby-Smith,

Burgoyne, & Araujo, 1999), and the learning organization (Pedler, Burgoyne, & Burdell, 1991; Senge, 1990; Watkins & Marsick, 1993).

An emphasis on learning underscores the essentially heuristic elements of educational planning in a dynamic, changing environment. No matter what is already known in the planning process, a model that underscores learning as a primary rubric assumes that changing contexts require ongoing learning. Since learning is multidimensional, it includes functional as well as empowerment elements. Because learning is systemic, stakeholders participate in co-constructing new knowledge. Making all steps of the process transparent through documentation, reflection, and communication supports inclusiveness. Programming that foregrounds learning requires a major shift in perception from a focus on the individual to a vision of a dynamic and fluid community of practice (Wenger, 1998).

Through learning, programs are enacted (Maturana & Varela, 1980, 1987) by praxis—purposeful, reflective awareness in the context of collaborative activity. In the learning model, phrases like "we make the road by walking" (Horton & Freire, 1990) and "learning our way out" (Finger & Asun, 2001) become operational. The learning approach represents a conceptual framework that guides the planning process. In the rapidly changing world, "learning" may provide a new perspective on the planning process. Practitioners who see themselves as learners will be able to move into uncertain contexts with a spirit of inquiry.

Program Planning in a Global Context

In this chapter, I have reviewed a variety of models for educational program and curriculum planning. Although each is unique, some emphasize more functionalist perspectives that focus on expert leadership, objective measurement, and clear step-by-step planning. Traditionally, the functional emphasis in curriculum planning in adult education is on the educator. Although the market continues to demand greater accountability in the planning process, the objective measures that accountability requires are problematic because of changing contexts. Others emphasize learners' experience and knowledge of their contexts. Increasingly, the role of the learner has received greater emphasis, leading to other approaches. For example, in the empowerment approach, learners' voices and active engagement are keys to effective planning. Yet the scope of who participates in adult education continues to expand. In a global environment where the implications and unintended consequences are often difficult to predict, how does the practitioner decide who should sit at the planning table? And from a marketing perspective, in a world where economies are driven less by national entities and more by international corporate interests, how does a planner respond to the wide variety of educational interests and at the same time, maintain a commitment to the democratic values of adult education? With the increasing power of the educational market (broadly understood) in driving the planning process, and the growing scope of that market, it is likely that the next generation of curriculum models will continue to stretch the assumptions of planners, incorporating elements of both the functionalist and the empowerment perspectives, yet depart from both in new ways. The models provide helpful guidance and continue to be important in understanding curriculum and program planning; however, in changing environment, no single generic model can guide practitioners in the real world of planning.

Whatever the directions these new approaches might take, it is likely that learning will be foundational to the process. As Eric Hoffer (1995) says, "In times of change learners inherit the earth while the learned find themselves beautifully equipped to deal with a world that no longer exists" (p. 32).

References

Apps, J. W. (1979). *Problems in continuing education.* New York: McGraw Hill.

Bergquist, W. (1993). *The postmodern organization: Mastering the art of irreversible change.* San Francisco: Jossey Bass.

Billet, S. (2001). *Learning in the workplace: Strategies for effective practice.* Crows Nest, NSW, Australia: Allen & Unwin.

Billett, S. (2002). Toward a workplace pedagogy: Guidance, participation, and engagement. *Adult Education Quarterly, 53*(1), 27-43.

Billett, S. (2004). From your business to our business: Industry and vocational education in Australia. *Oxford Review of Education, 30*(1), 13-35.

Boone, E. J. (1992). *Program development in adult education.* Prospect Heights, IL: Waveland Press.

Boone, E. J., Safrit, R. D., & Jones, J. (2002). *Developing programs in adult education: A conceptual programming model* (2nd ed.). Prospect Heights, IL: Waveland

Caffarella, R. S. (2002). *Planning programs for adult learners: A practical guide for educators, trainers, and staff developers* (2nd ed.). San Francisco: Jossey-Bass, Inc.

Cervero, R., & Wilson, A. (1994a). *Planning responsibly for adult education: A guide to negotiating power and interests.* San Francisco: Jossey-Bass.

Cervero, R., & Wilson, A. (1994b). The politics of responsibility: A theory of program planning practice for adult education. *Adult Education Quarterly, 45*, 249-268.

Cervero, R. M., & Wilson, A. L. (2006). *Working the planning table: Negotiating democratically for adult, continuing, and workplace education.* San Francisco: Jossey-Bass.

Cookson, P. S. (1998). *Program planning for the training and continuing education of adults*. Malabar, FL: Krieger.

Davis, D. C., & Ziegler, M. F. (2005, June). Learning our way out: A model of program planning for changing times. *Proceedings of the 46th Annual Adult Education Research Conference* (pp. 115-120). Athens: University of Georgia.

Dirkx, J. (1996). Human resource development as adult education: Fostering the educative workplace. *New Directions for Adult and Continuing Education, 72*, 41-47.

Doll, W. (1993). *A postmodern perspective on curriculum*. New York: Teachers College Press.

Easterby-Smith, M., Araujo, L., & Burgoyne, J. G. (Eds.). (1999). *Organizational learning and the learning organization: Developments in theory and practice*. Thousand Oaks, CA: Sage.

Egan, J. P. (2005). Local practice, local orientation: Grassroots program planning. *Convergence, 38*(1), 41-49.

Ely, M. L. (Ed.) (1936). *Adult education in action*. New York: American Association for Adult Education.

Faillos, C. A. (2006). Adult education and the empowerment of the individual in a global society. In S. B. Merriam, B. C. Courtney, & R. M. Cervero (Eds.), *Global issues and adult education: Perspectives from Latin America, Southern Africa, and the United States* (pp. 15-29). San Francisco: Jossey-Bass.

Finger, M., & Asun, J. M. (2001). *Adult education at the crossroads: Learning our way out*. London and New York: ZED Books.

Freire, P. (1970). *Pedagogy of the oppressed*. New York: Herder and Herder.

Freire, P. (1973). *Education for critical consciousness*. New York: Seabury Press.

Freire, P. (1990). *Pedagogy of the oppressed* (M. B. Ramos, Trans.). New York: The Continuum Publishing Company.

Fullan, M. (2001). *Leading in a culture of change*. San Francisco: Jossey-Bass.

Garrick, J. (1998). *Informal learning in the workplace: The subtle power of informal learning*. London:Routledge.

Gergen, K. (Ed.) (1992). *Organizational theory in the postmodern era. In rethinking organisations*. London: Sage.

Hoffer, E. (1973). *Reflections on the Human Condition*. Titusville, NJ: Hopewell Publications.

Heifetz, R. A. (1994). *Leadership without easy answers*. Cambridge, MA: Belknap Press of Harvard University Press.

Horton, M., & Freire, P. (1990). *We make the road by walking: Conversations on education and social change*. Philadelphia, PA: Temple University Press.

Horton, M. (1990). *The long haul*. New York: Doubleday.

Houle, C. O. (1972). *The design of education*. San Francisco: Jossey-Bass.

Houle, C. O. (1996). *The design of education* (2nd ed.). San Francisco: Jossey-Bass.

Hurst, J. (2002). Popular education, labor, and social change. In L. Delp, M. Out-man-Kramer, S. Schurman, & K. Wong (Eds.), *Teaching for change: Popular education and the labor movement* (pp. 9-18). Los Angeles: University of California, Center for Labor Research and Education.

Jarvis, P. (2004). *Adult education and lifelong learning: Theory and practice* (3rd ed.). London: RoutledgeFalmer.

King, K. P., & Wang, V. C. X. (Eds.). (2007). *Comparative adult education around the globe: International portraits and readings of the history, practice, philosophy, and theories of adult learning*. Hangzhou, China: Zhejiang University Press.

Lave, J., & Wenger, E. (1991). *Situated learning: Legitimate peripheral participation*. New York: Cambridge University Press.

Mansfield, G. P. (1999). *Development of a short duration Internet training program*. Retrieved August 22, 2007, from 24.148.8.218:81/~gregm/artifacts/ADED329-1.pdf

Maturana, H., & Varela, F. (1980). *Autopoiesis and cognition: The realization of living*. London: Reidl.

Maturana, H., & Varela, F. (1987). *The tree of knowledge: The biological roots of human understanding*. Boston: Shambhala.

Mayo, P. (1997). Tribute to Paulo Freire. *International Journal of Lifelong Education, 16*(5), 365-370.

Merriam, S. B., Courtney, B. C., & Cervero, R. M. (Eds.). (2006). *Global issues and adult education: Perspectives from Latin America, Southern Africa, and the United States*. San Francisco: Jossey-Bass.

Parker, F., & Parker, B. J. (1991). *Myles Horton (1905-90) of Highlander: Adult educator and southern activist*. Cullowhee, NC: Authors. (ERIC Document Reproduction Service No. ED336615)

Pearce, S. (1998). Determining program needs. In P. S. Cookson (Ed.), *Program planning for the training and continuing education of adults* (pp. 249-272). Malabar, FL: Krieger.

Pedler, M., Burgoyne, J., & Burdell, T. (1991). The *learning company*. London: McGraw Hill.

Pennington, F., & Green, J. 1976. A comparative analysis of program development processes in six professions. *Adult Education, 27*(1), 13-23.

Rivera, L. (2000). *Learning community: An ethnographic study of popular education and homeless women in a shelter-based adult literacy program*. Unpublished doctoral dissertation, Northeastern University, Boston, MA.

Senge, P. (1990). *The fifth discipline: The art and science of the learning organization*. New York: Doubleday.

Slattery, P. (1995). *Curriculum development in the postmodern era.* New York: Garland Reference Library of Social Science.

Smith, M. K. (1997). *Paulo Freire and informal education.* The encyclopaedia of informal education. Retrieved August 26, 2007, from http://www.infed.org/thinkers/et-freir.htm.

Sork, T. J. (1997). Workshop planning. *New Directions for Adult and Continuing Education, 76,* 5-17.

Sork, T. J. (1998). Program priorities, purposes, and objectives. In P. S. Cookson (Ed.), *Program planning for the training and continuing education of adults* (pp. 273-299). Malabar, FL: Kreiger.

Sork, T. J. (2000). Planning educational programs. In A. L. Wilson, & E. R. Hayes (Eds.), *Handbook of adult and continuing education* (pp. 171-190). San Francisco: Jossey-Bass Inc.

Sztomka, P. (1979). *Sociological dilemmas: Toward a dialectic paradigm.* New York: Academic Press.

Taylor, F. W. (1911). The principles of scientific management. New York: Harper Brothers.

Thayer-Bacon, B. J. (2004). An exploration of Myles Horton's democratic praxis: Highlander Folk School. *Educational Foundations 18*(2), 5-23.

Tyler, R. W. (1949). *Basic principles of curriculum and instruction.* Chicago, IL: The University of Chicago Press.

Umble, K. E., Cervero, R. M., & Langone, C. A. (2001). Negotiating about power, frames, and continuing education: A case study in public health. *Adult Education Quarterly, 51*(2), 128-145.

Wang, V. C. X. (2007). Chinese knowledge transmitters or western learning facilitators adult teaching methods compared. In K. P. King & V. C. X. Wang (Eds.), *Comparative adult education around the globe: International portraits and readings of the history, practice philosophy, and theories of adult learning* (pp. 113-137.). Hangzhou, China: Zhejiang University Press.

Watkins, K. E., & Marsick, V. J. (1993). *Sculpting the learning organization: Lessons in the art and science of systemic change.* San Francisco: Jossey Bass.

Welton, M. R. (1991). *Toward development work: The workplace as a learning environment.* Geelong, Australia: Deakin University Press.

Wenger, E. (1998). *Communities of practice: Learning, meaning, and identity.* New York: Cambridge University Press.

Wilson, A. L., & Cervero, R. M. (1996). Who sits at the planning table: Ethics and planning practice. *Adult Learning, 8*(2), 20-22.

Wilson, A. L., & Cervero, R. M. (2001). La Verneda-Sant Martí Adult Education Center: Adult education and the struggle for knowledge and power: Practical action in a critical tradition. *Proceedings of the 42nd Annual Adult Education Research Conference* (pp. 423-428.). East Lansing, Michigan State University. Retrieved August 27, 2007, from http://www.adulterc.org/Proceed-ings/2001/2001wilson.htm.

Wilson, A. L., & Hayes, E. R. (Eds.) (2000). *Handbook of adult and continuing education*. San Francisco: Jossey-Bass.

Yang, B., Cervero, R. M., Valentine, T., & Benson, J. (1998). Development and validation of an instrument to measure adult educator's power and influence tactics in program planning practice. *Adult Education Quarterly, 48*(4), 227-244.

Chapter 7
Developing Curriculum for Police Officers and Firefighters: Tips to Follow and Pitfalls to Avoid

Sandra R. Daffron, Gail M. Goulet, John L. Gray, and Jason X. Viada

Introduction

The very lives of police officers and firefighters depend upon proper training. Strategic approaches to curriculum development for their training can mean the difference between life and death for the public safety workers themselves and the public at large. This chapter investigates what is working and what changes ought to be made in the curriculum for these professionals.

The need for effective and efficient training of police officers and firefighters is pressing. In most parts of North America, there is a chronic shortage of qualified applicants for both professions as retirements surge, the population increases, and the economy offers more opportunities in the private sector for the top applicants. The challenges facing public safety are reflected in the continuing professional education of those who serve their communities. The demands are to create lasting solutions to complex problems, to fill the need for qualified leaders who possess the character to lead their organizations with integrity, and to keep up with the pace of change in laws, processes, and public expectations. These challenges affect every level of public safety organizations. With ever-changing threats to the public safety, and with less funding, the organization has to prevail, with fewer resources. The delivery of services to the public is predominately done, and will likely continue, by people in a face-to-face environment. The issue of developing a curriculum for training these public safety professionals, and then making meaning of the training, or transferring the learning into practice (praxis), becomes critical.

Baldwin and Ford in 1988 estimated that U.S. corporations spent up to $100 billion annually on training and education. Rowden reported in 1995 that training costs were even higher at $180 billion annually (p. 355). Awoniyi, Griego, and Morgan (2002) found, unfortunately, not more than about 10% of the information presented in these training programs actually transferred into practice. From these studies and figures, it becomes clear that program developers and trainers have an obligation to do more to ensure transfer of learning that results from their programs. This chapter addresses research conducted with police officers and firefighters about their training experiences, and offers tips and cautions for help-ing program developers, trainers, and the organization learn to design effective educational programs for professionals.

Background on Training Public Safety Workers

Public safety agencies have one thing in common, the mission to provide for the protection and safety of the communities that they serve. Within that context, the backbone of delivering this service rests squarely on the shoulders of the agency's personnel. Regardless of size and location of the agency, the personnel need the core skills to accomplish the mission. Fire personnel are battling fires, responding to emergency medical calls, and doing rescues. Police personnel are controlling events and people, investigating crime, and preventing disorder.

A challenge for the trainer of public safety employees is that most agencies have different hiring criteria for their first responders, including various educa-tional levels, various background standards, psychological screening, and a vari-ety of requirements resulting from written tests, physical performance tests, and medical standards. Though there is some uniformity within some states, most agencies have a broad latitude to determine the hiring criteria for their personnel. Some agencies require a college degree while others will accept a high school diploma or a General Education Degree (GED). Though federal laws require that testing be nondiscriminatory and used to determine qualifications for essential job functions, agencies can use the kind of testing they want to get the desired outcome.

Some agencies have rigorous physical fitness standards while others have none. Some agencies use psychological screening tools, a polygraph, and exten-sive background investigations, while others do little or none. Plus, the testing process continues to change and evolve resulting in employees within the same agency having experienced different testing processes. Therefore, the trainer and program developer cannot reliably make assumptions about the commonality of the educational preparation or abilities of the public safety employee. In public safety organizations, the trainer faces learners with a wide variety of skills, knowl-edge, and experiences. If the trainer or course developer assumes that a cookie-cutter approach to training, where one type fits all, will be adequate, the program will likely fail.

Culture

Each agency establishes a culture for training and the integration of informa-tion into its operations. This culture determines the training program's success and sets the tone for expectations by the management team, the agency's first-line supervisors and training officers. When the management team has low expectations, employees will not be expected to share, teach, or demonstrate what they have learned in training. The learning experience will remain the sole property of the learner and the organization, as a whole, may not benefit from it.

When skepticism about training or the importance of training is rooted in the agency's culture, the value of new tactics and information is often dismissed. One example is when a new employee has graduated from the academy and the field-training officer or first line supervisor says, "The first thing to do is to forget everything that you learned in the academy because we will teach you *our way of doing things.*" This culture of skepticism will not only stunt the learner, but will prevent the organization from growing, evolving, and being on the cutting edge of innovation and effectiveness.

For the trainer, the nonverbal cues by the learner will signal this skepticism. Because public safety employees receive a lot of mandated training and have the opportunity to learn about a host of complex topics, they often become critical consumers of training. When training is not current or when the instructor does not have the credentials or respect to conduct the program, learners will shut down and express their skepticism with silence, crossed arms, failure to return from breaks, or lack of engagement in class activities. When this occurs, the trainer needs to innovate, adapt, and rebuild the relationship with the participants.

Mandated versus Self-Directed Learning

Public safety personnel have a body of mandated skills and knowledge that they must master. Police officers must know criminal law, criminal procedures, search and seizure laws, and be proficient in weapons, defensive tactics, and driving skills. Firefighters must know the physical properties of fire, the safety procedures of responding to a fire, how equipment works, and how the firefighting team works as a team.

In addition to these areas of mandatory training, the sources of other mandated training often come from legislation, often inspired by a critical event, and mandates from professional organizations, risk managers, court decisions, lawsuits, and professional accreditation. Mandated training creates challenges in creating motivation to learn because it is viewed as "must do" rather than being self-directed by the learner. Some learners will participate in the training with an open mind but many more "occupy the seat" to earn the required hours to achieve the mandated training goal. Unfortunately, this negative thinking may prevent the learner from engaging in critical thinking skills that may create real learning. Examples of mandated training include recertification of first aid, skills using a breath test device that measures alcohol in a person's system, ability to use a confidential database, or specific kinds of rescue procedures. The skilled trainer will need to understand that some in the class are as knowledgeable as the trainer, while others will have little or no foundational knowledge. One solution to make this training more effective is to move the goal from clock hours of training to demonstrated competency.

Self-directed learning often comes after the mandated basic job skills are completed. Public safety training is complex, rich in topics, and rapidly changing due to emerging technology, innovation, the discovery of new solutions, and changing demographics. After initial training, the opportunities for self-directed learning for public safety employees are vast and include becoming a specialist in an area, promoting to a higher position within the profession, and instructing and mentoring. The profession often provides the resources for self-directed learning with Internet-based resources, distance learning, publications, conferences, and networking with other agencies

.

Different Models of Initial Training

In most states, the foundation of initial training is done at a formal institution that is commonly called an academy. However, in some states, the location of the training is done at a community college or university in a purely academic setting. In community colleges and universities, the training is available to any student who wants to attend the classes and pay the tuition. These learners are not typically prescreened by an employer for suitability. Training in the academic setting is commonly led and taught by professional educators and practitioners. In this setting, the student receives a certification or degree and is eligible to apply to public safety agencies for employment where the agency tests the applicant for suitability. If hired, the employee then receives the specialized training unique to that agency.

The challenge for the professional educator in the academic setting is that learners may have a desire to be in the profession but may not have the aptitude or will never likely be employed because of disqualifying past behavior, such as prior criminal convictions or history of illegal drug use. The professional educator in the academic setting is faced with learners with a wide variety of skills and motivation and it becomes difficult to keep the highly qualified learner engaged while not losing the lesser-equipped learner.

Another model for initial training is the academy that is conducted by public safety agencies. In some states and with nearly all state police agencies, learners attend a residential academy that is conducted by an agency whose mission is to train public safety employees. Typically, the learner is hired by a public safety agency and must meet minimum qualifications by testing before acceptance into these centralized academies. These academies are also more paramilitary in their form of training where students wear uniforms, conduct themselves in a military fashion, undergo stress training, and learn in a military-type of atmosphere. In this model, the learner is often a paid employee of an agency while attending the academy. The learner is not only evaluated on academic and skill performance but is also subject to discipline for conduct issues. For the trainer, the motivation of the learner is very high because failure means loss of employment. Program developers may have much greater control over the learning experience and have more opportunities to teach a variety of skill sets. Also, the breadth of aptitude and preparation is often narrower than in the academic setting.

These centralized academies are very expensive to operate and therefore have diminished in number. Some in the field criticize the paramilitary experience because they might not recognize it as applicable to public safety agencies and community problem-solving techniques that rely upon negotiation and collaboration skills.

The curriculum and delivery systems of these two models are often very similar and use lecture, discussion, traditional test taking, scenarios, and demonstrations. An emerging trend is using *problem-based learning* as a model to teach problem solving and use self-directed learning as principles for learners to find and explore the information and learning resources.

Field Training Programs

Following the completion of the more formal initial training is a structured on-the-job training program that can last weeks or months. A commonly used model provides 16 weeks of post academy training. The goal of the field training program is to build upon the knowledge and skills gained at the academy and within the context of where the work is performed and with the agency's specific ways to accomplish the mission. An experienced employee often delivers the field training instruction. The field trainer has expressed a desire to teach and usually has completed some specialized courses in adult learning. Learners are typically on probation during this field training program, and their employment may be terminated if their skills do not develop to meet the performance standards outlined in the field training program.

The performance and learning objectives of these programs are often tiered and therefore rise as a learner goes through the program. Training officers often use the teaching technique of tell-show-do or explain, demonstrate, perform, and give feedback, as they experience the variety of work in the field. In some programs, learners are evaluated every day by the trainer on a score sheet and the week's achievements and issues are summarized in a narrative. In some programs, learners write a journal of their reflections and help set goals for the coming training period.

Typically, the last part of the training program is characterized by the learner doing nearly all the work while the trainer assumes the role of the coach and only intervenes to prevent high-risk issues from occurring. Often, at the very end of the field training program, the student officer is in uniform and the training officer is not and acts as an observer. When done well, the field training program builds upon the academy training and transitions the learner to working in the field at nearly a full performance level.

The completion of the field training program often signals the end of the apprentice stage of job development and the beginning of the journeyman level. It is not uncommon for learners who did not excel in the academic setting of the academy to do very well in the field training program because of the applicability of the training. Conversely, it is not uncommon for "book smart" learners to find they are lacking "street smarts" as they struggle to apply concepts in a stressful environment with incomplete facts, changing circumstances, and unfolding events. That is to say that they must make quick decisions in less than ideal circumstances without time for reflection or discussion.

Field training helps to identify the employee's abilities. In one incident, which is not all that uncommon, a new employee with a four-year degree in criminal justice was hired by a police agency and excelled in the academy, earning top scores. However, in the field training program, the new employee could not apply the knowledge to situations consistently and quickly. As the performance expectations in the field testing rose, the employee's performance could not meet the standards and the employee was terminated.

Though the field training program may formally end, the learning and teaching do not. Learners become more self-directed in exploring the style of public safety service that works for them, the finding of new information and the lessons-learned from new experiences. Back at the station, the role of the trainer often shifts to supervisors, senior employees, and peers.

On-the-Job Training

Fire station and police station chiefs assign employees to provide on-the-job skills training. Decisions about the training rest with the station chief. The training can be routine practices to respond to emergencies or they can be specialized training. Sometimes critical events provide a need for practice. When the Columbine High School shootings took place in Colorado in 1999, and more recently, the Virginia Tech shootings in Virginia in the spring of 2007, police agencies around North America changed their 40-year-old tactics on responding to these active shooter events. Historically, the tactic was for patrol officers to contain, isolate, and control until Special Weapons and Tactics (SWAT) teams arrived. Now officers are to aggressively engage the shooters to prevent more victims from being injured. Firefighters hold sessions to respond to crucial events too and have changed their practices as a result of the September 11, 2001, disaster. The threat of terrorist attacks has led to a big increase in on-the-job training for all public safety agencies. Training has moved from the classroom to the hometown community with the creation of mock events that include volunteer actors. These mock events can take many hours of preparation and test the performance of members, teams, and agencies in their response to critical events.

Specialized Training

Specialized training is conducted in a formal setting with numerous topics that are ever changing to meet the challenges of providing for public safety. For policing, criminal investigation courses include interviewing, identifying and collecting evidence, interrogating suspects, and preparing the cases for court. Examples of more advanced courses include narcotics, investigating child abuse, death investigations, fraud investigations, and homicide investigations. Technical courses include deoxyribonucleic acid (DNA) evidence, composite sketching, computer forensics, blood spatter analysis, and technical accident reconstruction analysis. For firefighting, courses include chemical spills and explosions; mass evacuations; controlling the setting on land, sea, or air; containment; and multicause fires. Participation in these courses often requires completion of prerequisite courses and the approval from agency officials. Other tactical courses often require membership on a tactical team as well speed and strength endurance prerequisites. Instructor certification courses, such as handling of equipment, often have prerequisites that exceed standards for basic students.

Public safety agencies often provide for the professional development of supervisors and managers. Management studies personnel issues of hiring, evaluations, and discipline; liability and risk management; project management and decision making; leadership; budget development and fiscal control; and labor issues including contract negotiations and grievance procedures. Emerging topics for specialized training are homeland security, mutual aid, and command and control of regional emergency events.

Theoretical Framework

To study curriculum development of firefighters and police officers, we turned to the literature on transfer of learning. We wanted to identify the variables that need to be in place for the individual to implement the knowledge, skills, and information in the workplace. For this study we recognize transfer of learning as "the effective and continuing application by learners—to their performance of jobs or other individual, organizational, or community responsibilities - of knowledge and skills gained in learning activities" (Broad & Newstrom, 1992, p. 2). To make this transfer happen, we wanted adult educators to know if Knowles's principles and assumptions of the art and science of helping adults learn (andragogy) as the delivery system for continuing professional education were important for transfer. For program planning purposes, Caffarella (2002, p. 203) added a segment of "devising transfer of learning plans" to her interactive program planning model. Caffarella argues that educators have not paid much attention to how professionals could integrate what they learned at a continuing educational program into their practice. She provides techniques for the adult educator and lists potential barriers in curriculum development and program planning that could be overcome for transfer to take place.

We wanted to find factors that enhanced transfer. We also wanted to identify barriers that needed to be overcome for transfer to take place.

Methodology

We interviewed police officers and firefighters from various state, local, and national organizations in the United States and Canada. We used 15 interview questions to identify the variables in place in the program planning stages, during the presentation of the program, and in the post-program stages. For this study, the interview questions were grouped into four parts: the program planning process, the delivery of the program, the post-program phase, and suggestions and ideas to help with transfer of learning to practice. The questions were a compilation of studies on learning transfer from Baldwin and Ford (1988); Facteau, Dobbins, Russell, Ladd, and Kudisch (1995); Quinones, Ford, Sego, and Smith (1995); and Daley's (2001) study of four professions.

The compilation of studies led to four variables:

1. Variables within the pre-program process, which include the planning process and the characteristics and mind-set of the individual trainee before the training.
2. Variables within the delivery of the program including program design, methods of delivery, and involvement of the trainee in the learning process.
3. Variables in the post-training experience including informal learning methods with immediate application, the environment within the workplace, and support from the institution and peer support.
4. Barriers to transfer and suggestions for helping make transfer happen.

For the issue of bringing about a change to practice, Cervero (1985) posed the question of effectiveness of continuing professional education programs. He developed a model to examine a training program, the influence of the individual characteristics of the trainee on the learning environment, the nature of the proposed change, and the application within the work environment where the learning is to be practiced. Cervero's model was adapted for this study.

Participants

Approximately 300 police officers and 30 firefighters were asked to participate in this study. Of those, 270 police officers and 16 firefighters completed the surveys. Compared with the large sample of police officers, the sample of firefighters in the study was too small. The low number of participating firefighters may have affected any accurate conclusions we had to draw for this study. The participants were line officers, supervisors, managers, and executives from city and county agencies. Respondents were from Canada and the United States. Many of the police were chiefs and managers attending a nationally recognized police command school, School for Police Staff and Command, that is conducted by Northwestern University's Center for Public Safety. Participants were interviewed at their stations, completed surveys at their training site, or responded to an email request to complete the survey by email.

Data Analysis

Study Results

The police officers and firefighters responded in the interviews that for learning to transfer, they had to apply the skills and knowledge from the programs immediately into their practice, or learning would not take place. They very rarely discussed the concepts presented at the training programs with others when they returned back to their stations and they had to make up for the time they took away from the station for their training. They said they didn't always have time to incorporate the information that had been taught. The police officers and firefighters often expressed frustration with the lack of carry through of information when they were back at the station.

The numeric results of the 15 questions are shown here with the comments of the participants and a summary of the findings following each chart.

1. **Were you involved in the planning process of the program and if not, do you feel your needs for this program were represented and considered?**

Police

Yes, I was involved in the planning process. ------------------ 13 ------- 10%

No, I was not involved in the planning, but I feel all my

    needs were considered. -------------------------------------- 49 ------- 37%

No, I was not involved in the planning process, but my
   needs were mildly represented. ------------------------------- 27 ------- 20%
No, I understand participants were not directly involved
   in designing the program, but I did feel that in developing
   the curriculum, and refining it from year-to-year, my
   needs are represented and considered. -------------------- 35 ------- 27%
No, I was not involved in planning and feel my needs
   were not considered. -- 8 --------- 6%

                                                                    132   100%

Firefighter

Yes, I was involved in the planning process. -------------------- 5 ------- 38%
No, I was not involved in the planning, but I feel all my
   needs were considered. --- 3 ------- 23%
No, I was not involved in the planning process, but my
   needs were mildly represented. ------------------------------- 4 ------- 31%
No, I understand participants were not directly involved
   in designing the program, but I did feel that in developing
   the curriculum, and refining it from year-to-year, my
   needs are represented and considered. ---------------------- 1 --------- 8%
No, I was not involved in planning and feel my needs
   were not considered. -- 0 --------- 0%

                                                                    13   100%

A large majority of police officers and firefighters said they felt their needs were known by the program planners and incorporated into the training curriculum. A portion of those interviewed were police and fire chiefs and in management. They responded that they had a role in decision making on curriculum development. The firefighters overall felt their needs were met while 6% of police officers felt their needs were not met. Firefighters complained about the poor quality of Federal Emergency Management Training (FEMA) training.

2. **What motivated you to attend this program or why did you attend? Check all or as many as apply.**

Police

I attended this program to help me progress to the
   next level of advancement on my job or to be able to
   change jobs. --- 24 -------- 11%

I attended this program because I needed the skills
and knowledge it offered. -- 16 --------- 7%
I attended this program because my superior
recommended it. --- 34 ------- 16%
I attended this program because I needed credits for
my continuing professional education. ---------------------- 70 ------- 33%
This program was required as a part of my continuing
professional education. -- 71 ------- 33%

215   100%

Firefighter

I attended this program to help me progress to the
next level of advancement on my job or to be able to
change jobs. --- 5 ------- 31%
I attended this program because I needed the skills
and knowledge it offered. -- 1 --------- 6%
I attended this program because my superior
recommended it.   -- 2 ------- 13%
I attended this program because I needed credits for
my continuing professional education. ----------------------- 5 ------- 31%
This program was required as a part of my continuing
professional education.   --- 3 ------- 19%

16   100%

The motivation to attend the programs was usually not self-induced. Over half of the police officers reported they attended training because it was required or mandated and exactly one-half of the firefighters responded the same. Less than 1/2 of each group said they wanted the skills for their own knowledge or job advancement. We found this small amount of self-motivation to be troubling and one factor that hinders transfer of learning to practice.

3. **What was your mind-set or your expectations for this program and were they met?**

Police

My expectations were high--to gain the tools that are
necessary to actively manage my career. ------------------ 27 -------21%
My expectations were high—to gain the skills and
knowledge to better do my job. ------------------------------- 82 -------63%

My expectations were moderate—I didn't mind
attending but didn't have high expectations of
learning new information. -------------------------------------- 12 -------- 9%
I didn't have high expectations—this program was either
required or I knew I was expected to attend. ----------------- 8 -------- 6%
I had minimal expectations. ------------------------------------- 1 -------- 1%

130   100%

Firefighter

My expectations were high--to gain the tools that are
necessary to actively manage my career. --------------------- 4 ------- 44%
My expectations were high—to gain the skills and
knowledge to better do my job. -------------------------------- 2 ------- 22%
My expectations were moderate—I didn't mind
attending but didn't have high expectations of
learning new information. -------------------------------------- 1 ------- 11%
I didn't have high expectations—this program was either
required or I knew I was expected to attend. ---------------- 2 ------- 22%
I had minimal expectations. -------------------------------------- 0 -------- 0%

9   100%

When we questioned participants about their expectations, we were surprised that in spite of the low percentage of those who were self-motivated to attend, 84% of the police officers and 66% of the firefighters said their expectation to learn was high. They wanted to gain the tools and skills to manage their career and to do their jobs. Of the small group of firefighters 22% said they were there for the training because they had to be there and therefore weren't expecting much from the training.

Variable One: Involvement of the Learner in the Planning Process and Self- Motivation to Participate. The first three interview questions examined the preprogram planning process and the participants' involvement in the planning process. We wanted to know if the police officers and firefighters were involved in the planning process and if they felt they had been represented. We also wanted to know what their motivation was for participating in the program and if they had high expectations for learning.

In one of the basic assumptions of the practice of teaching adults, Knowles (1990) focuses on the involvement of the learner in the planning process as a crucial component for participation. Mathieu, Tannenbaum, and Salas (1992) in their study of transfer of learning say giving input into the program content is directly linked to motivation to attend and ultimately transfer of learning. What happens when, as our study shows, self-motivation is lacking?

Self-Motivation

Motivation to attend training occurs for a variety of reasons, but somehow, individuals must be motivated to attend. Does the motivation have to be intrinsic or extrinsic? Facteau et al. (1995) found the importance of pre-training motivation. They examined the factors related to pretraining motivation of 967 managers and supervisors. If the managers and supervisors understood the intrinsic incentives for the training, employees had higher levels of motivation to attend the training. Facteau et al. found that pretraining motivation was an important variable in transfer and that motivation would lead to transfer. Those who were required to attend training because of state requirements were less motivated and were less likely to transfer their learning to practice. That appeared to be true from the responses in this study. What is the result of transfer to practice if self-motivation is lacking but expectations for gaining information is high?

Expectations for the Training

Merriam and Leahy (2005) in a review of transfer of learning research found many studies in which learners with high expectations for the training demonstrate actual transfer of the learning. While this is an individual variable, this current study shows how positive past experiences with both the planning process and the training itself can influence the learners to have a high expectation for the program. Even though the motivation comes from extrinsic demands, can curriculum developers have any influence with the learner in shaping their expectations of the program and increasing their motivation to attend? Both self-motivation and high expectations for learning positively impact learning transfer.

4. **Was the program a positive learning experience for you? If no, why not? If yes, what was the most valuable part of the program? Check all or as many as apply.**

Police

Yes, networking opportunities were the most valuable. ------ 6 --------- 2%

Yes, I learned new skills that were valuable for my job. ---- 54 ------- 20%

Yes, it was a positive experience. I got information from
    experts in my field.   --- 77 ------- 29%

Yes, it was a positive experience because I had the
    opportunity to discuss the new information with
    my peers.   --- 73 ------- 27%

No, it was not a positive experience and a
waste of my time. -- 60 ------- 22%

270   100%

Firefighter --
Yes, networking opportunities were the most valuable. ------ 1 --------- 6%
Yes, I learned new skills that were valuable for my job. ------ 4 ------- 25%
Yes, it was a positive experience. I got information from
   experts in my field.   --- 4 ------- 25%
Yes, it was a positive experience because I had the
   opportunity to discuss the new information with
   my peers.   --- 4 ------- 25%
No, it was not a positive experience and a
   waste of my time. -- 3 ------- 19%

16   100%

We now turn to the program itself. We wanted to know if the participant felt the learning experience was or was not positive. While networking was not rated as the most valuable part of either the police officers' or firefighters' program experience, they did comment that they appreciated expanding their contacts with others as a result of the program. For both groups, approximately 75% said the program was a positive experience. They commented that the sharing of knowledge with their peers and instructors was valuable and led to a positive learning experience. Several commented on the important role of the instructor to "make or break" the program. Several others mentioned the difficulty of trying to teach a basic level and experienced level at the same time.

It is important to note that although 75% had a positive experience, approximately 1/4 of the respondents had a negative learning experience.

5.   **What methods of delivery did the instructors use? (for example: lecture, small group discussion, interactive projects, etc.) Check all or as many as apply.**

Police
Lectures, with time for questions and answers. --------------- 36 ------- 14%
Some lectures and some panels, with time for
   questions and answers. --- 75 ------- 28%
Lectures, panels and small group discussions;
   time for interactions with the speakers. --------------------- 59 ------- 22%

A variety of presentations and engaged the audience
in discussions, like case study, demonstrations, videos,
role playing. -- 27 ------- 10%
A variety of delivery methods with time for discussion of
new information with peers. ----------------------------------- 68 ------- 26%

265   100%

Firefighter

Lectures, with time for questions and answers. ----------------- 2 ------- 13%
Some lectures and some panels, with time for
questions and answers. --- 3 ------- 20%
Lectures, panels and small group discussions;
time for interactions with the speakers. ----------------------- 6 ------- 40%
A variety of presentations and engaged the audience
in discussions, like case study, demonstrations, videos,
role playing. -- 1 --------- 7%
A variety of delivery methods with time for discussion of
new information with peers. ----------------------------------- 3 ------- 20%

15   100%

---

6. How do you learn best?

Police

Lectures, with time for questions and answers. --------------- 13 ------- 10%
Lectures and/or panel presentations with time for
interaction with the speakers. --------------------------------- 14 -------- 11%
Through a variety of deliveries such as some lecture,
some small group, case studies, role playing,
videos. --- 87 ------- 66%
Small group discussions; interaction with my peers. ---------- 9 --------- 7%
My own research and reading with the ability to
ask questions. --- 8 --------- 6%

131   100%

Firefighter

Lectures, with time for questions and answers. ----------------- 0 --------- 0%
Lectures and/or panel presentations with time for
interaction with the speakers. --------------------------------- 1 -------- 11%

Through a variety of deliveries such as some lecture,
   some small group, case studies, role playing,
   videos. -- 8 ------- 89%
Small group discussions; interaction with my peers. ---------- 0 --------- 0%
My own research and reading with the ability to
   ask questions. -- 0 --------- 0%
                                                             9   100%

7.   How did the speakers involve you in the learning process?

Police
Not really interactive. --- 3 --------- 2%
Took questions, but did not encourage participation. ------- 14 -------- 11%
Encouraged participation through exercises.
   They gave real-world examples of their own
   experiences and how they overcame obstacles.
   Their advice is invaluable. ------------------------------------ 89 ------- 68%
Some preparation was required for the group
   discussions. The moderator involved the attendees by
   posing questions or answering any questions that
   emphasized the information presented
   in the session. --- 25 ------- 19%
The speakers involved us by taking questions
   throughout the session or by having audience
   participate in the presentations, like role playing. ----------- 0 --------- 0%
                                                          131   100%

Firefighter
Not really interactive. --- 1 -------- 11%
Took questions, but did not encourage participation. --------- 0 --------- 0%
Encouraged participation through exercises.
   They gave real-world examples of their own
   experiences and how they overcame obstacles.
   Their advice is invaluable. ------------------------------------ 7 ------- 78%
Some preparation was required for the group
   discussions. The moderator involved the attendees by
   posing questions or answering any questions that
   emphasized the information presented
   in the session. --- 1 ------- 11%

The speakers involved us by taking questions
   throughout the session or by having audience
   participate in the presentations, like role playing. ----------- 0 --------- 0%
                                                              9   100%

For questions 5, 6, and 7, we wanted to know what delivery methods were used by instructors, how the participants learn best, and if the learners felt the speakers involved them in the learning process.

The responses indicate that lecture was the primary delivery method for the programs with only 10% of the police officers' trainers delivering with a variety of methods and only 7% of the firefighters' trainers using other methods. However, about 1/4 of both groups said they were able to discuss the concepts with their peers.

When asked how they learn best, 66% of the police officers and 89% of the firefighters said they learn best with a variety of deliveries such as some lecture, small group discussions, case studies, role playing, etc. Both groups commented that lectures, Power Points, and reading information to them are overused and ineffective. Both groups prefer a variety of delivery methods, which is in keeping with the principles of adult education.

The speakers evidently used exercises and related to real-world examples as a means of discussion. However, none of the speakers in either group took questions throughout the session or used role playing. Respondents commented on group projects and were evenly divided on whether this was an effective method of learning.

Variable Two: Use of a Variety of Delivery Approaches, Andragogy, and Immediate Applicability on the Job. The emphasis on using a variety of delivery approaches for professionals is already apparent. Daffron and Davis (2005) in a study of Palestinian law professors found they made significant changes in their teaching styles, as a result of observation of other professors engaged in case study, problem solving and the Socratic method in their classrooms. Lectures to the Palestinian professors about changing their delivery methods did not bring about any change in their practice – transfer did not happen. But by observing and modeling other law professors, the Palestinian professors changed their long-time methods of lecture to a multimethod of delivery techniques. Transfer of learning occurred.

A study by Daffron and North (2006) of company professional software workers had similar results. The software workers said they learned very little from the instructors who lectured and used Power Points. The software professionals said they were able to incorporate the new information into practice if they could try it at the program and if case studies and problem solving were taken from their field's practice.

A study of state court judges by Daffron, Cowdrey, and Doran (2007) found judges transferred learning only if they could discuss concepts of the program with each other and with the instructor—at the program site. They did not have the opportunity to do this when they returned to the bench. Therefore, discussion, problem solving, and case studies had to be presented at the program for the judges to analyze the information and to either put it into practice or disregard it.

These three studies illustrate the importance of matching delivery methods to the way learners prefer to learn. Because adults learn in a variety of ways, the delivery methods should be a variety too.

Use of Andragogy

The directors of the academies told us they provided training for their instructors with the application of adult education principles. We wanted to know if the trainers and instructors actually used these principles, and if an andragogical approach to training was used in the programs. Knowles (1980) lays out the principles and assumptions of andragogy:

- The environment for learning is safe, comfortable, and encouraging.
- Adults have knowledge and experience and learn best when they can share and exchange the information with others.
- Adults are motivated to learn, usually without external direction.
- Instruction is planned to meet the needs of the individual.
- Adults learn in a variety of ways.
- Adults learn best when information is tied to their work or personal life, is meaningful to them, and can be immediately applicable.
- Adults are self-directed and make their own decisions about learning.

The responses from the survey shows that some instructors used the principles of andragogy but most did not. The police officers and firefighters said they wanted the programs to use a variety of techniques for presentations but the reality was, instructors felt most comfortable with lectures and Power Points followed by a brief discussion. Others said it will take a real effort to make a change in the way the programs are delivered to fit the andragogical principles and assumptions.

One of the few studies about training public safety workers comes from New South Wales by Rushbrook et al. (2001) and mentions the application of adult education methods. Adult methods of teaching were introduced in the Police

Recruit Education Program within the New South Wales Academy in the 1990s. The article says that instructors began using . . . "experiential learning, case studies, educational contextual studies, and emphasis placed on a practicum component" (p. 3). The plan was to produce reflective practitioners.

The curriculum developer and program planner must work together to incorporate principles of andragogy, or a variety of delivery methods into professional continuing education programs. Baldwin (1992) in a study of business students said they responded positively to classes using a variety of delivery methods. Merriam, Caffarella, and Baumgartner (2007) cite studies about the variety of ways adults learn and emphasize the need to deliver programs with various methods. Finally, Tallman and Holt (1987) indicate it isn't enough to deliver programs with a variety of methods, the instructors have to do it with examples related to work and with exercises and discussion related to practice. A good andragogical approach to curriculum development and program planning is needed with this profession and is requested by the firefighters and police officers.

Making Meaning

Transfer of learning is all about how students use the new information they have gained through training and make meaning out of it. Daley (2001) says that a case can be made for "meaning-making" and states that

> . . . in the process of using information, the professionals changed what the information meant to them based on the results they observed. In other words, incorporating new knowledge is a recursive, transforming process, rather than a simple, straightforward transfer of information from one context to another. (p. 50)

For the next set of questions, we wanted to know if the respondents made meaning of the information.

8. Have you used the skills and knowledge from the program in your job?

Police

Yes they were immediately applicable to my work. ---------- 74 ------- 56%

They will be useful in the near future on my job. ------------- 33 ------- 25%

They may be helpful to me someday, but are not
    immediately applicable. --- 22 ------- 17%

I don't need this information now, but have posted the
    information in a file for the future. ------------------------------ 2 --------- 2%

I don't see the need for this information in the future. --------- 1 --------- 1%

                                                                                132   100%

Firefighter

Yes they were immediately applicable to my work. ------------ 3 ------- 33%

They will be useful in the near future on my job. -------------- 0 --------- 0%

They may be helpful to me someday, but are not

    immediately applicable. --- 6 ------- 67%

I don't need this information now, but have posted the

    information in a file for the future. ------------------------------ 0 --------- 0%

I don't see the need for this information in the future. -------- 0 --------- 0%

                                                                      9   100%

Did the new information transfer to practice and was it used on the job? Of the police officers, 81% said the information was either immediately applicable or would be useful in the future. Of the firefighters, 67% said the information might be helpful someday and only 1/3 said it was immediately useful. The written comments helped to clarify the issues. Respondents listed barriers to transfer as not applicable, too busy upon return to use skills, and a lack of support of management to incorporate information into practice.

9.   Have you changed the way you handle your job as a result of this program?

Police

Yes. -- 51 ------- 39%

Definitely. I plan to change my approach to my job in the

    near future as a result of this new information. ------------- 30 ------- 23%

Maybe, I may use this information in the future,

    but am not sure.   --- 28 ------- 21%

Not really. --- 21 ------- 16%

No, and I do not plan to handle my job any differently

    as a result of this program. ------------------------------------ 2 --------- 2%

                                                                      132   100%

Firefighter

Yes. -- 3 ------- 33%

Definitely. I plan to change my approach to my job in the

    near future as a result of this new information. --------------- 1 ------- 11%

Maybe, I may use this information in the future,

    but am not sure. --- 5 ------- 56%

Not really. --- 0 --------- 0%

No, and I do not plan to handle my job any differently
as a result of this program. ------------------------------------- 0 --------- 0%

9   100%

Even though 81% of police officers said they have used the new skills and knowledge on the job, the reality is not as many have made changes in their practice as a result. The number of firefighters (1/3) who said they have used the information on the job is the same as those who have changed their behavior or will change in the future. While it is possible to use the new information on the job, the real test of transfer comes when a person changes behavior or practice on the job as a result.

10. Were you expected to share what you learned at this program with other colleagues? If yes, what did you share?

Police

I was not expected to share what I learned. ------------------- 30 ------- 23%
No, I was not expected to share what I learned but think
   there is good information to share. --------------------------- 60 ------- 46%
Maybe, but no one told me what they were expecting. ----- 26 ------- 20%
Yes, my supervisor asked me to make a report
   when I returned. --- 7 --------- 5%
Yes, I am expected to present an oral report or to set up
   a workshop for my colleagues on what I learned from the
   program. --- 8 --------- 6%

131   100%

Firefighter

I was not expected to share what I learned. --------------------- 2 ------- 22%
No, I was not expected to share what I learned but think
   there is good information to share. ----------------------------- 3 ------- 33%
Maybe, but no one told me what they were expecting. ------- 2 ------- 22%
Yes, my supervisor asked me to make a report
   when I returned. -- 0 --------- 0%
Yes, I am expected to present an oral report or to set up
   a workshop for my colleagues on what I learned from the
   program. --- 2 ------- 22%

9   100%

What happens when the police officer or firefighter completes the training and returns to the job? We wanted to know if the organizations had a role in making transfer happen. First we wanted to know if the employee was expected to share the information with colleagues. Only 5% of the police officers were expected to give a report to their supervisor and none of the firefighters said they had to report to their supervisor. Several said they were expected to share with colleagues.

11. Were there any resources from the program that you have used? Check all or as many as apply.

Police

Networking; I have contacted the speaker/s or
    others I met at the program to discuss implementation
    of information presented at the program. -------------------- 13 --------- 5%
I have used the program materials. ----------------------------- 57 ------- 22%
I have used online resources. ----------------------------------- 44 ------- 17%
I have filed the program material for later use. ---------------- 81 ------- 31%
I have not used resources from the program. ----------------- 63 ------- 24%
                                            258   100%

Firefighter

Networking; I have contacted the speaker/s or
    others I met at the program to discuss implementation
    of information presented at the program. --------------------- 2 ------- 15%
I have used the program materials. ----------------------------- 1 --------- 8%
I have used online resources. ------------------------------------- 4 ------- 31%
I have filed the program material for later use. ------------------ 5 ------- 38%
I have not used resources from the program. ------------------ 1 --------- 8%
                                            13   100%

The program resources and materials are being used by all but a few of the firefighters. However, 24% of the police officers say they do not use the materials.

12. Are you encouraged to attend these kinds of programs? Who encourages you?

Police

Yes. My supervisor. -- 53 ------- 40%

Yes. My colleagues encourage me. ----------------------------- 9 --------- 7%
No one encourages me, I decide what to
    attend myself. --- 40 ------- 30%
We have mandatory requirements for our continuing
    professional education and this program fulfills
    some of the mandatory requirements. ----------------------- 23 ------- 17%
I usually am discouraged from attending programs like
    this due to time and money constraints.   -------------------- 7 --------- 5%
                                                                                    132   100%

Firefighter
Yes. My supervisor. --- 3 ------- 33%
Yes. My colleagues encourage me. ----------------------------- 2 ------- 22%
No one encourages me, I decide what to
    attend myself. --- 1 ------- 11%
We have mandatory requirements for our continuing
    professional education and this program fulfills
    some of the mandatory requirements. ------------------------ 3 ------- 33%
I usually am discouraged from attending programs like
    this due to time and money constraints.   -------------------- 0 --------- 0%
                                                                                      9   100%

When we asked who encourages participation in the programs, 40% of the police officers said their supervisor encouraged them to participate. Fewer firefighters, or 1/3 received encouragement from their supervisor to attend the training program. But 22% of the firefighters said their colleagues encouraged them and another 1/3 said the programs they attended were mandated. The same information was supported by the comments. Both groups said they attended programs due to supervisor or colleague encouragement or because the training was mandated.

Variable Three: Recognizing the Context for Learning in a Professional Practice. Daffron and North (2006) posit a good tool for transfer of learning is to expect the trainee to share the information with peers and/or management upon return from the training class. Many of the studies on transfer of learning cite organizational support as critical for transfer to practice. When Factaeu et al. (1995) examined the role that organizational support played in transfer, they found if the organization emphasized the importance of the training, then employees were likely to pay more attention to the learning situation and return to put the information into practice. In this study, like studies of other professions, we were told that organizations did not give any indication that the employee was expected to share the information gained from training with others on the job. Organizations seem to encourage participation in the training, but the encouragement stops there.

Quinones, Ford, Sego, and Smith (1995), in a study of 118 graduates of an Air Force training program, identified the most crucial variable affecting transfer of learning as the support of the supervisor and the organization's expectation that the trainee would be able to perform the tasks on the job after the training was completed. They found that successful transfer occurred when trainees knew before the training that they would be expected to recall and demonstrate the skills and knowledge learned on the job. The study illustrated that transfer also depended upon individual motivation, ability, and personality characteristics. They conclude, "It is also possible that individuals performing more tasks (or more complex tasks) are perceived more positively by their supervisor. More positive attitudes on the part of the supervisor would then result in greater opportunities to perform trained tasks" (p. 43).

Xiao (1996), Campbell and Cheek (1989), Vroom (1964), and Noe (1986) examined the link of trainee motivation to learning to employer expectations. Noe found trainees will be more motivated to learn if a high effort leads to high performance and if high performance leads to high job performance, then the high job performance is tied to desirable outcomes. In Xiao's model, KSA (the utilization of knowledge, skills, and attitudes gained in the training setting) was encouraged by the organizations for electronics workers in China. The facilitation for learning was tied directly to the organizations' expectations of the workers.

13. Were there any factors, personal or professional, that prevented you from incorporating the ideas presented by the program into your job?

Police

No, I incorporated the ideas.	53	40%
No, I plan to incorporate the ideas when I have time.	9	7%
No, I could incorporate the ideas but the material isn't relevant so I won't take time to use it.	40	30%
Yes, but when I returned back to my job, I was too busy to incorporate the ideas.	23	17%
Yes, but there were other reasons why I didn't incorporate the ideas into practice.	7	5%
	132	**100%**

Firefighter

No, I incorporated the ideas. --------------------------------------- 3 ------- 33%
No, I plan to incorporate the ideas when I have time. --------- 2 ------- 22%
No, I could incorporate the ideas but the material isn't
   relevant so I won't take time to use it. -------------------------- 1 -------- 11%
Yes, but when I returned back to my job, I was too
   busy to incorporate the ideas. ---------------------------------- 3 ------- 33%
Yes, but there were other reasons why I didn't
   incorporate the ideas into practice. --------------------------- 0 --------- 0%
                                       9   **100%**

It is possible that in spite of all efforts to encourage transfer to practice, there are real barriers to implementation. For the police officers, lack of relevancy of material, lack of time, and interference by politics were formidable forces for 52%. In the comments police officers said policies and supervisors who were resistant to changes were strong factors preventing transfer. Firefighters had similar comments with some reporting strong enough barriers to prohibit implementation.

14. **How have others helped you to put the information you learned into practice? How have others made it difficult to put the information into practice? Check all or as many as apply.**

Police

My supervisor helped me put the information
   into my practice. --- 4 --------- 2%
My colleagues have helped me put the information
   into my practice. --- 25 ------- 15%
Speakers at the program or others who attended the
   program have served as a resource to help me put the
   Information into my practice. ----------------------------------- 53 ------- 32%
Use of the information in my practice is on hold
   pending approval or a change in policy. -------------------- 50 ------- 30%
My supervisor doesn't want me to use the information
   in my practice. --- 32 ------- 20%
                                       164   **100%**

Firefighter

My supervisor helped me put the information
   into my practice. --- 0 --------- 0%
My colleagues have helped me put the information
   into my practice. --- 1 --------- 8%
Speakers at the program or others who attended the
   program have served as a resource to help me put the
   information into my practice. ------------------------------------- 4 ------- 33%
Use of the information in my practice is on hold
pending approval or a change in policy. ------------------------ 5 ------- 42%
My supervisor doesn't want me to use the information
in my practice. --- 2 ------- 17%

                                                          12   100%

The results of this question supports question 13. It is often difficult to implement information into practice and the supervisors, those who encourage participation in programs, cannot be counted on to assist with implementation. This is a huge problem.

Variable Four: Barriers to Transfer of Learning. One study of police training, Rushbrook et al. (2001) found that the emphasis on creating a learning organization in the workplace cited by Marsick and Watkins (1990) seemed to pass by the public safety profession. In recent years, the emphasis has been on implementing learning within the organizational context. Rushbrook et al. say,

> *This assumes that organizations are prepared for change, anticipate the future, develop structures that are more responsive to the ideas of individuals, and capture the synergies available in teams. There is now a realization that learning in organizations occurs at the individual, team, and organizational levels, and in the way that organizations interact with both their internal and external environments.* (p. 5)

This effort to promote a change and to have a vision for what the organization can become as a result of organizational training, works optimally when it is top down and coordinated within the organization. This last step cannot happen by accident. The vision or plan for organizational learning or training works when it is known and accepted by all employees of the organization.

Harris and Volet (1997) also emphasized the need for an organization to establish a culture for learning. Like Rushbrook et al. they found senior management set the plan in place for systemic learning in the workplace. The systemic learning should include:

- A strategic approach that provides an implementation framework for the vision and direction of the organization
- A number of systemic features which facilitate continuous learning within the organization
- A number of interrelated factors in the workplace learning culture that support the learning process (p. 46).

Harris and Volet emphasized the importance of establishing this kind of culture because of the very nature of police work. They say, "In an organization that values brotherhood and loyalty in potentially life-threatening situations, the concept of police culture has greater significance than that embedded in private corporations or less publicly exposed government organizations (p. 46). Chan (1996) also discusses the role of the police culture as a brotherhood that guides the officers' work 24 hours a day, not just during work hours.

Tips for Curriculum Development and Pitfalls to Avoid

15. What advice would you offer for continuing professional educators, to make sure information presented at a program gets put into practice? Check all or as many as apply.

Police

Make sure the information is relevant to the issues
  facing attendees. --- 61 ------- 19%
Focus on key themes and continually reinforce them in
  as many ways as possible. The more exposure one has
  to the information, the more it is put into practice. --------- 62 ------- 19%
Ensure that attendees incorporate the information
  into their practice as much as possible after the
  program. -- 25 --------- 8%
Allow for plenty of time for questions, small group
  interaction, and discussion among attendees. ------------- 70 ------- 21%
The ability to involve the attendees in the learning process
  is crucial. The lecture setting, while effective in conveying
  basic ideas, tends to alienate those who "think" they
  know the info's and then feel it's a waste of time. -------- 110 ------- 34%
                                                                    328   100%

Firefighter

Make sure the information is relevant to the issues
   facing attendees. --- 9 ------- 30%
Focus on key themes and continually reinforce them in
   as many ways as possible. The more exposure one has
   to the information, the more it is put into practice. ----------- 4 ------- 13%
Ensure that attendees incorporate the information
   into their practice as much as possible after the
   program. --- 4 ------- 13%
Allow for plenty of time for questions, small group
   interaction, and discussion among attendees. -------------- 6 ------- 20%
The ability to involve the attendees in the learning process
   is crucial. The lecture setting, while effective in conveying
   basic ideas, tends to alienate those who "think" they
   know the info's and then feel it's a waste of time. ----------- 7 ------- 23%
                                                    30   **100%**

Question 15 gave the police officers and firefighters a chance to report suggestions for putting curriculum and training together for transfer to occur. The data is reported in 10 tips and 4 pitfalls to avoid.

Tips for Curriculum Development

1.   Conduct a needs assessment prior to program planning. Each training program ought to fit into the ultimate plan for the organization, and take the organization toward accomplishing its mission. Before meeting with a stakeholders' group or conducting a needs assessment, first determine the mission of the organization. Then do the following:

    a.   Create a stakeholders group of those who are invested in the outcomes and use this group for ideas and direction.
    b.   Do a needs assessment that is driven by both the needs of the agency and the needs of the learners.
    c.   Use the stakeholders group to pilot test the needs assessment to ensure the results are correct.

Determine which available training fits within the mission, and what types of training must be created to achieve the long term and short term goals of the organization. Determine which members of the organization ought to attend particular training by centrally organizing past, present, and future training in the organization. By understanding the mission of the organization, using advice of the stakeholders, conducting a needs assessment, and then checking the results of this effort, the organization is left with a list of training needs targeted to the exact needs of the organization.

2.   Empower learners to control their own training plan. Give learners the opportunity to write a plan for their career path and determine which training will be consistent with their career goals and the agency's mission. Also, at the beginning of each training class, provide learners with an opportunity to tell the instructor what they want from the class.

It is empowering for employees to feel they have some control over their training. The management of the organization benefits by having training targeted for each individual and can then put the information into the broader picture of the organization. The employees and supervisors determine together what training will be needed to achieve those goals. Training ought to be planned at appropriate intervals and milestones throughout the learners' careers. To help keep the learner matched with the training goals, it is helpful at the beginning of each training session for trainers to ask the learners what they want to get out of the class. As learners participate by stating what they want, the instructor then can positively reinforce their participation by writing the suggestions on a white board or poster size chart. This genuine demonstration of giving control of the class to the learners fosters an environment in which transfer of learning will occur.

3.   Create a training focus foremost on safety. Safety is the top priority for all peace officers, firefighters, and emergency medical personnel. In some ways all training needs to incorporate the importance of safety for the public and/or safety of the employees.

Establish an environment where learners believe training is very important. Society employs peace officers, firefighters, and emergency medical personnel so that they can keep the public safe. In order to do this, public safety workers must be safe themselves and that happens through focused training. The management of the organization ought to communicate this important focus to all employees at the outset so they will understand that training is vital, and each employee will commit to learning, not just listening.

4.   Maintain skills through refresher courses. Many skills learned by public safety employees are perishable and must be practiced to prevent loss of skill. Schedule annual or quarterly refresher courses as indicated by skill and content. Public safety employees must learn and maintain a variety of tasks essential to the completion of their jobs. Many tasks are not frequently performed, but when the situation dictates, the task must be performed without hesitation. Public safety workers, often under stress in risky, chaotic, uncomfortable situations, and suffering from fatigue, have to perform these tasks. It is important that safety employees frequently practice these tasks. It is also important to make the distinction here that the initial explanation, demonstration, and rehearsal of tasks occur in ideal conditions that foster transfer of learning. Only as the task is repeated over and over and the resulting skill becomes part of the employee's working knowledge, should scenarios be introduced with these difficult situations. The result is self-confidence in one's ability, praxis, and often, survival.

5. Provide an opportunity for information sharing. Foster an environment in the organization in which employees are encouraged to pass on information in formal and informal sessions.

Much of the training that occurs for public safety workers is formal. Learners can become certified instructors by attending train the trainer courses. Certified instructors pass on information to learners during formal in-service training. In addition to that, learners who go to specialized classes can return to their agencies and provide formal summaries of the information they have gained for their peers. Informal information sharing among small groups and between individuals is also to be encouraged. Each time this information exchange takes place, the information is mentally and verbally rehearsed. This helps solidify the learning for the person passing the knowledge to others. Overall, this is an important part of fostering a workplace of learning and preparing for the demands of public safety professions.

6. Use adult education principles in training. Take the time at the beginning of each training session to discuss how the employees will apply the material to their work. Begin immediately with relevant material and make it applicable to the work setting.

Learners must recognize the need to learn before they will learn. Often the learners identify the courses they want to attend, and other times, the organization identifies the course the employees will attend. Either way relevancy to the job is key to transfer of learning. The learner needs to understand the importance of the training and the material presented. Sometimes it is the role of the management and/or the instructor to point to the reasons for the training.

7. Determine readiness to learn and the skill level of the trainee. Training classes ought to confirm to the demands of the public safety workers' hours.

a. Public safety employees often work nonstandard schedules, so training ought to be scheduled with a variety of times to suit the readiness of the learner.

b. The skill levels for all classes should be set and stated.

In many professions, it is not unreasonable to set training class hours as 9:00 am-5:00 pm. In the profession of public safety workers, a scenario like this is more likely than not.

The worker leaves home for a 12-hour shift on a Sunday night. Things quickly become so hectic there is barely time to use the restroom, much less to eat a meal, and all the while sweat builds inside the less than comfortable gear, equipment, and boots. Then by 7:00 am Monday morning, the worker would most likely be thinking about the balance between sleeping and spending time with family. Heading for a Monday 9:00 am-5:00 pm training session would be the last thing on the list.

Training is often scheduled without regard to these kinds of schedules. Readiness to learn is blocked by the schedule. Most public safety employees do their jobs because they want to, because they have something inside of them that drives them to be protectors. They want to come back Monday night for their next challenging shift. These circumstances are common for public safety workers, and they do not want to be in a class on Monday morning. If they are forced to follow a schedule that is comfortable and convenient for the instructor but not for them, they will hate the class and learning is unlikely, no matter the quality of instruction. It is important to offer a variety of scheduled training sessions to accommodate the problems of 12-hour shifts.

The other part of readiness to learn is to plan the curriculum to meet the needs of a specific knowledge base. One of the comments made by quite a few public safety workers in this study is that all levels and abilities of skilled workers are in the same classes. An effort ought to be made to rate the classes by skill level, then advertise the skill level to help guide the learner to the proper level.

8. Use hands-on and skill demonstrations. Generally, public safety training is about being able to perform difficult tasks routinely and without hesitation. After learners have heard about and observed the completion of the tasks, allow them the opportunity to demonstrate their ability to complete the tasks during the training. This can happen best in a hands-on approach with demonstrations.

Once learners know what is expected, provide the opportunity for them to practice and then demonstrate their skills. It is not enough to know about cardiopulmonary resuscitation (CPR) and how it might work; all public safety workers must be able to perform CPR without hesitation and with precision. Lives depend upon it.

9.   Update training in a timely manner. The body of knowledge available to public safety personnel continually changes and is updated. Updates in areas such as law, science, and technology require the organization to keep up with the knowledge and to pass it on to all employees.

The orientation into a public safety occupation typically includes a large block of initial training in an academy. The academy curriculum is a process, but not the ultimate destination. New laws are enacted, case law changes, science advances, technology improves, and the curriculum must keep up with it all. The training received by an entry- level employee in 1990 is generally radically different from the training received by an entry-level employee in 2000. It is the responsibility of each local organization to keep each employee updated and training usually can't wait for the opportune moment.

10. Create a learning organization. In many instances, training can be given in sessions that are attended by all employees of varying ranks. In other instances it is important for administration to first provide the information to mid-management, then to first line supervisors, and finally to line personnel in order to ensure that undermining does not occur and all learn.

In order for an organization to accomplish its mission, the employees must continue to learn, to train, to practice, to update. This takes a series of commitments at all levels of the bureaucracy. Administration must support training and education with encouragement, flexible schedules, funding, and resources. This support has to move through the organization's mid-managers, first line supervisors, and line personnel. At times, new material can be delivered to each level of an organization while ensuring that the members at each level understand the importance of the material. Unfortunately, this study has found no short cuts or ways around management seizing the responsibility for transfer of learning. The management creates a learning organization by intent and has a vision that places training as of utmost importance to the organization, or transfer to practice becomes haphazard or nonexistent. Again, there seems to be no way around this important commitment to learning.

Pitfalls to Avoid
1.   Send all public safety workers to training because it is the right thing to do and they will learn something that will be useful on the job. This study points to the problem of sending workers to programs because they need training without regard for their need for the information. With so much pressure on the public

safety profession today, supervisors ought to take time to put together individual educational plans for their employees and then send them to appropriate training, on their level, with a plan for advancing their skills and knowledge. With mandated training hours, a real pitfall is a training session that fills the hours without providing useful or necessary skills for the learner.

2. Leave the training up to the experts and send public safety workers to the academy for training. A good supervisor will see the need for a vision or a plan for the organization and take hold of the training culture and the learning. This study shows employees who attend training outside of their station rarely share the information with others at the station. Transfer of learning can quickly multiply in a station with a plan or a vision for sharing information and knowledge. The supervisor can easily make a plan for the station to be a learning organization at every opportunity.

3. Instructors can effectively deliver most information by using lectures. This study shows public safety workers are like other adults, they learn in a variety of ways. Only those who learn best through oral deliveries will benefit from straight lectures. The others will retain only about 10% of the information given in a program. Creating a "fun" learning environment or one that is a positive culture for learning only takes some thought and effort to focus on the learner. All instructors can become excellent instructors by choosing a variety of delivery methods.

4. Time is money and with resources so limited, the public safety worker should get right to work after a training session rather than waste time talking about the training. For learning to transfer, the information should be immediately applicable to the job. This means the learner needs to use the information as soon as possible on the job. The temptation for the supervisor is to have the trainee make up for the time taken away from the job by the training. However, the results of this study show that the information is lost and not transferred because of lack of opportunity to use it, to apply it, and to share it with others. Supervisors would do well to make sure the trainee has the opportunity to apply the learning within the first few days back on the job.

Implications for Future Practice

We have determined for purposes of this study that transfer of learning is the application of knowledge and skills gained from an educational setting into practice at the workplace. The literature shows that this transfer occurs only in the minority of cases, or about 10% of the time. Merriam and Leahy (2005) reviewed the literature and in turn made a compelling argument for continuing professional educators to understand the strategies needed in program planning and curriculum development to bring about transfer. We agreed with them and conducted this study to identify tips for curriculum developers for police officers and firefighters and also to list pitfalls to avoid in the process.

First, we found public safety workers like to attend training and think it is important. Their encouragement and motivation come from their supervisors and colleagues. Others attend training because it is mandated. They also go to training with the expectation they will learn skills and knowledge useful to their work.

Second, the instructors receive adult education training but appear to choose the lecture as their main delivery mechanism. There is a wide inconsistency in the professional qualifications of instructors in public safety work. The public safety workers tell us they like to learn in a variety of ways but the delivery of the programs is usually with a lecture. A question for further study is to look at the training and qualifications of instructors of public safety workers to determine what kind of tools and assistance they need to use a broader array of delivery methods.

Third, there are different models for public safety instruction. Some instruction is delivered in an academic setting with certificates and degrees. Others are in academies with centralized training, some with a paramilitary delivery and content. A question for further study is to examine the short-term and long-term effectiveness of these models.

Fourth, a problem occurs when the trainee returns to work. This study shows that back at the station public safety workers rarely report what they learned and usually do not share the information with others. This is a loss of opportunity for others to benefit from the trainee's experience and it can also mean the trainee doesn't get the opportunity to transfer learning to practice.

As Daley (2001) found in her research and this study shows, for knowledge to become meaningful in professional practice, the educator needs to understand the context for learning to take place, and then put it into place. For this group of public safety professionals, the context is to have each local station become a learning organization with a vision for learning for each employee, and then to build upon the opportunities to put new learning into practice.

References

Awoniyi, E. A., Griego, O. V., & Morgan, G. A. (2002). Person-environment fit and transfer of training. *International Journal of Training and Development, 6*(1), 25-35.

Baldwin, T. T. (1992). Effects of alternative modeling strategies on outcomes of interpersonal skills training. *Journal of Applied Psychology, 77,* 147-154.

Baldwin, T. T., & Ford, J. K. (1988). Transfer of training: A review and directions for future research. *Personnel Psychology, 41,* 63-105.

Broad, M. L., & Newstrom, J. W. (1992). *Transfer of training: Action-packed strategies to ensure high payoff from training investments.* Reading, MA: Addison-Wesley.

Caffarella, R. S. (2002). *Planning programs for adult learners: A practical guide for educators, trainers, and staff developers* (2nd ed.). San Francisco: Jossey-Bass.

Campbell, C. P., & Cheek, G. D. (1989). Putting training to work. *Journal of European Industrial Training, 12*(4), 32-36.

Cervero, R. M. (1985). Continuing professional education and behavioral change: A model for research and evaluation. *The Journal of Continuing Education in Nursing, 16,* 85-88.

Chan, J. B. (1996). *Changing police culture: Policing in a multicultural society.* Melbourne: Cambridge University Press.

Daffron, S. R., & Davis, W. (2005). Lessons learned from Palestinian law professors about transfer of learning. *Journal of Legal Education, 55*(4), 571-583.

Daffron, S. R., Cowdrey, D., & Doran, J. (In press). Transfer of learning for state court judges: Maximizing the context. *International Journal of Lifelong Education.*

Daffron, S. R., & North, M. W. (2006). Learning transfer: Tips from software company professionals. *PAACE Journal of Lifelong Learning, 15,* 51-67.

Daley, B. J. (2001). Learning and professional practice: A study of four professions. *Adult Education Quarterly, 52*(1), 39-54.

Facteau, J. D., Dobbins, G. H., Russell, J. E. A., Ladd, R. T., & Kudisch, J. D. (1995). The influence of general perceptions of the training environment on pretraining motivation and perceived training transfer. *Journal of Management, 21*(1), 1-25.

Harris, L., & Volet, S. (1997). *Developing a learning culture in the workplace.* Brisbane, Queensland: ANTA.

Knowles, M.S. (1980). *The modern practice of adult education.* New York: Cambridge University Press.

Knowles, M. S. (1990). *The adult learner: A neglected species* (4th ed.). Houston: Gulf.

Marsick, V. J., & Watkins, K. E. (1990). *Informal and formal learning in the workplace.* New York: Routledge.

Mathieu, J., Tannenbaum, S., & Salas, E. (1992). Influences of individual and situational characteristics on measures of training effectiveness. *Academy of Management Journal, 35,* 828-847.

Merriam, S. B., Caffarella, R. S., & Baumgartner, L. M. (2007). *Learning in adulthood* (3rd ed.). San Francisco: Jossey-Bass.

Merriam, S. B., & Leahy, B. (2005). Learning transfer: A review of the research in adult education and training. *PAACE Journal of Lifelong Learning, 14*, 1-24.

Noe, R. (1986). Trainees' attributes and attitudes: Neglected influences on training effectiveness. *Academy of Management Review, 27*, 736-749.

Quinones, J. A., Ford, J. K., Sego, D. J., & Smith, E. M. (1995). The effects of individual and transfer environment characteristics on the opportunity to perform trained tasks. *Training Research Journal, 1,* 29-48.

Rowden, R. (1995). The role of human resource development in successful small to mid-sized manufacturing businesses: A comparative case study. *Human Resource Development Quarterly, 6*(4), 355-373.

Rushbrook, P., Browne, R., Maxwell, J., Booth, A., Gillies, D., Caddy, A., et al. (2001). *Organizational learning and the New South Wales police service probationary constable practicum program: A project outline.* In a paper prepared for the 9th International Conference on Post-Compulsory Education and Training (pp. 1-8). Gold Coast, Queensland.

Tallman, D. E., & Holt, M. E. (1987). Moving learning from workshops to work. *Continuing Higher Education Review, 51*(1), 15-31.

Vroom, V. (1964). *Work and motivation.* New York: John Wiley.

Xiao, J. (1996). The relationship between organizational factors and the transfer of training in the electronics industry in Shenzhen, China. *Human Resource Development Quarterly, 7*(1), 55-73.

Chapter 8
A New Model for Effective Learning: Moving Beyond Analysis, Development, Design, Implementation and Evaluation (ADDIE)

Judith A. Cochran

Introduction

Individualized instruction, analysis, development, design, implementation, and evaluation (ADDIE) are instructional strategies based upon pragmatic and behaviorist learning theories. Their 50 years of classroom implementation is described along with examples of ADDIE's disappearance from international instruction. A new learning theory, principles, and instructional strategies now provide educational processes that are culture-free and effective in engaging adults in their own learning.

Analysis, development, design, implementation, and evaluation, or the ADDIE model of instruction, can involve adults in their own learning. The advocates of ADDIE claim it expands the way to achieve practical business results. It assists adults in the transfer of learning to the job, the community, or subsequent classes. The use of ADDIE promises to counteract the effects of traditional adult courses and trainings that are assumed to have become events where information is delivered but not necessarily transferred outside of the seminar, workshop, or conference. Adult educators may not share the same educational background nor are they likely to engage with other educators in extended discussions regarding their methods of instruction. As a result, training providers for businesses tout ADDIE as an exciting new training approach to increase the transfer and the leverage of instruction (Brinkerhoff, 2002). While some adult educators apply these supposedly new concepts to corporate settings, the train has left the station. The definitions of adult learner, the learning environment, and instructional processes have traveled to a new country. The ADDIE model of instruction will be described for those who are not familiar with it. For others, the new model of adult education currently in place will paint a landscape of the new educational territory.

History of ADDIE

The idea of involving adults in their own instruction began with John Dewey in the early 1920s with the pragmatist educational movement (Dewey, 1997).

Individuals would decide upon projects that were functional and significant in their lives. On the job or in a seminar, they would learn the skills necessary to develop these projects. Today, this form of education is found mostly in vocational training for adults. For example, students build a house for the class project and in the process, learn to frame, put up sheet rock, and paint it. The evaluation of the house is whether it can be used as a home. Does it work? Since Dewey's time, vocational educators have added evaluation criteria of cost effectiveness and organizational productivity to this pragmatic philosophy. The leverage of training resulting from the transfer of house-building skills occurs when the learner works on another house. In short, involving the adult in the instructional process is not new in pragmatic or vocational seminars.

In another philosophy, andragogy, advocates first described ADDIE instruction in the same sequence as behaviorist Robert Gagne (1988), only 30 years earlier.

They described the instructional process according to following principles:

- Create mechanisms for mutual planning among students, teacher, etc.
- Arrange for a diagnosis of learner needs and interests (analysis).
- Enable the formulation of learning objectives based on the diagnosed needs and interests (development).
- Design sequential activities for achieving the objectives (design).
- Execute the design by selecting methods, materials, and resources (implement).
- Evaluate the quality of the learning experience while re-diagnosing needs for further learning (evaluate).

In andragogy, learning is primarily individually directed with the ideal instruction delivered in an informal learning environment (Knowles et al., 2005).

Learning is no longer taking place in courses with content crammed into a designated time filled with lectures and discussion. In short, ADDIE is not used extensively as an instructional model. Instructional delivery has significantly changed in continuing education, adult basic education, vocational programs, prison courses, hospital clinics, and language institutes. The time has come for the multiplicity of adult educators to communicate with each other about instructional models and processes that support newer definitions of the adult learner, the expanded learning environment, and instructional strategies currently in use.

Redefining the Adult Learner

In the past, *adult learner* was a generic term for someone of a specific age, ignoring new identity characteristics that include ethnic, racial, religious, and patriotic commitments. The earlier definition ignored the community and culture where the adult interacted. Other areas of neglect have been neurological, experiential, and performance identities. The importance of these neglected areas can be observed in the example of the marginalized adult learner. Such individuals have experienced repeated underemployment or unemployment and poverty. If the marginalized learner is narrowly defined as a learner of a specific age, such learners might take responsibility for their condition and blame themselves for their unemployment (Burman, 1988). Obviously, the initial belief system of the marginalized adult has frequently been altered by negative work experiences. The definition of the adult learner has also expanded to include work values. In view of these considerations of the adult identity, programs are developed such as work values instruction programs to help the marginalized adult learner become a more effective employee. In short, the expanded definitions of adult learners have impacted the development of education programs.

Most importantly, adult identity is now also defined by shared memories of a common past—around events, seen as crucial, in recorded, remembered, or sometimes imagined history. Adults are not only individuals of a certain age but of a certain experience. For example, a Jewish person who remembers the founding of Israel may not have been alive in 1949 or live in Israel, but considers the event to be fulfilling the ancient prophesy of rebuilding the Jewish kingdom given to the Jewish tribes by God. The same event, the founding of Israel, is remembered by Palestinians and neighboring Arabs as *nakha* or the calamity. The nakha occurred when 10% of the population which was Jewish created a government for the Palestinian population which comprised 90% of the inhabitants of the area (Lewis, 1998). Each community's collective memory or imagined history of this event is a part of shared adult identity. Shared memories like this example of ethnic, religious, and patriotic commitments greatly influence the adult learner's perception of instruction.

After 9/11, the author taught a course on the Middle East with students who were Jewish, Hindu, Muslim, Christian, and agnostic. The textbook, a series of readings, was rejected by some of the students most of the time. Their collective memory influenced perceptions of textbook learning as well as their own experiential memories. Furthermore, teachers are generally very effective instructors when they come from the same cultural, ethnic, and, religious commitment as their students. They "understand" their students. More likely, they share the collective memory, cultural restrictions, and perceptions of the learners. For these reasons, it is important that teachers and students analyze their own biases and belief systems as they relate to instruction.

Collective narratives also simplify what are often complex, contested interpretations as presented in the example above about the founding of Israel. The narratives found in textbooks and classroom instruction typically present knowl-

really happened." And the framing devices that organize the ac-
eally happens are typically "transparent." Another example is that
....s, part of the female identity is to experience mathematics as difficult. This is a transparent framing device that influences how women approach
math. In the past, many women had this collective memory and did not study more
advanced mathematics, so they did not seek jobs that required it. As a result of this
framing, most women did not major in mathematics, contributing to the fact that
today's women often do not see fields such as engineering as female occupations.
Those using the framing devices look through them and fail to recognize how they
fundamentally shape our understanding of the past and also the future (Wertsch,
2003).

Particularly in totalitarian governments, history is interpreted and made simple
rather than complex. These narratives can be used to introduce perspectives and
interpretations as found in communist countries. In this manner, those in political
power use education and narratives to veil their authority, finding instruction an
ideal instrument for political socialization. Collective narratives can be used to
socialize students without their being aware of what has occurred. When adults
encounter others who have a different account of the past, it is hard not to presume
they have been misled or even "brainwashed," or perhaps they are simply trying to
provoke others by making blatantly false arguments (Wertsch, 2003, p. 17). For
example, the author encountered a young Russian in Moscow who did not believe
what she had heard broadcasted on Radio Free Russia. She was so upset that she
went to the library to check the information. When she did not find any documentation outside that of the collective narrative she knew, she felt validated. She
knew the broadcast was false. Adults, more than younger learners, are less likely to
understand how humans are divided up into collective memory communities.
These are a part of their culture. Thus, when individuals are instructed in a specific
area, it is important to recognize the collective memory communities of adults
who might appear to be the same age, gender, and profession. The redefined adult
identity factors influence how individuals analyze, develop, design, implement,
and evaluate learning. Collective memory is a significant part of the cultural
definition of the adult learner. Adult identity components include aspects of ethnic, racial, religion, nationality, and collective memory components.

The Theoretical Context of ADDIE

The educational environment and instructional strategies used with adult
learners should be informed by learning theories. The question then is what theory
provides the best student engagement and transfer of learning? Theories of learn-

ing support multiple concepts that are supposed to predict effective learning. Learning theories, however, are culture-bound and dependent upon the memory communities of its advocates.

Adult education in some countries continues to follow historical traditions. Documented history of educational theory dates to 4500 B.C. when the Heroditus described the University of Ur as the site of the most learned of men (Cochran, 2008, p. 11). Learning in ancient times used written dialogue delivered orally by tutors to an elite population of adult males. Many today study some of these dialogues in the Torah or Koran or Bible, especially the latter's books of Proverbs and Psalms. The Egyptians have the *Books of Instruction* that date from approximately 3300 B.C. (Cochran, 2008, p. 12). The Chinese have instruction on how to teach dating from 1300 B.C. Early learning theory assumed adults were best educated when the students listened to the texts being read, then wrote and memorized them. Adults were expected to learn religious and civil regulations by rote memory. This ancient learning theory continues today in many cultures, especially those with a Confucian heritage.

Educational learning theory is included in all teacher certification courses. The content of the courses include behaviorism, pragmatism, cognitivism, and brain-based learning. Called educational psychology, philosophy of learning, or learning theory, the courses cover contemporary theories of learning developed from the 1890s to the present. Each theory reflects the collective narrative of the culture and historical experiences of its developers and advocates. ADDIE is an instructional model based upon behaviorism.

Behaviorism and Instruction

Behaviorism, an outcome of the scientific impact of the industrial revolution, identified learning as a result of environmental responses to positive or negative conditioning. Skinner (1965) was the American psychologist who is frequently credited with the articulation of the behaviorist learning theory. He stated if the instructor controls the reinforcement and punishment in the classroom, he or she changes behavior and ensures learning. This theory places the control of learning called conditioning upon the teacher's segmentation of content into "steps" and intermittent positive or negative conditioning in the classroom. Learning can then be monitored in measurable changes. The behaviorist classroom has students controlled by the teacher who delivers content orally or through the textbook or computer. The teacher is responsible for delivering and measuring all learning. The computer can replace the teacher by controlling student learning with negative or positive reinforcement. All learning in behaviorism can be observed as taking place in the external environment. In behaviorist learning theory, adult involvement in analysis, development, design, implementation, and evaluation (ADDIE) is based upon the skill of the teacher/technology in eliciting and controlling student responses through consistent conditioning.

Gagné (1998) and other behaviorists as early as 1974 clearly identified the ADDIE sequence described below in step-by-step instruction.

1. Analyze the type of learning outcomes desired.
2. Establish the learning hierarchy or sequence.
3. Identify internal conditions.
4. Identify external conditions.
5. Record learning continuum.
6. Record curriculum of learning.
7. Select media.
8. Motivate by incentives, task mastery, or achievement.
9. Summarize evaluation.

Called instructional systems design (ISD), Gagné's structure was well accepted, followed, and extended by others (Rossett, 1987). It proved to be a useful organizer for design and development of training methods, models, and tools. This sequence became the basis for the packaged training and education programs delivered by media and instructors or trainers. This model continues in use today by business training developers. However, it is neither a new nor a particularly innovative instructional model for high impact learning.

Cognitivism and Constructivist Instruction

Cognitivism became the dominant psychological force in the 1960s replacing behaviorism and pragmatism as an increasingly popular learning theory. Cognitive psychology is an expansion of behaviorism accepting internal and external learning experiences as appropriate to analyze and examine. Constructivism views learning as a process in which the learner actively constructs or builds new ideas or concepts based upon current and past knowledge. In other words, learning involves constructing one's own knowledge from one's own experiences. The three primary propositions are that individuals should understand their interaction with the environment, know that disequilibrium is the stimulus for learning, and understand that knowledge evolves through the evaluation of the viability of individual understanding (Savery & Duffy, 1995). Constructivist learning is a very personal endeavor, whereby internalized concepts, rules, and general principles are applied in a practical real-world context. Now the teacher no longer controls learning but acts as a facilitator who encourages students to discover principles for themselves and to construct knowledge by working to solve realistic problems.

Knowledge construction is viewed as a social process rather than the teacher-controlled process identified in behaviorism. Students attempt to clarify and organize their thoughts so that they can communicate them to others. Students share their views with others as they elaborate on what they learn. As they express their thoughts, other students discover some thinking flaws and inconsistencies while validating others.

Early cognitivists such as Bandura (1986), scholars and researchers have suggested that collective memories mediate knowledge, expectations, and actions. They assert that reflection and challenge cause individuals to evaluate and adjust their thinking and turn from "what is subjectively reasonable for them to believe to what is objectively reasonable for them to believe" (Fenstermacher, 1979, p. 159). The process of accommodating new information and developing beliefs is thus a gradual one of taking initial steps, accepting and rejecting certain ideas, modifying existing beliefs systems, and finally accepting new ideas. Learning is viewed as an interactive experience between external and internal events.

Problem solving is a strategy frequently used in cognitivist seminars. There are multiple ways to discuss and solve it but the learner must develop ownership for the overall problem. Learners can discuss with others their thinking processes as they consider the complexity of the problem. In constructivism students can explore and learn within a given framework or structure. For example, in language learning, the problem is how to greet a new person. There are multiple greetings that students can select to learn within the framework of an introduction. The students discuss and speak their introductions in a social context, picking the greeting they feel is most appropriate. This is a simplified example of learning as perceived by cognitivists.

Ages and Stages Theories

Other learning theories further define self-directed learning. Some target ages and stages of development. For example, stage theorists focus on distinct, qualitative differences in modes of thinking at various periods of adult life. The expectations for self-directed learning differ at each stage. Theorists such as Loevinger (1976), Kohlberg (1969), and Kegan (1982) clarified what they determined was the stage-mode of thinking for adults. They gave each stage a label. Kohlberg (1969) described the stages of adult moral development where orientations toward authority, others, and self changed with different stages in the life cycle. According to Kohlberg (1969) and his followers, the most evolved adult would be one who no longer followed authority or norms of behavior of others. Kegan (1982) described the stages of adult mental development and Loevinger (1976) identified stages of ego development. A critical aspect of understanding and giving credence to each of these learning theories are the community narratives or memories their authors share. All are American, all but one are male and all were born in the early 1900s (Kohlberg in 1927; Loevinger in 1918; Kegan in 1944). For them, democracy, collective interaction and independence are paradigms for understanding adult learning in the culture and time during which they live/lived.

Final categories of adult learning theories are called functional theories, considering the adult's experience and his selection of learning as the primary focus in his or her education. This is individualized, self-directed learning exemplified by efforts of older adults to learn after retirement in areas such as music, dance, gardening, or yoga. The content of learning began in the 1920s from being controlled by teachers in behaviorism to pragmatism and cognitivism's individual experience and self-control in the 1960s.

In the more recent theories, the democratic components of self-selection and cooperative learning are significant aspects of instruction. According to andragogy, learning is best when it is self-selected, and classrooms do not easily fit this theoretical principle. To functional or pragmatic theorists, the computer could replace the teacher with the student choosing his or her own learning contract and educational experiences, including accessing content from resources on the Internet, in the environment, and from experts. In andragogical educational theory, better learning is considered to take place in cooperative settings. Educational outcomes of cooperative learning indicate no overall effects on academic achievement or student preference (Thompson & Chapman, 2004). The collective narrative of more recent educational theorists included the exceptional value of independence which partially explains their collective theoretical emphasis upon self-directed learning. Many of the behaviorist, pragmatist, functionalist, and cognitive theorists were from an Anglo-American background and were males born and educated in the first half of the 1900s.

After the principles of learning theories are presented to prospective teachers, they have concerns. Which theory is the most effective in predicting learning for most adult learners? As an instructor of multiple students, how does one teacher translate any or all theories into a manageable system of classroom practice? What learning theories consider the collective memory of learning communities that differ from those of American males? When they don't experience any specific learning theory in their preparation, adult educators turn to research. There they can find directives that are impossible to execute:

> *Teachers of adult learners should respect adult experiences and apply them to current situations to produce good educational results. Adult learners are motivated to learn if the subject matter is relevant to their current role and transition period. Finally, for most effective learning to occur, participation in learning should be voluntary. . . . The developmental stages of students gen-*

erate different conditions for learning and what is learned should be related to the students' developmental changes and life roles. (Trotter, 2006, p. 11)

Following these directives and principles would put adult educators in great difficulty. For example, "the most effective learning should be voluntary." When students are allowed to learn only when they want to do so, students would not come to class. Their absences would erase the economic base of most educational efforts. While a teacher could argue students are learning effectively when they come, their absence due to employment or family needs could guarantee low enrollment and high dropout and reduce the number of paid teaching positions. In this example, the research advice is a very difficult principle for the adult educator to follow.

Another problem is the vague generalities adult educators read as demonstrated by Wendt (1999):

The fire service instructor should view himself as a facilitator. When instructing adult learners, strive to guide them according to each class member's knowledge instead of spoon-feeding raw facts. Facilitate learning by incorporating students' experiences, observations of others, personal ideas and feelings into the lesson. Strive to foster an atmosphere of trust and acceptance of different ideas and values. (p. 3)

This is an example of how an adult educator understands cognitive learning theory but does not tell others how to operationalize it in the classroom beyond striving to guide them according to each class member's knowledge. Adult teachers can't learn how to imbed learning theory into instruction when they have not witnessed it in their own teaching preparation. Furthermore, they often get little assistance from professional articles. For example, if prospective teachers hear a lecture on a cooperative learning classroom, they do not know how to monitor learning groups, change instructional delivery, and evaluate individual learning and other factors that occur in this change of instructional strategies. They must experience these situations to understand the complexity of this process. Furthermore, the principles described in behaviorist, cognitive/constructive, and functional learning theories are not universal, may not be applicable beyond a single discipline, and in some cultures, poorly predict future behavior. Because they have limited experience of alternate learning theories in their teacher preparation, most instructors do little but move page by page through textbooks that tell them how to teach content such as foreign languages, math, or literacy. Unfortunately, the instruction in textbooks is not necessarily related to international, national, or local evaluation measures or standards. Without a connection to educational theory and employment contexts, teaching that follows textbook content frequently lacks relevance. Thus models such as ADDIE seem to offer a means for learner involvement and subsequent high impact learning.

The ADDIE Model of Instruction

Analysis

The first aspect of involving the adult learner in instruction is analyzing the learner's needs. Analysis is defined as breaking a larger whole into component parts. The skills of analysis exist among the competencies of adult learners. But what components are lacking in the adult learners? Because self-needs are difficult to diagnose, instructors often make the first analysis of student needs when beginning a training course. Self-directed instruction in andragogy necessitates that the adult analyze personal learning needs. Ways to accomplish this include taking interest inventories, career aptitude tests such as the *Strong Campbell*, or academic tests such as the *Nelson Denny Adult Reading Test*. The adult can also take tests that identify learning preferences such as the *Meyers Briggs* or the *Gregoric Learning Style Test*. These describe preferences for each learner in how instructional material should be organized along with the learner's social relationship requirements. In some cases, once the learning preference tests have been taken, the adult involvement in learning analysis is completed as the results provide the needed information for instructional development and design.

Other learning theories require analysis of individuals and the outcomes wanted for the course, community, or business. These outcomes also can determine expected individual and perceptual results such as increased self-confidence or rejection of a specific career direction. Within the framework of analyzing the individual, unit, and community, there must also be rewards for external and internal success for all of the groups. If rewards are to be effective, they must be individualized. For example, male winners would not enjoy a box of pantyhose. Likewise, the female award recipients would not appreciate a gift certificate to a golf shop with no women's merchandise. In order to be effective, relevant internal and external rewards need to be a part of the learning analysis.

In research and program development, learner needs are the first step in involving the student in learning before developing and designing a program. The following paragraph indicates the amount of effort put into the analysis of student needs for a nursing program (Meeker & Beyers, 2003):

> To assess statewide needs, the university's school of nursing surveyed hospitals, veterans' administration facilities, health departments, and long-term care and skilled nursing facilities to determine their need for advanced prac-

tice nurses (APNs) and their desired practice competencies. The Healthcare Executive Needs Survey, created by the authors, was distributed to 399 recipients. Surveys were returned from 54 of the state's 67 counties. (p. 3)

Many instructors assume adults can employ self, content, or community analysis skills without knowing content standards or using a diagnostic tests. If the adult does not know how to proceed, analysis must be taught as a part of the course. For example, in literacy, self-analysis can be done by repeatedly analyzing oral reading of written paragraphs. In terms of involving adults in mastering analysis skills when reading material, the issues are often complex. For example, in a *Time* article in April 16, 2007, reading comprehension was difficult. "In 2000, the number of illiterate Chinese was 80 million. The number of illiterate Chinese in 2005 was 116 million. This is an increase of 30 million illiterates. 1,500 Chinese characters need to be known in order for a Chinese citizen to be considered literate" (p. 18). It would seem from the sequencing of sentences that the increase in illiterate Chinese citizens is related to the number of Chinese characters that the adult must know. Has the number of recognizable Chinese characters increased in the five years between the two measurements of illiterate citizens? Can one assume that the Chinese population has gotten less educated, less intelligent, or grown more rapidly? All could be interpreted from the two facts presented. However, they do not provide a satisfactory analysis of the paragraph. Multiple interpretations could be deduced from the facts presented. Although the three facts are included in the same article, perhaps they are not related to each other. As presented in this example, analysis begins with understanding the facts, considering their veracity, and then determining which components have the greatest importance to the learner. As determined by this simple example, analysis is not an easy skill for the adult learner to acquire. With the ADDIE model, adult learners are involved in analysis at the beginning of the instructional process through the analysis of themselves and their individual learning needs. In some cases, they might have to be instructed in how to apply the process of analysis to their own living and work environment.

Development
Development of training, seminars, workshops, or courses requires sophistication in multiple areas of educational construction. Instructional development in the past focused upon deciding on program ideas, prioritizing these ideas, researching the resources available for the ideas, identifying and writing objectives for learning them, and determining the forms for the evaluation of the mastery of the ideas. Today, the development of adult education programs has become interactive with the community and the learner in a variety of forms. For example,

in St. Louis, Missouri, there is a community action group involved in developing academic, social, athletic, and parent programs for students at the high school in the Tower Grove area. These programs are directed by the community education director of the St. Louis public schools. Those leading the development of programs include artists, religious leaders, directors of nonprofits, and the high school principal. This is an example of how adult education program development has expanded beyond the classroom and into the community.

Adult learning programs frequently develop on local and national levels, particularly involving stakeholders in health care, emergency responders, and literacy initiatives. Adult education programs are being developed throughout the world. Egyptian literacy programs for adults demonstrate the variety of development initiatives that have emerged in a single area of instructional need in one country. The development of these programs serves as a model for other countries that also have concerns regarding their citizens' literacy levels.

Development Utilizing International and Community Resources

Egypt is a poor country with one of the lowest literacy levels in the Middle East (Heyneman, 1998). The descriptions included here come from recently funded reports and personal observations (Cochran, 2008; Iskandar, 2005; UNPDP, 1998-1999). Egypt is one of the largest recipients of financial aid from the African Union, the United States and the European Union. Since 1990, Egypt has developed an extensive array of literacy programs demonstrating how the development of resources, objectives, and the evaluation of learning can take a variety of forms in adult education (Cochran, 2008). Egypt also demonstrates program development that involves adults in instruction in ways that incorporate and move beyond the ADDIE model.

In Egypt, the community is seen as a contributor to adult literacy programs. Voluntary literacy teachers were created through no-cost contracts with prospective undergraduate teachers enrolled in the colleges of education, with unemployed graduates of university colleges, and students in religious institutes. Voluntary teachers were given financial bonuses and incentives in the form of free housing and meals. Volunteers and literacy teachers were requested to educate adult illiterates who were classified according to their ages and professions. The national Egyptian literacy organization provided free books and necessary teaching aids. After an instructional period of at least six months, the illiterates sit for exams and if successful, they are given promotion certificates. The program of voluntary literacy through free contracts was executed in 2006 with 5000 contractors helping 10,000 persons to become literate (20 persons per class).

A second innovative use of community resources was the mobile schools. Mobile educational caravans were developed for villages and remote areas in which thinkers and intellectuals were asked to participate in literacy education by raising the awareness on the importance of literacy and encouraging illiterates to join classes held around the caravans. Moreover, intellectuals were asked to promote educational services in the most deprived areas, as well as providing health, social, and environmental information and services to the people. Local intellectuals such as judges and other religious leaders also encouraged the production of literacy materials related to learning about the environment. Egyptian government officials had also previously developed literacy curricula called "Learn and Get Enlightened." Four hundred educational caravans were sent to villages and hamlets in 2006.

Furthermore, local businessmen were invited to combat illiteracy in their villages. At the same time, centers for vocational training were established in order to link career training to literacy. Vocational centers participated in the establishment of community learning cooperatives that included educational, vocational, cultural, health and sport activities. Businessmen were invited to support these vocational centers as a social investment in their communities.

Continuing to use the extended communality as an educational resource, the government used television channels and radio broadcasting to deliver distance education. Government literacy lessons were combined with educational drama to engage adults in literacy learning. Broadcasting offered on different schedules to enable illiterates to follow programs regardless of employment commitments covered most governorates. The Egyptian Literacy Organization provided textbooks in illiterates' homes to permit students to follow programming. Literacy programs were offered on all channels in order to increase availability. Preparation is in place for all areas to receive the transmission of the thematic Nile Sat literacy educational channel Egyptian Nile-Sat. Other literacy programs with innovative initiatives utilizing different communities included:

1. Supporting and generalizing from the pilot experiences of nongovernment organizations in literacy and adult education fields to maximize the role played by community participation in literacy.
2. Encouraging self-learning through recording literacy lessons on tapes and distributing them with literacy books.
3. Printing literacy books in Braille to serve blind illiterates.
4. The establishment of multipurpose centers for literacy, vocational training, library, kindergarten, and health care.
5. Expansion of group witness clubs to increase the number of beneficiaries and providing adults with techniques necessary to receive literacy educational channels.
6. Opening literacy classes in prisons, orphanages, health units, women's clubs,

hotels, worship institutions, youth centers, public clubs, and homes.

7. Making all effort to conduct instruction at times suitable for the students. Teachers are provided. Notebooks and educational aids are distributed at no cost.

8. Preparing and qualifying 121,758 individuals to work as teachers in literacy classes during the period from 1993 to 1999; the total number of supervisors and inspectors amounted to 7,630 trainees.

9. Using new and encouraging marketing such as the "educated village" and the "educated family" to encourage self-learning.

10. Requesting pioneer women as well as the educated women and the agricultural and health care guides to assist in the eradication of illiteracy of rural women. (UNPDP, 1998/99)

Development of Literacy Curricula

Literacy and adult education curricula were developed according to the objectives identified by the government's General Plan of Literacy and Adult Education. Curricula contain the following:

1. Teaching in the work locations should be carried out whenever possible.

2. The curricula contain evaluation and assessment systems in order to improve student application and recognize the goals.

3. Reading materials are added to the curricula related to adults' social, educational and cultural needs. New educational aids have been created especially for literacy teachers (literacy packages, educational aids, creative teacher manuals, and magnetic blackboards). (CDELT, 2006)

The General Organization of Literacy and Adult Education started developing curricula by issuing a textbook series entitled "Learn and Get Enlightened." It consists of three books which focus on the following subjects: life activities, human rights, problems resulting from overpopulation, related aspects of how to look after and develop the environment, and the role of the women as active participants in society. In addition, branches of the government literacy organization in the governorates were requested to prepare reading materials based on the environment in which the illiterates lived in order to meet their survival needs. Calligraphy programs were also included as one of the subjects of the literacy curricula to improve the skills of writing. The government delivered teachers' kits that were used extensively as they contained computers, posters, maps, enlarged educational models, and cards of letters and words. Other improved teaching aids like the magnetic boards were included in the teachers' kits.

Cooperation with United Nations Educational, Scientific and Cultural Organization (UNESCO) provided financial assistance for the publication of six post-literacy books and the production of an education kit for literacy teachers. In order to enhance linkages between literacy programs and vocational training to provide illiterates with vocational skills, the Egyptian Literacy Organization has undertaken the responsibility of providing illiterates with training on some handicrafts according to their individual abilities and desires, with the aim of increasing production and promoting the living standards of their families. These handicrafts include manual carpet weaving, leather and wood productions, sewing and hand embroidery works for the females—carpentry and electric works, house maintenance and other activities for the males. All target illiterates to help them acquire the skills of running small-scale projects that increase income. One hundred and fifty multipurpose centers have been started in the last 10 years that combine literacy programs and vocational training.

Cooperation with another literacy program exists regionally between the General Organization of Literacy and Adult Education and the Arab League Educational, Cultural and Scientific Organization (ALECSO). The program was entitled "Read, in the Name of God" containing material based on learning and writing some verses of the Koran and the Prophet's speeches. Another form of cooperation among institutions is manifested in the integrated experimental project in the Village (Alsatamony) in Dakahleya Governorate. It targeted a scheduled comprehensive development for the village in education, training, women's activities, cultural activities, and guidance activities in agriculture, health, and environment.

Other collaborative literacy efforts were developed among different Egyptian Ministries. In cooperation with the Ministry of Social Affairs, 1,808 literacy classes were conducted in 2006 through 688 participating nongovernment organizations. The numbers of participants totaled 39,606 illiterate males and females. Efforts were also undertaken by the National Council for Motherhood and Childhood within the Council's project for the Comprehensive Development of Literacy for Women from ages 16 to 35. This project targeted 50,000 female illiterates attempting to obtain the certificate of the first stage of basic education. And finally, the Ministries of Defense and Interior cooperated with each other by providing literacy instruction to soldiers in their units (Egyptian Ministry of Education, 1997). The greatest national literacy program has been the National Campaign of Literacy. TV announcements were broadcast to inform illiterates and urge them to get enrolled in literacy classes. Local TV channels transmit literacy lessons in order to give illiterates an opportunity to follow these programs. Sixty drama episodes have been transmitted on the literacy lessons as a part of "Learn and Get Enlightened." Newspapers and media coverage highlight the activities undertaken by the Literacy Organization and its affiliated centers in the governorates (Egyptain Ministry of Education, 1997).

Beyond Basic Literacy Curriculum

In Egypt, adult literacy education is no longer considered as beginning and ending within the classroom. As preparation for the fulfillment of lifelong continuous education, the organization encourages adult students to find better circumstances in order to improve their living conditions. The curriculum focus is upon ensuring the transfer and utilization of acquired skills and knowledge. The General Organization of Literacy and Adult Education encourages students to continue their education through preparatory education (the second stage of basic education). The age of enrollment in the first preparatory grade has been raised to 18 years old. By 1997 about 9,935 were enrolled in the preparatory stage. Enrollment increased by 36,149 during the period from 1997 to 1999. A newspaper named *Enlightenment* continues to be issued for distribution for classes and centers of literacy and among literacy graduates. In addition, 100 libraries with postliterate reading materials have been established in the governorates in order to encourage reading for all (UNPDP, 1998-1999).

The General Organization of Literacy and Adult Education has established a special department for literacy program graduates within its premises and at its centers in the governorates. These departments organize training courses for teaching English, computer uses, and word processing. Other training courses for women's activities are held in order to increase female awareness and education. There are special training courses teaching adults how to begin projects that provide more income by promoting recent literacy skills and providing services for agricultural activities, health, and environmental conservation.

The organization has a schedule for the completion of the integrated system of information and support of decision making. During 1999, in addition to the various systems, the central information system linked the organization with its affiliated centers in the governorates. This network of computers has a database containing the numbers of illiterates and participants in all adult programs. The Social Fund for Development supports the governorates with computers according to another plan. Plans exist to connect this system with the Internet in order to get information on the world activities in the field of literacy and adult education. The country has addressed all of the concepts normally found in the ADDIE model of instruction and gone beyond it in the inclusion of community, government, and international resources. While individualized instruction is described, many other diverse literacy programs were developed. Egyptians obtained facilities and external resources; built a base of support in the communities, the government, and international agencies; increased enrollment; established and communicated schedules for illiterates and staff on site and in the media; developed program ideas, objectives, and curriculum; and made all available to teachers and adult learners. The needs of adult learners were recognized through the cultural focus, content, and flexible scheduling. And finally, Egypt established articulation, integration, and centralization of instruction through governmental bodies charged with executing the goals of the programs.

Furthermore, the innovation of Egyptian literacy programs began in 1986 following the guidelines of engaging the adult in ADDIE and more recent instructional processes. The programs recognize adults are most interested in content that has immediate relevance to their jobs or personal lives. Egyptian programs focus upon improving the economic, environmental, and social conditions of the illiterate adult. Throughout the adult education programs, there are reminders of the significance of learning to the Muslim culture in the titles of some literacy programs and materials and in the encouragement of students to participate. The collective memory and culture are taken into account in program development. The profiles of Egyptian adult literacy programs extend beyond having the adult learners engaged in the programs themselves. Most of those without the ability to read cannot earn a living at the level of those who are literate. So for both economic and personal reasons, improving the literacy rate has been a primary objective of the Egyptian government with the international support of private and nongovernment organizations. For example, Egypt's cooperation with the British Federation of International Cooperation (DFID) is designed to cover the training of literacy teachers and activation of the role of vocational training centers in literacy programs. It is difficult to determine any greater variety of programs directed at literacy. In short, the development of literacy programs in Egypt is a description of an interactive model of program planning.

The interactive program development model is also used by organizations such as the Academy of Educational Development that has many adult education programs throughout the world. Examples include: A Professional Training Program for the Hashemite Kingdom of Jordan; Advancing Learning and Employability for a Better Future (Morocco); Diaspora Skills Transfer Program for Southern Sudan; Guatemalan Conflict Resolution Program. Without considering the cultural and economic context, building a solid base of community support, and devising transfer of learning plans, these educational programs would exist only as training events and not as individual and community changing programs.

The development of adult education programs makes a connection of content to individual and community needs, resources, and outcomes. The community outcomes are integrated through the social and economic mandates. The multiplicity of needs in the development of adult education necessitates a clear system for designing and implementing instruction. Evaluation or the collection of data must indicate how those needs have been met. The execution of the programs by the Academy of Educational Development and the Egyptian government must be followed by evaluation systems that document community involvement and adult learning. Otherwise, the instruction is without impact for the participant and the community.

Design

To the surprise of many, designing an educational program is preceded by analysis of student and cultural needs and then the development of resources in the economic and social support for the program. One does not merely open the book and start teaching. Adult instructional design first targets program and learning outcomes. These outcomes are stated in what is known as objectives. Program objectives provide the road map of the contributions of the program to the participants, the community, and perhaps the country. For example, the program objectives for literacy in Egypt include the importance of increasing adult literacy for the economic development of the country. Learning objectives describe what personal skills, knowledge, or attitudes the individual will acquire. The roots of program and learning objectives come from behaviorism theory of the 1920s where it was mandated the outcomes should be measurable, clearly articulated, and comprehensible. Learning to write objectives that meet these criteria is not an easy task and often takes three or four weeks to teach prospective teachers in curriculum methods courses. For this reason, some instructional materials come with the objectives written by program planners or textbook writers rather than teachers. In short, program design begins with the identification of program and learning objectives.

If the course is teacher-directed, the teacher then selects and sequences the content. For example, if nurses are returning for staff training in the operation of a new heart monitoring machine, the adult educator would decide what concepts needed to be taught about the machine and in what order. Likewise, a professor teaching about Indians of the American Southwest would need to decide what cultural concepts were most important for students to learn and which should come first, second, and third. In a cognitive-based course, objectives can "flow naturally as if the concepts were their own architects and their revelation engineered by their own processes of evolution" (Granger, 1998).

In a class where the students direct their own learning, they decide the content and the sequence. This is assumed to be a means of making the curriculum relevant to adult learners. Many students in adult basic education programs cite the lack of connection between taught curriculum and their lives as a primary cause for dropping classes (Quigley, 1997). One way to ensure the curriculum's appropriate selection and sequencing is to conduct formal and informal needs assessments with potential and participating learners. In some programs, learners meet weekly to discuss their needs and interests and their feedback is often incorporated into future curriculum development plans. In a family literacy program serving the Latino immigrant community, staff was paid to attend various community activities to solicit ideas and opinions from potential participants. This information was then used to identify areas of interests and to determine sequencing and scheduling of course objectives. The underlying assumption is that if a curriculum is relevant to its participants and reflective of their needs, they would be more motivated to participate, despite their busy schedules. In both examples, it is significant to note the students do not decide and sequence the curriculum, they merely have input acquired through program administrators and teachers.

Obviously, students may or may not know what would be most beneficial for them to learn and how they could most easily master the physical development, new skills, new knowledge, or new attitudes. Cranton (1992) argued for three kinds of attitude changes: change in assumptions, change in perspective, and change in behavior. Implicit in Cranton's transformational outcomes is a change in self-identity. Likewise, instructional developers and teachers do not have knowledge regarding necessary attitude changes before they begin instruction. For example, English as a second language instruction usually begins with basic assumptions of minimal language proficiency. In Turkey, the author had a student who had never spoken a word of English, having acquired all his language proficiency from the radio. As this example demonstrates, until the students arrive and are assessed, assumptions about content proficiency cannot be made accurately. In all cases, selection and sequencing of instruction should be based upon the criteria of content importance and relevance to the student and more recently, to the community.

The selection and sequencing of content in program design cannot ignore a critical issue of acquiring knowledge—access. Knowledge has, in the past, been a defining difference between the rich and the poor, the elite and the downtrodden. For some cultures and countries, adult education is an attempt to fix the problems resulting from limited access of all citizens to elementary and secondary schooling. As described by Lyotard (1984), access to knowledge is becoming controlled like the access to money:

> *It is not hard to visualize learning circulating along the same lines as money, instead of for its "educational" value or political (administrative, diplomatic, military) importance; the pertinent distinction would no longer be between knowledge and ignorance but rather, as is the case with money, between "payment" knowledge and "investment" knowledge—in other words,*

between units of knowledge exchanged in daily maintenance framework (the reconstitution of the work force, "survival") versus funds of knowledge dedicated to optimizing the performance of a project . . . One could imagine flows of knowledge traveling along identical channels of identical natures, some of which would be reserved for the "decision makers," while the others would be used to repay each person's perpetual debt with respect to the social bond. (p. 6)

A frequent response to concerns regarding access to content is that knowledge is readily available through the Internet, local libraries, and the media. This is more the case in democratic countries but not necessarily true elsewhere. However its availability is determined, access to knowledge is another critical consideration when designing adult education.

Selecting Instructional Activities

Instructional activities are the means of delivering instructional content. They range from the simple memorization and recitation of knowledge to case studies and simulations. Teacher preparation textbooks such as *50 Strategies for Teaching English Language Learners*, by Herrell and Jordan (2008) come with instructional DVDs showing how teachers use some of the instructional activities. Such resources are very helpful in selecting instructional activities.

Instructional activities in themselves do not deliver knowledge, improve thinking, develop motor skills, or change attitudes. They merely have the capability of involving the learner in high, medium, or low engagement activities. For example, in a lecture to 300 students, the students may or may not be listening or engaged. In one such classroom at Harvard, the author sat between one student writing a short story in Spanish and another one taking notes. Both appeared the same to the instructor who could barely see them anyway. Taking notes from a lecture could be categorized as a low involvement instructional activity.

Each of the activities listed below must be modified and evaluated in view of student competencies. High student engagement is expected and encouraged in most instructional activities. A small sample of potential instructional activities are listed below.

1.   Total physical response.
2.   Book clubs.
3.   Shared dyads.
4.   Leveled questions.
5.   Conceptualizing with model development.
6.   Learning centers.

7. Cooperative learning groups.
8. Integrative learning projects.
9. Reciprocal teaching.
10. Role playing.
11. Simulations.
12. Case studies.
13. Learning style grouping.
14. Skills grouping.
15. Video instruction.
16. Educational software.

A cooperative learning group activity is described by Brown (2004) providing an example of program objectives that instigate cultural change:

> *Together with others in the class who chose the same non-monolithic group to study in depth, adult learners conduct the class on a given day. Students are expected to assign and distribute additional readings so that they can present the history of that group's educational experience in the U.S. (including the circumstances that brought or made them inhabitants of the U.S.), and how they were treated. The program objective is to help class members understand how the group has been treated in this country and how the history lives on and affects the present (e.g., philosophically, economically, politically, socially, and culturally). Adult learners' presentations include: (a) information regarding the values considered representative of the majority of people in that group; (b) a discussion of their schooling experiences; and (c) any other issues that they deem important (e.g., stereotypes, inequitable treatment, successful pedagogical strategies). As part of the class, students could also have a one-hour panel presentation from at least three people from that group. Panel members introduce themselves, engage in a sharing of their educational experiences, and participate in an informal question and answer session with all members of the class. Cultural values, lessons taught, schooling experiences and misperceptions experienced are discussed, as well as suggestions in working more effectively with community members from all cultures.* (p. 3)

The major instructional activity in all situations is the interaction and verbal responses between teachers and students. In a recent example, the teacher of an adult education class was removed from her course midsemester as she had caught a student cheating and some of her interactions with students offended the cheating student and others. The importance of this removal is that it had nothing to do with the learning in the course or following university policies. Such growing emphasis on the happiness of adult learners while ignoring knowledge mastery demonstrates the importance of verbal interaction as a learning activity. Furthermore, this example of student-teacher interaction demonstrates the significance of student complaints regarding how they demand to be treated in the classroom.

Gathering Instructional Materials

Sometimes the gathering of instructional materials seems overwhelmed by the objectives. The description by Spatz and Erwin (1996) that follows would make gathering instructional materials quite difficult. "This project had the essential community-based education for adult learners, built on a strong theoretical foundation, which combined health education, learning styles, brain hemispheric and anthropology concepts" (p. 2). Once the objectives, content, and sequence of content and activities have been determined, instructional materials have to be found. The obvious choice would be to open the book and start on page one and select questions or problems from the back of the book. These questions would be placed on a handout for students if they did not have a book. In this simple format, the instructional materials are inexpensive, readily available, and lack variety. Nevertheless, financial constraints often mandate that the teacher make do with whatever is available.

Distance education is a different instructional design influencing adult education. Web-based instructors have multiple individuals telling them of the materials they should include in course content. The following materials were cited for an English class by DuCharme-Hansen and Dupin-Bryant (1989). This example gives the scope and sequence of gathering material. The lesson topic is to learn to use the research process. The objectives are: to identify types of information required for a writing topic; to be able to identify sources that are credible and current; to gather information from appropriate sources; to prepare accurate summaries of information gathered from sources; to document sources. The materials gathered for this lesson plan are:

1. Post handouts on information types.
2. Post examples of credible and current sources for content.
3. Post examples of sources that are not credible and current.
4. Post reading "How to Gather Information" for class reading and then discussion.
5. Post audio lecture on "Common Mistakes When Gathering Information." (p. 32)

The obvious and frequent difficulty for all teachers is often where to find these materials and how to select them. There are no references for the audio lecture on "Common Mistakes When Gathering Information." This must be a teacher-made instructional material. Further, "post examples of credible and current" sources for content are not in the textbook so they must be found in other textbooks or written by the teacher. In addition, there should be several examples for students to examine.

Videos, if not available from the local library, are expensive and do not necessarily follow the program and learning objectives developed. How many videos are there on the research process? The next difficulty is taking the time to find additional readings that are relevant to the content. The materials gathered for this example do not cover the last two objectives of preparing summaries and documenting sources. Many embarrassing problems can occur when assignments are made with objectives and materials that are not covered in the course material. And when gathered, the instructor should vet the instructional materials in order to address the attitudes, new knowledge, new skills, physical development, and background of the participants. It is questionable whether students writing their own lesson plans can do this. Likewise, finding material that will address all of the instructional objectives is a difficult mandate requiring the instructor's time and expertise. In short, money and time and availability are frequent constraints when gathering instructional materials.

Implementation

Putting instruction into action is more complex than often expected by adult educators. Implementation means determining the relationship among teacher, learners, and content. In most cases, this means constructing a lesson plan for each day of instruction. The general format for lesson plans include the time allotted and the listing of objectives (program and learning), the initial motivating event listed that engages students in the topic, the learning activities, and form of evaluation (Serdyukov & Ryan, 2007). This content is usually taught in curriculum methods teacher preparation courses.

The classroom results of the combination, sequence, and/or implementation of objectives and strategies are not stress-free. Because learning and the accompanying change can be volatile and frightening, learning can actually pose threats to psychological security as it challenges comfortably established knowledge, beliefs, and values, including those that may be central to self-concept (Mezirow, 1990). Adults, unlike youth, have established their cultural identities, loyalties, and knowledge base. Educators have identified certain processes of knowledge development within the context of adult learning: "First, learning is experiential since it co-emerges with environment, individuals, and activity. Secondly, some understanding is embedded in the conduct and relationships among the participants, rather than the minds of individuals. Thirdly, learning is a continuous process of invention and exploration that is linked to disequilibrium and dissonance and amplified with feedback loops" (Fenwick, 2002). The notion of learning from the interaction of the teacher, students, and objectives is widely accepted in ethnographic studies of learning in the workplace and in the context of organizational change that may lead to conflict, fear, antagonism, when there is a departure from familiar and comfortable routines (Grossman, Wineburg, & Woolworth, 2001; Lomax, 1999).

Learners' cultural values, socialization processes, academic expectations, and acquired learning styles intersect to shape adults' learning processes and outcomes. Erikson (1987) further noted that the cultural gap between learners' native culture and educational culture, if perceived to be unfit or inferior by their teachers, would negatively affect students' achievement and dropout rate. Learners' socio-cultural contexts play a crucial role in shaping the teaching-learning dynamics. Adult educators, when interacting with students from different ethnic and racial backgrounds, should critically examine personal cultural assumptions rather than judging students' behaviors through their own cultural lenses. A range of factors may contribute to a student's behaviors in classrooms including a lack of language skills, preexisting learning styles, appropriate gender behavior, or avoidance of losing face when unsure of the correct response. Students' mysterious behaviors are likely related to cultural learning styles rather than a lack of interest or ability (Lee & Sheared, 2002). Unfamiliarity with certain cultural values and behavior norms prevalent may prevent teachers from accurately understanding student needs as they develop daily lesson plans. Thus the teacher's cultural knowledge and communicated respect of students are unstated but inherent parts of the implementation process.

Regardless of the strategies used, implementation needs to be carefully planned over a series of sessions, with adequate opportunities for debriefing or feedback, in a structured setting where people adhere to agreed-on guidelines for safety and confidentiality. Implementing instruction in the ADDIE's model should also factor in community context. One example of community context is adult ethnic schools that provide unique learning space for immigrant learners whose cultural values, experiences, and methods of understanding are viewed as the norm and serve as a foundation for teaching (Sheared & Sissel, 2000).

While researchers argue that the cultural difference between a learner's home and school are harmful to the student (Guy, 1999), adult ethnic schools continue to stand as a community-controlled site that embrace the cultural-linguistic codes the learners call their own. In the past, the purpose of education was to prepare immigrant youth to understand, learn the language, and become a citizen in the predominate culture. The outcome was a homogenized society. Today's educators suggest that teachers and program administrators, who work with adult immigrant learners to form a partnership with immigrant communities in order to develop relevant lessons, enhance understanding of the served immigrant population and increase awareness of immigrant learners' socio-cultural history. In this way, education is relevant and serves the minority culture, rather than creating a unified culture. The outcome is hoped to be a society that accepts and does not attempt to change minority cultural values, languages, and beliefs. Immigrant population partnerships between schools and the immigrant community obviously extend adult instruction beyond the classroom and the ADDIE model.

Lewis and Varbero (1995) suggest some strategies for creating minority school partnerships that enable programs to create a working relationship with the immigrant communities. Their first suggested step is to gain support from local elected officials by inviting them to serve as board members who are directly involved in decision-making processes. The second strategy is to have bilingual assistants who have access to the community and its cultural knowledge to help create a greater awareness of the program as well as inviting community members to participate. As active members of the community themselves, the bilingual assistant staff members are effective in utilizing and expanding their existing social networks for student recruitment and retention. To have a staff that is fully representative of the learners' ethnicity is difficult, particularly for programs that provide courses to more than one immigrant community. A third possibility is to engage learners in classroom activities that include writing about their life experiences and concerns regarding their resources, their biography, and their current social and economic situation in the host country. These activities invite learners to document and share their past and current socio-cultural and linguistic context while creating an experience-based learning context, engaging learners to reflect on the role literacy and education play in shaping their lives (Weinstein-Shr, 1995).

In addition, some educational areas such as nursing and management education require the implementation of interactive-distributive learning methods to efficiently meet student and health care education and agency needs. Interactive-distributive learning programs encompass a variety of teaching formats, including live classes, interactive television classes, and media-enhanced and Web-based instruction. Implementation also is not a simple process. Students who are involved in instructional implementation need to be knowledgeable about how to develop lesson plans, schedule and select learning activities, and evaluate community influence on program delivery.

Evaluation

One of the greatest weaknesses in adult instruction can be the failure to evaluate learning in a meaningful manner. Meaning is determined by asking the question of what relevance the evaluation has to classroom instruction (Popham, 2000).

If instruction is targeted to nationalize tests as in the Test of English as a Foreign Language (TOEFL) exam, then standardized tests are meaningful to classroom instruction. In some subject areas, learning is measured internationally to provide comparisons with other countries and to determine the level of content mastery. Today, there is the National Assessment of Adult Literacy (NAAL) and other standards that establish levels of proficiency in reading and writing. These standards assist countries in developing appropriate policies and instruction.

International and national evaluations are necessary. For example, despite the repeated reporting of 30, 60, or 90 million adults with inadequate literacy skills as measured by the U.S. Department of Education and the National Governor's Association in both 1993 and 2003, some 95 percent of adults surveyed reported that they did not think they have a literacy problem (Strict, 2007). In addition, federal policies in the management of adult literacy programs appear to have led to a loss of some 1 million enrollments in programs since 1993. Additionally, investments in the Adult Education and Literacy System (AELS) in 2007 barely exceed $200 per enrollee, less than 3% of the $6,500 provided for each child in the federal Head Start program. Such comparisons suggest that we need to rethink the nature of our national assessment of adult literacy and what our national and state policies ought to be in the light of what new assessments reveal (Strict, 2007). Adult educators must be aware of the national assessments conducted that give an international context for understanding the success and failures of their students.

The second level of evaluation is on a program level to determine the effectiveness of the instruction for the local group in meeting content standards, determine quality and initiate improvement. In the United States, there is a National Reporting System (NRS) that collects data on learning gains and several outcomes such as secondary degrees/certificates awarded, transition into further education/training, and employment. However, there are not yet national standards for program quality or comparable national assessment tools that would make valid comparisons of how well different programs and different states are performing. Further, the NRS data on learning do not include pre- and post-test scores so that gains in learning can be estimated more accurately (Strict, 2007).

Such program evaluation is important but sometimes limited in other countries. Evaluation frequently does not extend beyond documentation of the number of illiterates. Continuing with the example of Egypt, adult literacy programs are well funded by external and Egyptian sources. Law No. 8 was issued in 1991 for literacy and adult education with the aim of mobilizing a comprehensive national campaign. The law stipulated the establishment in 1992 of the General Organization of Literacy and Adult Education. The organization started carrying out the various planning responsibilities as well as the executive, educational and coordinating efforts among different institutions involved in the implementation

Table 8.1
Illiteracy in Egypt 1996

Education Status	Urban	Rural	Total
Illiterate	5,245,554	12,102,191	17,347,745
Proportional distribution	30.25%	69.76%	100%

of the National Plan of Literacy and Adult Education scheduled for the decade 1992–2001 through its branches in 26 governorates and in 251 educational idaras, covering 1,047 main villages and 20,945 hamlets. The Egyptian equivalent was modeled after the American National Assessment of Adult Literacy and the Adult Education and Literacy System. Not only national data but also international evaluations identified a need for literacy education based upon national program data collected by UNESCO, World Bank, and the United States (Heyneman, 1998).

Table 8.1 indicates statistics of illiteracy in the total population in 1996 related to their distribution during the next 10 years. This table indicates that illiterate citizens in rural areas doubled those in urban areas. For this reason, the Egyptian Ministry of Education, in addition to the General Organization of Literacy, expanded efforts to eradicate illiteracy in rural areas and the places deprived of educational service. Their measurement of literacy provides models for other countries demonstrating the importance of national educational evaluations.

National assessments indicate literacy programs for adults have not reached the total adult population, as 31% of the rural were literate in 1996 compared to 49% in 1992 (UNPD, 1998/1999). All national evaluation rates continue to indicate a wide gap between males and females, with more literate males than literate females.

Table 8.2 shows that illiteracy rates in Egypt have been reduced from 1986 to 1999. What is not evaluated is the effectiveness of the type of program, the level of literacy that was achieved by graduation, and the employment that follows departure from the program. Furthermore, there is no description of the pre-tests and exit tests that determine the reduction in illiteracy. According to Strict (2007), the same data is not available on illiteracy in the United States. It appears that nationally and internationally, evaluation of adult literacy is in an embryonic stage.

The final area of evaluation is individual assessment that collectively gives measures of program efficiency. There is no better means for engaging adults in their learning than by having them develop their own tests. However, test taking

Table 8.2

Indicators of Illiteracy Reduction in Egypt, 1986–1996

Year	Illiteracy Rates Males	Illiteracy Rates Females	Total Percentage of Illiteracy
1986	37.8	61.8	49.4
1990	35.5	55.2	47.1
1996	29	50.2	38.6
1999	23.2	43.4	33.1

has been the primary instructional method of engaging students in instruction. Continuing with the area of literacy as an example, adult learners can be evaluated by standardized, competency, and informal tests. The standardized tests compare student results to that of the statistically developed bell-shaped curve averages of scores. The competency tests identify levels of proficiency in areas assessed such as vocabulary, comprehension, and fluency. The informal tests usually measure percentage of correct and incorrect answers from textbook or teacher-made tests. The knowledge responses can vary from essay to short answer to multiple-choice responses. When evaluating online courses, the format again changes. No longer is the student evaluating learning with a particular instructor. In the online environment, the instructor's role is only one part of a much broader experience such as the technology, the user interface, the design of the content, and the modes of delivery (Conceicao, 2007).

No matter the format that evaluation takes, international, national, and individual scores are used for a variety of purposes: student entrance, placement, entrance, and graduation, program modification, material selection, and diagnostic decision making.

Technology

How can educators translate data from student performance into meaningful and valuable information? Today, technology is being used to transform large- and small-scale educational assessments into accessible data. The interpretation of the data is where program and individual development begins. The questions consistently asked are, What do teachers and programs need to do to be more effective in their work. How can adult educators provide it?

Some of the newest computer programs help teachers and administrators measure academic progress and improvement and analyze and report student data. Programs such as POWERSOURCE target specific competency levels and content areas for students. The assessments on this program are designed by a team led by

David Niemi to motivate students and assist them in organizing their knowledge of subjects such as algebra. Each assessment aligns with mathematics standards, builds on recent cognitive research, and provides frequent information about how well students are performing so that teachers can make immediate adjustments as necessary (Engle, 2007). International assessments of mathematics and science competencies such as the Third International Math and Science Studies (TIMSS) provide a baseline for levels of achievement that can be expected for students in different countries. For example, North Korea, Palestine, and Egypt are countries with equivalent levels of poverty when compared on TIMSS. Surprisingly, these three countries do not have the same average algebra score for eighth graders (Martin & Associates, 2000).

Knowles, Holton, and Swanson (2005) believed that adults are most interested in learning subjects that have immediate relevance to their careers or personal life. How is relevance in personal life evaluated? In the course taught by Grimmett (2000), "Women in Educational Leadership," the evaluation was ongoing during the entire course development and delivery. Course content and activities were evaluated among the professors and participants after every class session. Recommendations for modifications of content and activities were considered in subsequent classes and courses. Post-course evaluations indicated that participants felt the course was relevant, addressing the issues surrounding their interests, needs and values (p. 37).

In Scotland, technology has been developed as another means to measure relevant self-directed learning (Kelly & MacKay, 2003):

> *It encourages a disciplined approach to learning, promotes thought about learning needs and increases the ability of general practitioners to learn from everyday experiences. In some instances, users were able to apply what had been learned.* (p. 358)

From a random sample of 40 adult learners, 23 subjects returned completed data. The small completion rate does not support the effectiveness of the software in evaluating self-developed instruction. It does, however, indicate technology is being explored as a tool for evaluating adult self-learning in addition to making it easier to access and interpret collected data.

Conclusion of ADDIE Model

The ADDIE model of instruction has existed under different names for the past 30 years. Called the Instructional Systems Design by Gagné in the 1970s, teachers and program developers segmented learning into categories. Now, trainers are suggesting the adult learners structure their own education following the

ADDIE model in order to transfer learning to their own specific situations. Multiple difficulties have been described when adults are engaged in structuring their own instruction. First, self-diagnosis or analysis is not easy or always accurate. In some cases, analysis skills must be first taught to the learner. Secondly, the ADDIE model does not include aspects of self-identity that are often unrecognized such as the influence on learning of collective memory, transparent interpretational frameworks, cultural values, and community context. The definition of the adult learner has greatly expanded.

Adults can possibly become engaged in the development and design of their educational experience. However, a personal perspective may be limited. As individuals, they may not have access to the national standards established in some areas such as mathematics, literacy, second language learning, science, and vocational or career requirements. Furthermore, instructional development often needs interagency cooperation or external resources. Examples of multiple partners and stakeholders in health care, emergency relief, and vocational education are extensive. Furthermore, for the individual to become competent in instructional development and design takes more than one experience to understand and operationalize. Adults may be partially involved in constructing their educational experience but they cannot master it in a single assignment.

And finally, implementation of learning can be managed by lesson plans, educational software, and distance education. In all cases, the adult needs to determine the scope and sequence of the experience, which is often not easily determined. The reaction of adult learners to their own lesson plan could be positive. However, many learners want external involvement that cannot be constructed without cooperation of other people. The process of developing lesson plans is complicated and time consuming. There is the necessity of determining appropriate learning activities, gathering resource material, and selecting appropriate evaluation procedures.

And finally, distance education has introduced diverse instructional formats and delivery and evaluation systems to the ADDIE model. Evaluation now considers not only the instruction provided by the teacher but also the effectiveness of the methods of content delivery and the quality of the technology. Distance education requires more time from instructors in program analysis, development, design, implementation, and development. It is questionable whether adult learners want to step into these new responsibilities. Perhaps they might only want teachers to "do their job" and "teach me." Expectations of students and teachers will have to change when adults are engaged in their own learning. The assumption that adults will set the highest standards for learning and its transfer has yet to be documented.

The Next Evolution

Adult learning is described in theories that reflect the cultural context in which the theories were constructed. Behaviorism evolved from the industrial marketplace when human's actions were controlled in assembly line concepts. One of the earliest behaviorists, Frank Gilbreth, followed concepts to such a degree that he used them in parenting his 12 children as described in the book *Cheaper by the Dozen* (2005). After behaviorism, the educational theory evolved into cognitivism where individual internal and external behavior was described as important to learning and the psychology of instruction. When stated in educational principles, cognitivism became complex. Behaviorist and cognitivist learning theories were followed by pragmatism or functionalism targeting learning that can be verified by experiences in the environment. Functionalism was followed with a format for individualizing instruction through self-directed learning. This process, called andragogy by some educators, enabled adults to construct learning contracts that met their own needs with resources not necessarily identified by the instructor. Thus, the emphasis in learning conditions has gone from focusing on analysis in behaviorism to individual development in cognitivism to individual transfer to the marketplace in functionalism. And recently the emphasis on learning conditions has been on strategies of design in andragogy.

The next evolution of adult learning theories now reflects the scientific advances that have enabled researchers to electronically map the operation of the brain when learning is taking place. Neurological functions that can be mapped have been matched to the environmental conditions that exist when new meaning is absorbed. Some researchers call this theory constructivism while others refer to it as brain-based learning. It is considered a new territory that recognizes the uniqueness of individual mental experiences. Physiological processes have become the basis for describing learning and the conditions where it occurs. The benefits of this new paradigm are that the concepts are culture free, individual, and applicable to all normal adults. The following principles have been proposed to expedite learning and accelerate its retention.

The author has simplified the principles listed below for the purpose of applying them to adult learning.

1. All learning is physiological.
2. Social context is a part of learning.
3. The search for meaning is innate and constant for all adults.
4. Meaning occurs through recognizing patterning.
5. Emotions are critical to patterning

6. The brain processes parts and wholes simultaneously.
7. Learning involves both focused attention and peripheral perception.
8. Learning always involves conscious and unconscious processes.
9. There are at least two approaches to memory; archiving individual facts or skills and making sense of experience.
10. Complex learning is enhanced by challenge and inhibited by threat associated with helplessness. (Cain et al., 2005, pp. 1-190)

The principles are exemplified in the following instructional situations (Jensen, 2000):

1. Engage learners physically in learning by connecting movement and learning. For example, the jigsaw learning activity is successful in student learning because it utilizes the principle that all learning is physiological.
2. Adults' primary communication skills are language-driven. Speaking, reading, and writing enhance knowledge and retention for adults when presented in a social context such as play or skit production.
3. Lesson plans should include objectives built around themes, student emotions, and interdisciplinary relationships to help learners to understand and comprehend.
4. Identifying mathematical patterns is a good activity for adults. Sudoko is an example of obtaining meaning through patterns.
5. Students should enjoy coming to class. Teachers often interpret this to mean they should feed adult learners. Food and a variety of learning activities are ways to create positive emotions and an excitement and love of learning.
6. Multipath, simultaneous learning is visual, auditory, kinesthetic, conscious, and nonconscious. The best learning incorporates the immense variety of experience from rich, multisensory, real-life stimulation. Having students participate in the addition of more music, writing, dance, and art to instruction will only improve learning.
7. There are cycles and rhythms of learning meaning that attention is not constant. Hormones, diet, emotions, and body chemistry trigger fluctuations in attention, memory, and learning cycles.
8. Students learn better by alternating focus and diffusion of content with a variety of choices as to when to learn.
9. Memory is defined by the type of knowledge retained. For example, there are emotional memories; declarative, explicit and event related (episodic) memories; procedural, implicit memory for learned skills; priming; and associative conditioning.
10 Students should know the type of memory they are to use with the assignments made.

11. Threat, anxiety, and induced learner helplessness impair learning in many ways. They reduce the brain's capacity for understanding, meaning memory, and higher order thinking skills. Learners feel threatened by loss of approval, helplessness, use of rewards, criticism, lack of resources, and unrealistic deadlines. Reduce these conditions in the instructional process.

12. Assessments should measure meaning construction through model development, methods of solving problems, enhancement of individual insight and action, and perceptions of interdisciplinary relationships. (p. 49)

The importance of these principles and their utilization in educational situations is that their prediction of learning behavior can be replicated. These principles are not conjectures of intelligent educators trying to make meaning from the behavior they observe. These concepts can be demonstrated by positive emission topography (PET) scans and other physiological measures. Following this new model enables teachers to increase adults' learning. The future could demonstrate how adult educators can use biological understanding regarding optimum learning conditions.

References

Bandura, A. (1986). *Social foundations of thought and action: A social cognitive theory*. Englewood Cliffs, NJ: Prentice Hall.

Briggs, K. C., & Myers, I. B. (1953). *Myers Briggs type indicator*. New York: Rowan Bayne.

Brinkerhoff, R. (2002). *High impact learning*. New York: Basic Books.

Brown, J., & Fischo V. V. (1993). *Nelson Denny adult reading test*. Rolling Meadow, IL: Riverside Publishing.

Brown. K. (2004). Leadership for social justice and equity: Weaving a transformative framework and pedagogy. *Educational Administration Quarterly*, *40*(1), 79-110.

Burman, E. (1988). *The assassins*. Rochester, VT: Inner Traditions International.

Cain, R. N., Cain, G., McClintic, C., & Klimlek, K. (2005). *12 brain/mind learning principles in action, the fieldbook to making connections, teaching and the human brain*, New York: Corwin Press.

Center for Developing English Language. (2006, Summer). *English language symposia: History and language*. Retrieved July 29, 2007, from http://net. Shams.edu.eg

Cochran, J. (2008) *Educational roots of political crisis in Egypt*. New York: Rowman and Littlefield Publishers.

Conceicao, S. C. O. (2007). *Setting directions for the future of online and adult education*. New Directions for Adult and Continuing Education, *113*, pp.

41-50. Wiley Periodicals, Inc. Retrieved August, 16, 2007, from www.inter science.wiley.com

Cranton. P. (1992). *Working with adult learners.* Toronto: Wall & Emerson, Inc.

Dewey, J. (1997). *Experience and education.* New York: Free Press.

DuCharme-Hansen, B., & Dupin-Bryant, P. (1989). Distance education plans: Course planning for online adult learners. *TechTrends, 49*(2), 31-39.

Egyptian Ministry of Education. (1997). *Egypt and twenty-first century.* Cairo: ARE.

Engle, S. (Winter, 2007). Eva Baker: Improving assessment and accountability systems in schools. *Forum, 9*(1), 4.

Erickson, F. (1987). Transformation and school success. *Anthropology and Education Quarterly, 18*(6), 335-355.

Fenstermacher, G. D. (1979). A philosophical consideration of recent research on teacher effectiveness. In L. S. Shulman (Ed.), *Review of research in education* (pp. 157-185). Itasca, IL: F. E. Peacock.

Fenwick, T. J. (2002). *New understandings of learning in work: Implications for education and training.* Report submitted at the conclusion of a Coutts-Clarke Research Fellowship. Retrieved August 14, 2007, from http://www.u alberta.ca/-tfenwick/ext/coutts-clark.htm

Gagné, R. (1988). *Principles of instructional design.* Fort Worth, TX: Holt Rinehart and Winston.

Gilbreth, F. B. (2005). *Cheaper by the dozen.* New York: HarperCollins.

Granger, C. (1998). History—the foundation for curriculum and cognition engineering—using the naturalistic educational theory to increase science literacy. *Journal of Thought, 31,* 85-96.

Grimmett, P. P. (2000). Breaking the mold. In T. R. Carson & D. Sumara (Eds.), *Actionresearch as a living practice* (pp. 157-163). New York: Lang.

Grossman, P., Wineburg, S., & Woolworth, S. (2001). Toward a theory of teacher community. *Teachers College Record, 103*(6), 942-1012.

Guy, T. C. (1999). *Culture as context for adult education: The need for culturally relevant adult education. A challenge for the twenty-first century.* New Directions for Adult and Continuing Education, No. 82. San Francisco: Jossey-Bass.

Hansen, J., & Campbell, D. (1981). Strong Campbell interest inventory. New York: John Wiley and Sons.

Herrell, A. L., & Jordan, M. (2008). *50 strategies for teaching English language learners.* Upper Saddle River, NJ: Merrill/Prentice Hall Publishers.

Heyneman, S. (1998). The quality of education in the Middle East and North Africa (MENA). *International Journal of Educational Development, 17,* 449-446.

Iskandar, N. L. (2005). *Egypt: Where and who are the world's illiterates?* Paper commissioned for the EFA Global Monitoring Report 2006, Literacy for Life by the United Nations Educational, Scientific and Cultural Organization, Community Institutional Development.

Jensen, E. (2000). *Brain facts*. San Diego: The Brain Store.

Kegan, R. (1982). *The evolving self: Problem and process in human development*. Cambridge, MA: Harvard University Press.

Kelly, D. R., & MacKay, L. (2003). CELT: A computerized evaluative learning tool for continuing professional development. *Medical Education, 37*, 358-367.

Knowles, M. S., Holton, E., & Swanson, A. (2005). *The adult learner* (6th ed.). Boston, MA: Elsevier Butterworth Heinemann.

Kohlberg, L. (1969). Stage and sequence: The cognitive developmental approach to socialization. In D. A. Goslin (Ed.), *Handbook of socialization theory and research* (pp. 347-380). Chicago: Rand-McNally.

Lee, M., & Sheared, V. (2002). Socialization and immigrant students' learning in adult education programs. In M. V. Alfred (Ed.), *Learning and sociocultural contexts: Implications for adults, community, and workplace education* (pp. 211-219). New Directions for Adult Continuing Education, No. 96. San Francisco: Jossey-Bass.

Lewis, B. (1998). *Multiple identities of the Middle East*. New York: Schocken Books, 18.

Lewis, N., & Varbero, C. (1995). Connecting through culture brokers: Promise and pitfalls. In G. Weinstein-Shr & E. Quitero (Eds.), *Immigrant learners and their families* (pp. 33-42). McHenry, IL: Delta Systems.

Loevinger, J. (1976). *Ego development: Conceptions and theories*. San Francisco: Jossey-Bass.

Lomax, P. (1999). Working together for educative community through research. *British Educational Research Journal, 25*(1), 5-21.

Lyotard, J. (1984). *The Postmodern Condition*. Manchester, UK: Manchester University Press.

Martin, M. O., & Associates. (2000). *TIMSS 1999 internal science report: Findings from IEA's report of third international science study at eighth grade*. Chestnut Hill MA, Boston College: TIMSS International Study Center.

Meeker, P., & Byers, J. F. (2003). Data driven graduate curriculum redesign: A case study. *Journal of Nursing Education, 42*(4), 186-8.

Mezirow, J. (1990). *Fostering critical reflection in adulthood: A guide to transformative and emancipatory learning*. San Francisco: Jossey-Bass.

Ministry of Education. (2006). *General plan of literacy*. Cairo: ARE.

Popham, J. W. (2002). *Classroom assessment: What teachers need to know* (3rd ed.). Boston: Allyn and Bacon.

Quigley, A. (1997). *Rethinking literacy education*. San Francisco: Jossey-Bass.

Rossett, A. (1987). *Training needs assessment*. New York: Educational Technology Publishing.

Savery, J. R., & Duffy, T. M. (1995). Problem based learning: An instructional model and its constructivist framework. In B. Wilson (Ed.), *Constructivist learning environments: Case studies in instructional design* (pp. 18-27). Englewood Cliffs, NJ: Educational Technology Publications.

Serdyukov, P., & Ryan, M. (2007). *Writing effective lesson plans: The 5-star approach*. New York: Allyn & Bacon.

Sheared, V., & Sissel, P. (Eds.). (2000). *Making space: Merging theory and practice in adult education*. Westport, CT: Greenwood Publishing.

Skinner, B. F. (1965). *Science and human behavior*. San Francisco: Free Press, New Impressions Edition.

Spatz, T. S., & Erwin, D. O. (1996). Witnessing to save lives! *Adult Learning, 96*(7), 6.

Strict, T. (April 7, 2007). Strategies for evaluating the effectiveness of adult literacy programs: An update from 1990. *NLA Forum*, 7-11.

Thompson, J., & Chapman, E. (2004). Effects of cooperative learning on achievement of adult learners in introductory psychology classes. *Social Behavior and Personality*, 32(2),139-146.

Trotter, Y. (Winter, 2006). Adult learning theories: Impacting professional development programs. *The Delta Kappa Gamma Bulletin*, 8-13.

United Nations Planning Development Programme.(1998-1999). *An education for the future: A human development perspective*. New York: United Nations Publications.

Warner, J. (2002). *Gregoric learning style test*. New York: HRD Press, Inc.

Weinstein-Shr, G. (1995). Learning from uprooted families. In G. Weinstein-Shr & E. Quitero (Eds.), *Immigrant learners and their families* (pp. 105-119). McHenry, IL: Delta Systems.

Wendt, G. A. (1999). Using adult learning techniques in instruction. Fire Engineering, 152*(5), 5-10.*

Wertsch, J. (2003). *Caucasus context*. Tbilisi, Georgia: US-Caucasus Institute Publishers.

Curriculum Development for Adult Learners in the Global Community

Volume II
Teaching and Learning

Edited by
Victor C. X. Wang

KRIEGER PUBLISHING COMPANY
Malabar, Florida

Contents

Acknowledgments

As editor of the book, I must express my heartfelt thanks to many people in the field. As soon as I finished composing the proposed chapter titles, I sent them to scholars and practitioners (who have taught adult learners around the globe) in the field of adult education. To my great surprise and delight, I received responses within two weeks from many of our first-rate professors and practitioners in the field. Therefore, I wish to thank my friends, colleagues, and mentors who contributed to this volume. Without your contribution, this book would not be a reality. It has been my utmost pleasure working with each and every one of you and I am so proud of your insightful chapters. A special thank you goes to Kathleen P. King and John A. Henschke who invited Patricia Cranton and Edgar Boone to provide reviewer letters. Patricia Cranton and Edgar Boone are experts' experts in the field. Their letters definitely confirm the value of this book.

I extend a huge thank you to Shannon Ryder of Krieger Publishing Company for her timely encouragement and support. The users and our students should be happy about the professionalism our publisher can provide! Worthy of note is the fact that Krieger Publishing Company is one of the authoritative publishers in publishing books in adult education around the globe. Not only are they professional, but they also provide first rate editors (Mary Roberts is one of them) for books in the field of adult education. Their efforts will undoubtedly add to the quality of our book. Thank you again, Shannon and Krieger Publishing Company! May our cooperation continue for many years.

Victor C. X. Wang

The Editor

Victor C. X. Wang, Ed.D., is an assistant professor/credential director of vocational and adult education at California State University, Long Beach. Wang's research and writing activities have focused on workforce education, the foundations of adult education, adult teaching and learning, training, transformative learning, cultural issues in vocational and adult education, distance education, and curriculum development. He has published more than 10 books and dozens of chapters and refereed journal articles and has been a reviewer for three journals. He has won many academic achievement awards from different universities in China and in the United States. He taught extensively as a full professor in China in places such as universities, radio stations, and China Central TV (CCTV) prior to coming to study and work in the United States in 1997. He has taught adult learners English as a second language, Chinese, computer technology, vocational and adult education courses, research methods and curriculum development for the past 18 years in university settings. In addition, he has served as a translator/narrator for national and international leaders both in China and in the United States. The videotapes and DVDs he published for national and international leaders are played all over the world for both educational and investment purposes. He coedited two books (*Comparative Adult Education Around The Globe; Innovations in Career and Technical Education: Strategic Approaches Towards Workforce Competencies Around the Globe*) with Fordham University's Professor Kathleen P. King, which have been adopted as required textbooks by major universities in the United States and in China.

The Contributors

Mary V. Alfred is an associate professor of adult education and associate department head in the Department of Adult Education and Human Resource Development at Texas A&M University. Her research interests include learning and development among women of the Diaspora, welfare reform as it relates to women's economic development, and diversity issues in higher education and the workplace. She is the 2003 recipient of the Commission of Professors of Adult Education Early Career Award and a recipient of the Cyril O. Houle Scholars Research Grant for Emerging Scholars in Adult Education. She is the coeditor of *Adult Learning* and holds membership on several adult education journal editorial boards. She is the author of two books, *Immigrant Women of the Academy* and *Learning in Sociocultural Contexts*. She also coedited a special issue of *Adult Learning* titled "Immigrants in Adult and Higher Education." She has served on the steering committee of the annual Adult Education Research Conference and on the executive committee of the Commission of Professors of Adult Education. Alfred earned her Ph.D. in educational administration with a focus in adult education and human resource development leadership from the University of Texas at Austin.

Talmadge C. Guy is an associate professor of adult education at the University of Georgia. He was formerly associate vice chancellor for adult and basic education at the City Colleges of Chicago. He graduated with a doctor of education degree from Northern Illinois University. His research interests include African American adult education, popular culture, and race. He has published papers in scholarly journals on multicultural education and institutional change, African American adult education history, and culturally relevant adult education. He edited the volume *Culturally Relevant Adult Education: A Challenge for the Twenty-First Century.* Guy travels internationally and has conducted numerous workshops on cultural awareness and multiculturalism.

Barbara P. Heuer is an assistant professor and coordinator of the masters program in adult education and human resource development at Fordham University, New

York City. She holds an Ed.D. from the University of Georgia and an M.L.S. from Rutgers University. Her areas of interest center around access issues in informal learning and information literacy. She coedits with Kathleen King, *Perspectives, The New York Journal of Adult Learning.*

Kathleen P. King, Ed.D., is a professor of adult education at Fordham University's Graduate School of Education in New York City. King's major areas of research have been transformative learning, professional development, distance learning, and instructional technology. Her experience in adult learning has spanned these fields in diverse organizations including community-based organizations, business, higher education, career and technical education and numerous partnerships. Her recent endeavors continue to explore and develop learning innovations and opportunities to address equity, access, and international issues. She is the author of 10 books and numerous articles. King is the editor in chief of *Perspectives, The New York Journal of Adult Learning* and research board member for several national and international academic journals. In addition to receiving numerous academic and professional awards in the field of adult learning, her coedited book about distance education, *Harnessing Innovations Technologies in Higher Education*, received the Frandson Book Award from the University Continuing Education Association in 2007, and she was recently nominated for the International Adult and Continuing Education Hall of Fame.

Fredrick M. Nafukho is an associate professor of human resource development and chair, HRD Program of the Department of Educational Administration and Human Resource Development, College of Education and Human Development, Texas A & M University. He holds a Ph.D. in human resource development, Louisiana State University, where he was a Fulbright Scholar, an M.Ed. in economics of education, and B.Ed. in business education and economics from Kenyatta University, Kenya. In his 16 years of experience working in higher education, he has also served as associate professor and assistant department head, University of Arkansas, Fayetteville, and head, Department of Educational Administration and Curriculum Development, Moi University, Kenya. Nafukho has published over 120 articles, chapters, and books. His primary area of research has been aligned with investment in human capital, enrollment modeling and prediction in higher education, E-learning, and performance improvement. He served as proceedings editor and chair of the Academy of Human Resource Development Annual Conferences, 2006-2007. He is a board member of the AHRD Executive Board, and serves as an editorial board member of *Human Resource Development Quarterly, Advances in Developing Human Resources,* and *Journal of Eastern Africa Research* *and Development.* He teaches courses in adult education and human resource development.

Wei Zheng, Ph.D., is an assistant professor of human resource development from the Department of Counseling, Adult and Higher Education at Northern Illinois University. She received her Ph.D in human resource development from the University of Minnesota, and her bachelor's degree in English language and literature from Beijing University. Her research areas include social dynamics of innovation, knowledge management, and international human resource development. She has won awards for her scholarship from the Academy of Human Resource Development and the Academy of Management. She has taught English to both children and adults in China, designed and implemented learning programs for working professionals, and worked as human resource development consultant for a variety of organizations.

Introduction

Victor C. X. Wang

As a common Chinese proverb goes, without rice, even the cleverest house-wife cannot cook (Yuan, 2007). The implication is that without the right material, no matter how good you are as a cook, you may not accomplish the cooking task. Similarly, Westerners posited that knowledge of curriculum is, by definition, central to the professional teacher and an essential orientation for all professional responsible beginners (as cited in Print, 1993, p. 1). Two lines of thought from totally different cultures have confirmed the importance of curriculum development for professional teachers. What are the compelling reasons why adult learners want to teach others? Over the years, adult learners have accumulated such a rich reservoir of experience that they are ready to obtain teaching credentials from a university in order to teach their occupational skills to others. Without teaching credentials, they are not authorized to teach others. By teaching their knowledge, skills and attitudes to others, adult learners become professional teachers and trainers. However, having sheer knowledge in one's occupation does not automatically grant a person the power to teach in the field. A great deal depends on one's knowledge in curriculum development. This is probably why a course in curriculum development in all vocational and adult education credential programs is offered in almost every state in the United States. By credential laws and regulations, all teachers are required to be equipped with knowledge in curriculum development.

Curriculum development can be considered as both art and science although most scholars consider curriculum development as a process that can be described as more akin to art than science (Iwasiw, Goldenberg & Andrusyszyn, 2005, p. 2). Further, it is a complex process characterized by interaction, cooperation, change, and possibly conflict (Iwasiw et al., 2005, p. 2). Some argue that curriculum development has neither beginning nor end, indicating that curriculum is an ongoing activity in any established field (Iwasiw et al., 2005, p. 2). It is also true that curriculum development is influenced by personal interests, philosophies, judgments, and values. As I continue to teach courses such as the core course titled "Curriculum Development for Designated Subjects" in the state of California, I have examined and compared many books regarding curriculum development available in the field of vocational and adult education including some international books in this field.

What I have found about these books on curriculum development is the sheer fact that most books reflect behavioral philosophy in curriculum development. These books address traditional aspects of curriculum development such as planning, designing, managing, and evaluating for a sound lesson plan. These approaches support behavioral philosophy in curriculum development. Some books even address Bloom's 1956 taxonomy, needs assessments, task analysis or even the four steps of instruction (e.g., motivation, presentation, homework, and follow-up). It is obvious all these approaches work well with behavioral philosophy. While behavioral philosophy in curriculum development is a well-established method, other philosophies, judgments, and values have been virtually ignored. In the field of vocational and adult education, not only do we need behavioral philosophy in guiding our teachers and/or administrators to develop curriculum, but also we need other philosophies such as humanistic, progressive, liberal, radical, and analytic philosophies. Although our adult learners do not oppose a behavioral philosophy, they embrace other philosophies such as humanistic and progressive philosophies. As adult learners learn to develop curricula to teach other adult learners, theories of adult learning can offer to help them develop sound curricula for other adult learners. Leaders in adult education indicate *andragogy* (*the art and science of helping adults learn*) reflects humanistic and progressive teaching philosophies. Therefore, other adult learning approaches together with the use of andragogy in curriculum development should be considered given the nature of our adult learners. This book has been written to provide a current, practical, international, and adult learning based approach to designing and developing curriculum in the field of vocational and adult education.

The demands of both public and private schools in America and society today are such that teachers with international, adult learning based curriculum skills are highly valued. This book seeks to provide a vital source for teachers who wish to develop their skills in the field of curriculum design and development in the larger field of vocational and adult education. As Zumwalt suggests, "Given the view that professional teachers should have the knowledge to enable them to create sound educational programs... it is essential that teachers have knowledge of some planning process that enables them to think about curriculum beyond the individual lesson" (as cited in Print, 1993, p. 93). To go beyond the individual lesson, professional teachers need to take into consideration different variables and models that can help them with their planning process. With this goal in mind, the contributors and editor of this book have addressed in detail how these variables and models can equip professional teachers with knowledge and skills to build sound, practical, adult learning based curriculum for adult learners.

In addition, this book seeks to address:

- How do you design meaningful curriculum for economically and culturally disadvantaged adult learners?
- How do you derive curriculum from adult learners themselves?
- What are the fundamentals of curriculum development?
- What are the generic models that can be applied to adult learners?
- What do you do to design and implement E-learning curriculum for adult learners?
- How do you use principles of adult learning to develop curriculum for adult learners?
- What about learners in the global community? How do they challenge curriculum developers in vocational and adult education?

These are but a few of the many questions we ask our adult educators when they are engaged in developing curriculum for other adult learners in the field. To help adult learners receive their teaching credentials and to enable them to teach their occupational skills to others in the field, such questions need to be addressed in detail. This volume and VolumeI have provided answers to the above and other questions related to curriculum design and development in the larger field of vocational and adult education.

One final factor to consider when developing curricula for adult learners is that we draw adult learners from around the globe. These adult learners from the global community come to adult educators not just for teaching credentials. More importantly, they come to adult educators to acquire the basic knowledge and skills of curriculum development. To develop meaningful and practical curriculum for adult learners in the global community, one has to take into consideration theories and principles of adult learning— powerful approaches other than just a behavioral philosophy. As globalization brings different cultures together, adult learners are positioned in a global community, defying existing curriculum development approaches that may not serve them well. Over the years, the theories of adult learning have been applied to various fields. Why not use them for the sake of curriculum development in the field of adult education itself? They can prove to be a powerful tool in assisting curriculum developers design useful curricula for adult learners.

As I continue to teach curriculum development in the field, I also notice one phenomenon, that is, books on curriculum development have not been written by experts in the field of adult education. They have been written by people in other fields. To paint the picture bleaker, courses in curriculum development are not taught by people with a background in adult education, but rather by people from other educational fields. Small wonder only behavioral philosophy has been taught. Should such a situation continue, we will definitely fail to serve both our educators of adults in training and our adult learners. To rectify such a situation in the field, both scholars and practitioners (who have taught adult learners around the globe) have contributed chapters to this book and to Volume I.

Volume II consists of two parts. **Part I** "Curriculum Development in the Global Context" contains three chapters. These three chapters address cultures and demographic changes and how cultural and social forces affect curriculum development for adult learners in the global context. Guy (Chapter 1) focuses on a number of prominent models that are available for educators to incorporate multicultural content into curricula. He indicates that a culturally relevant approach to curriculum development requires educators to incorporate learners' cultural practices and values in the teaching and learning process.

Alfred (Chapter 2) writes about demographic change and how it has significantly transformed the student population in higher education in the country. In her words, these demographic changes result from more permeable transnational borders, thus calling for the internationalization of curricula in higher education. Her chapter explores the impact of immigration and globalization on the adult education curricula and ways by which adult educators can plan and design instructional programs for more global learning. In addition, it addresses the need for instructional designers to consider the sociocultural contexts of learners, particularly those whose prior socialization to schooling happened in nonwestern cultures.

Zheng (Chapter 3) introduces English-language education in China, its challenges, and curricular implications. First she describes and analyzes English-language education in China against the broader background of English-language education and adult education in general. The current practices of English-language education are described, and the social, cultural, and economic forces that underlie the practices are explained. Second, a historical review of the curricular evolution of China's English education is presented. A set of challenges are explained, and suggestions are provided for improving curriculum based on principles of curriculum development in a global context.

Part II, "Teaching and Learning in the Global Community," revolves around four chapters. The purpose of curriculum development is to provide meaningful materials for teaching and learning. Without addressing this purpose, teaching and learning in the global community would be meaningless. The four chapters discuss how adult educators can help adult learners learn best, using digital technologies and in the global context.

King (Chapter 4) provides insight into understanding globalization, global communities and their meaning for learners and educators. She presents specific recommendations for learner's competencies, educators' instructional strategies, and educators' continuing professional development. Through her in-depth analysis, King emphasizes the utmost importance of using digital technologies to facilitate adult teaching and learning in the global community in the 21st century.

Heuer (Chapter 5) describes issues, aspects, and approaches of information literacy that help adults learn "how to learn." She argues that information literacy, the ability to find and fathom good information, combines technological skills with critical thinking habits and has emerged as a crucial coping skill in the 21st century for adult learners.

Nafukho (Chapter 6) argues that educators as designers and implementers of curricula are being challenged to be innovative and to incorporate technology in the instructional processes for adult learners with diverse learning needs so as to promote learning and not to discourage learning. His chapter examines the role of the teacher in E-learning courses and identifys the standard features of E-learning courses. His chapter further demonstrates the relevance of constructivism philosophy in E-learning course design and delivery, and assessment of the learning process.

Wang (Chapter 7) presents an empirical study that focuses on whether andragogy can be implemented in a different social context, such as in China. Wang's chapter indicates that the Western style of education characterized by the use of andragogy clashes with many factors such as influences from a few individuals, political and educational directives, and preferences of adult learners from an authoritarian culture such as in China. In terms of who can develop curricula for adult learners in China, it has to be the higher authorities rather than adult educators or adult learners themselves.

As we read through the pages of this book, we will learn that curriculum development takes on new meaning according to educators' individual and collective values and beliefs about education, teaching, and learning. Our contributors maintain that curriculum development is shaped by contextual realities, and even politics. As globalization has become a reality, it is becoming all the more important that we address developing curriculum development for adult learners by crossing cultural boundaries, instructional design and the transactional adult learners, and curriculum development for other major cultures such as in China. As decentralization remains the norm in curriculum development in the Western culture, what about centralization that is extensively implemented in other cultures? Both American adult learners and adult learners from other countries need to be equipped with knowledge in curriculum development from other cultures. Once adult learners have acquired the knowledge and skills on how to develop meaningful curriculum, they need to learn how to teach adult learners in the global community. They also need to learn methods of helping adults learn in the

21st century. Can the theories of adult learning be implemented in every culture around the globe? Such topics make this book especially relevant and compelling for today and the future.

This book is designed for the teacher-practitioner and is written from both a scholar's and a practitioner's perspective. The book falls naturally into two volumes. Individual chapters can be selected according to readers' specific needs and interests.

References

Iwasiw, C. L., Goldenberg, D., & Andrusyszyn, M. A. (2005). *Curriculum development in nursing education*. Sudbury, MA: Jones & Bartlett Publishers.

Print, M. (1993). *Curriculum development and design*. Australia: Allen & Unwin.

Yuan, H. W. (2007). *Chinese proverbs*. Retrieved August 30, 2007, from http://www.wku.edu/~yuanh/China/proverbs/q.html.

Index